LUIGI GALLEANI

THE MOST DANGEROUS ANARCHIST IN AMERICA

LUIGI GALLEANI
THE MOST DANGEROUS ANARCHIST IN AMERICA

ANTONIO SENTA

TRANSLATED BY **ANDREA ASALI** WITH **SEAN SAYERS**
FOREWORD BY **SEAN SAYERS**

© 2019 Antonio Senta
© Translation 2019 Andrea Asali and Sean Sayers
Foreword © 2019 Sean Sayers
This edition © 2019 AK Press (Chico, Edinburgh)
Originally published by Nova Delphi, Rome, Italy, 2018
This edition published by arrangement with the Author

ISBN: 978-1-84935-348-9
E-ISBN: 978-1-84935-349-6
Library of Congress Control Number: 2019933789

AK Press	AK Press
370 Ryan Ave. #100	33 Tower St.
Chico, CA 95973	Edinburgh EH6 7BN
USA	Scotland
www.akpress.org	www.akuk.com
info@akpress.org	ak@akedin.demon.co.uk

The above addresses would be delighted to provide you with the latest AK Press distribution catalog, which features books, pamphlets, zines, and stylish apparel published and/or distributed by AK Press. Alternatively, visit our websites for the complete catalog, latest news, and secure ordering.

Cover illustration by Clifford Harper
Cover design by John Yates | stealworks.com
Printed in the USA on acid-free, recycled paper

CONTENTS

EPILOGUE
Return to Italy

Acknowledgments

This work is the result of a long period of research begun a decade ago, when I set out to perform a study on Italian-language anarchist periodicals published in the United States. That project did not materialize, but my interest in the subject continued and led me, first, to edit the Italian edition of Paul Avrich's essential book, *Sacco and Vanzetti: The Anarchist Background*, released by Nova Delphi in 2015, and then to participate in a series of conferences, conventions, and volumes by multiple authors commemorating the ninetieth anniversary of the execution of Sacco and Vanzetti.

The book you hold in your hands aims to reconstruct the life and ideas of Luigi Galleani. Starting with his individual experiences and original points of view, it also aims to reconstruct the social and cultural climate subversives lived within for fifty years (1880–1931), in Europe as well as the United States. An exciting tableau emerges, and every reader will make their own independent evaluation of it. The events are framed by the complex relationship between insurgents and the exploited, or in other words, between a political vanguard and the labor movement. Galleani continually addresses a proletariat among whom his propaganda takes root, in different places and times. Even the most extreme positions, and consequent actions, are not extraneous to the context and struggles of workers. My hope is that the following pages will help the reader better understand many historical aspects of the anarchist movement and its underlying principles, so we can avoid hasty judgments on subjects considered obscure, odd, or marginal.

This is the second biography on the insurgent from Vercelli, after the one written in the 1950s by Ugo Fedeli, activist, archivist, and autodidact historian whose life and papers I studied for several years.

No archives dedicated to Luigi Galleani have survived to this day, not even a book archive. The heritage of a life spent roaming has been irremediably lost, particularly due to continuous police attention and repression. Nevertheless, I was able to retrace written material by and about him in various archives.

About seventy original letters written in French and unpublished, conserved in the Jacques Gross Papers at the International Institute of Social History in Amsterdam, were first and foremost useful. Several folders from the Ugo Fedeli Papers, also kept at the Institute in Amsterdam, likewise shed light on the subject, containing the material Fedeli used to prepare his biography on Galleani. The *L'Adunata* fund at the Boston Public Library was helpful as well. Police documents kept at the Central State Archives in Rome, the State Archives in Massa and Turin, the Historical Archive of the Ministry of Foreign Affairs of Rome and the National Archives in Washington, in addition to periodicals and other printed material found in Amsterdam, Boston, the Archiginnasio Library in Bologna, the Berneri-Aurelio Chessa Family Archives in Reggio Emilia, and the Gallica of Paris, today partly digitized and available online, were all of service.

Although critical literature and secondary sources were duly considered, I wanted to give primary attention to the perspective of the "most dangerous anarchist in America," insomuch as I could deduce from the sources most closely linked to him, his writings, letters, accounts from his comrades and family members. This seemed to me the most interesting and meaningful way to reconstruct the kind of life he led.

It would have been much more difficult to write this book without the generous contributions of so many people. Sean Sayers followed the research step by step and inspired me on many an occasion, helping me, among other tasks, to source material in the archives of Boston and Massa, and sharing documents, photos, and family memories. Fiamma Chessa made available the documentation kept at the Berneri-Chessa Archives. Tomaso Marabini did the same with his historical popular archive. Jack Hofman helped me with the research at the International Institute of Social History in Amsterdam, as did Anna Manfron at the Archiginnasio in Bologna. Over several years, Tobia Imperato sent me what he found on and by Galleani. Gino Vatteroni shared his research on emigration from Carrara to the United States. Davide Turcato was always available to provide recommendations and advice, as well as bibliographical suggestions. Marianne Enckell, Gianpiero Bottinelli, Edy Zaro, and Davide Bianco were very helpful in reconstructing the periods Galleani spent in Switzerland and France. I exchanged information and impressions on Galleani's time in Turin with Marco Scavino, and received information on Galleani's years spent in exile in Pantelleria from Sandro Casano and Giuseppe La Greca. I discussed the anarchist movement in the United States and the role of activists such as Galleani, Alfonso Coniglio, and Umberto Postiglione with Edoardo Puglielli, and the role of the press in Italian-language political transatlantic emigration with Andrew Hoyt. David Bernardini helped me understand several aspects of German-language anarchist emigration to New York. Giorgio Galleani from Ventimiglia shared information on the noble origins of the Galleani lineage. Robert D'Attilio, through Sean Sayers, also encouraged my research. Thanks to Ferdinando Fasce for the epistolary exchanges on the subject of Italian immigration in the United States, Enrico Ferri for information on the Armenian revolutionary movement, the Giuseppe Pinelli Archive collective of Milan and Franco Schirone for bibliographical information, and Massimo Ortalli for having publicly encouraged me, several years ago, to write a biography on Galleani. The aforementioned Sayers, Imperato, and Turcato had the patience to review a draft of the book and provide feedback, as did Carla De Pascale and Elena Suriani. I would like to acknowledge and thank everyone mentioned, with the shared awareness that only I am responsible for what is written in the following pages. I dedicate this work to Jacopo, the newest arrival.

Antonio Senta
(December 2017)

Foreword

I am Luigi Galleani's grandson, he was my mother's father. I did not know him, he died well before I was born. My mother told me only a little about him. She was not at all unwilling to talk about him, but she would do so only when asked; and, with the arrogance of youth and to my great regret, I did not ask much about him. So when I was growing up I had only a sketchy awareness of his life and activities, and it was not until after my mother died that I started to become interested in his life. When, at last, I did begin to look into my family's history, one of the first steps I took was to look to see if there was anything about him on the Internet. I was amazed to discover how much there was there, and to realize what an important person he had been and what a remarkable life he had led.

As Antonio Senta describes in these pages, he was born in 1861, in Vercelli (Piedmont), one of four children in a respectable middle class, Catholic family. His father was an elementary school teacher. Galleani was evidently a spirited and independently minded person even in his youth. According to family legend, he was pressured by his father against his wishes into studying law at the University of Turin, but he didn't take his degree, by that time he was already actively engaged in radical politics.

He became a leading activist in North West Italy as well as in the Lunigiana area, around Carrara (Tuscany), the site of the famous marble quarries. A series of strikes and demonstrations by quarry workers were put down with brutal military force by the government. To avoid arrest Galleani fled to France, but he was expelled from there and moved to Switzerland. When he returned to Italy he was arrested and charged, under the Crispi government's notorious Article 248, with thirty-five others with "conspiracy," and sentenced to three years imprisonment. From prison he was sent directly into internal exile (*domicilio coatto*) on the tiny and inaccessible island of Pantelleria, between Sicily and Tunisia.

Pantelleria is now a fashionable resort. In the 1890s, when Galleani was exiled there, it was poor, bleak, and extremely remote. This was the harshest of punishments: the prisoners called themselves "*i morti*" in a newpaper with that title that they managed to smuggle out. Among its articles was one by my grandfather with the title "*manet immota fides*," the Latin for "the faith remains unchanged" (he was fond of Latin quotations). That became his motto.

On Pantelleria, he met a remarkable young woman named Maria Rallo, from a local family. My mother said that they owned a vineyard. By the time they met, Maria was already a widow with a son and an infant daughter. She and Luigi became lovers and she became my grandmother. Then Galleani decided to escape. According to my mother, Maria's family helped him to get a little boat, in which he made the perilous crossing to Tunisia. From thence he made his way to Alexandria in Egypt, where he was joined by Maria and her two children (Salvatore Errera and Ilia). By then she was eight and a half months pregnant with a third child (Cossyra).

In Egypt, they were threatened with extradition back to Italy. So, in 1900, the family made its way, via London, to the USA, where Galleani had been invited to become Editor of *La Questione Sociale*, the leading Italian American anarchist paper at that time, based in Paterson, NJ.

Soon after the family arrived, however, there was a major strike by the local silk workers, many of whom were Italian immigrants. Galleani was injured by the police in a demonstration, and then charged with incitement to riot. Before the trial, he managed to escape to Montreal, across the border in Canada. When the hue and cry died down, he slipped back across the border under an assumed name, and settled with his family in Barre, Vermont.

Barre was a congenial place for them. There is a huge granite quarry on the outskirts of the town that employed a large number of Italian quarry workers and stone cutters, many from Carrara where Galleani had been active. Even before Galleani arrived, it had a strong radical tradition, and this endures still: its Senator is Bernie Saunders, the socialist candidate who did so well in the 2016 Primary elections for the Democratic Party presidential nomination.

Soon after settling in Barre, in 1903, Galleani started his own newspaper, *Cronaca Sovversiva*. It was lively and provocative and it rapidly built up a large following. In time it became the best-selling anarchist periodical in North America. Galleani was a brilliant and powerful orator and he made frequent lecture tours around the country to spread his ideas.

Eventually, in 1907, he was betrayed to the New Jersey authorities and extradited back there to stand trial on the charges arising from the demonstration in 1902; but there was a hung jury and he was acquitted. He returned to Barre to a triumphant homecoming.

By this time, the family was made up of two daughters (Ilia, Cossyra) and three sons (Salvatore, Olimpio, Balilla). In 1909 their youngest child, my mother, Mentana (always known as "Tana") was born in Barre. Three years later, Galleani relocated *Cronaca Sovversiva*, to Lynn, Massachusetts, near Boston, and the family moved to Wrentham, Massachusetts—a small and typical New England town, also near Boston, where there was a large population of Italian workers, and where Galleani had many followers. He soon gained more—including, most famously, Nicolo Sacco and Bartolomeo Vanzetti, whose visits to the family's farm outside Wrentham my mother remembered and talked about.

Galleani's comrades, together with other anarchists and radicals in America, had always been the targets of persecution and attacks. These grew much worse in 1917 when the US entered World War I and with the upsurge of radical activity that followed the Russian Revolution. Galleani opposed the war with the slogan, blazened across his newspaper, "*contro la Guerra, contro la pace, per la rivoluzione.*" He tacitly advised his followers not to register for the draft, which was compulsory even for foreigners, some of whom, including Sacco and Vanzetti, moved temporarily to Mexico. The government and the Press whipped up a vicious anti-anarchist and anti-red scare, a hate-filled, xenophobic and racist campaign demonizing radicals and foreigners. Italians and other recent immigrants were treated as dangerous and evil.

The government repeatedly tried to close down *Cronaca Sovversiva*. They banned it from the mail, but its supporters distributed it by hand. They raided its offices, seized its distribution lists and intimidated and arrested its subscribers. Indeed, subscribing to *Cronaca Sovversiva* was treated as a ground for deportation.[1] My mother remembered frequent police raids and searches at the family home, and interrogations of the family and neighbors.

The government wanted to deport Galleani, but they could not do so. The law as it stood did not allow the deportation of anyone who had family born in the US, who had been a resident for more than six years, and who hadn't broken the law. So they brought in a new law: the Immigration Act of 1918. Galleani and literally thousands of other foreign immigrants suspected of being anarchists and radicals, were rounded up and deported without charge or trial in what became known as the "Palmer Raids" after the Attorney General, A. Mitchell Palmer, who ordered them.

My mother remembered visiting her father in prison while he was awaiting deportation. She brought some chocolates, which the guards cut up into little pieces to check that nothing was hidden in them. A police report describes the way that her older sister Ilia, who became a distinguished doctor, was treated on one such visit. The file is headed "In re: Bomb outrages … (anarchistic matter)." Bureau of Investigation agents had been interrogating a neighbor of our family, who said, "My husband goes to church and he knows Galliani [sic] and got some books from Galliani [sic] and he burned them because we did not want to get in trouble."[2] The report continues,

> When Agents got through with this lady, we noticed that
> the girl in the waiting room desired to see Galliani [sic].

When questioned she said that her name was Ilia Galliani [sic]; that she ... is about 22 years of age now, ... that her father's name was Louis Galliani [sic] and that he was now in the detention room awaiting deportation.

Then they questioned her:

Q. Do you believe in the American form of Government?
A. I came here to see my father: I did not come here to answer any questions. I don't see why I should answer questions at all.
Q. We are Government Officers and we expect you to answer that question.
A. I don't see why I should answer that.
Q. Do you believe in the over-throw of the Government?
A. I don't interest myself in such questions....
Q. Do you believe in the trickeries of anarchism?
A. I haven't formed any idea. I have not adopted any form of ideals.[3]

I am struck by the calm way that my aunt handled herself, although no doubt she and other members of the family were used to being treated in this sort of way.

Galleani was deported to Italy in 1919. There, he immediately began political activity again and restarted Cronaca Sovversiva, bringing out some further issues, but it was closed down for the final time in 1920. In 1922, Mussolini and the fascists came to power; Galleani was imprisoned for writing anti-military articles, and then he was sent into internal exile again—this time on Lipari, another small island like Pantelleria off the coast of Sicily.

In 1930, he was released back to the mainland. His health had deteriorated, he was suffering from diabetes. He lived in Caprigliola, a small hilltop village in the Lunigiana area where he was guarded twenty-four hours a day by the police who reported daily on his activities. He died of a heart attack on his regular afternoon walk in 1931, age seventy. He is buried in the cemetery nearby.

When Galleani was deported, his family (Maria and their six children) was left in the US. Maria still had a young child (my mother, Tana, who was only ten years old), but she had to get a job; she found work in a local knitwear factory. According to my mother she met new people and got to like it. One of her daughters (Cossyra) went back to Italy to look after Galleani. The oldest daughter, Ilia, became a pioneer of birth control and a doctor to the anarchist community in the Boston area (they always called her "*la dottoressa*").

My mother loved and revered her father who was suddenly taken away from her. In a brief memoir recorded at the end of her life she said, "When my father was to be deported, my parents were discussing it and I went up to their bedroom and said to him, 'why don't you say you don't believe any more?' I'll never ever forget the look on his face. Now, I'm so glad he lived the way he did and believed in what he did."

She was proud of him, she was inspired by him. Eventually she became a communist. Although there is often bitter antagonism between anarchists and communists, she felt that she was continuing his work, fighting for the same ideals. She moved to New York where she met and married my father, an Irish writer who had moved to America in the 1930s. My younger brother and I were both born in New York in the 1940s.

After the end of the Second World War there was another anti-red scare in America, McCarthyism. My father was working in TV. He was blacklisted and couldn't get work. We left America. We lived for a while in Ireland and Italy before settling in London in 1949.

I went to school and university in England and then I became a university teacher of philosophy. My work focuses on Hegel and Marx. I was inspired by my mother and by my grandfather. I am proud to be his grandson. I would like to think that I too, in a small way, am continuing his work.

A few years ago I began doing more systematic research on my grandfather. This started almost accidentally. I was on holiday near Carrara and decided to visit the local state archive to see whether they had any information about him. At first they were suspicious of me and would hardly open the door, but when I mentioned Galleani's name, they produced a thick file of police records on him for the eighteen months he lived in the area at the end of his life.

The police reported on him every day, even when there was nothing significant to report; they opened his letters and—very helpfully—typed them out before sending them on to him. This inspired me to visit other archives and it whetted my appetite to learn more. I started to learn Italian in order to read these documents and his writings.

As I discovered what an important and interesting figure he was, I formed the plan to write a biography, and begun reading and collecting other material; but I was working on my own, and I was soon overwhelmed by the sheer quantity of information that I was accumulating and the difficulty of the task I had embarked upon. I was starting to despair when I was put in touch with Antonio Senta, who was also doing research on Galleani and who wanted to write a biography of him. He is much better qualified than I am to do so, and we rapidly agreed that he would write the biography and I would help with research as and when I could. This book is the excellent result.

***

In Galleani's time, anarchism was a powerful and important political movement. Indeed, until the Russian Revolution, it was more influential on the far left than Marxism or communism.[4] Then, and even to some extent still now, there was a widespread view that anarchism is a purely negative and destructive philosophy, an arbitrary and irrational sort of nihilism. The popular image of anarchists in this period was that they were conspiratorial, bomb-throwing terrorists, bent on causing chaos and destruction. This is an image that was successfully spread by widely read novels such as Dostoyevsky's *The Possessed* and Conrad's *The Secret Agent*.

This picture must be set aside completely if one is to understand Galleani. He was not in the least conspiratorial or secretive, he proclaimed his views to the world in a fearless and forthright manner. Those who heard him testify to his power and eloquence as a speaker, even the police reports regularly mention this. He was also a prolific writer of trenchant and persuasive prose. He wrote (and no doubt spoke) in an elaborate and strongly rhetorical style; he peppers his paragraphs with Latin sayings and quotations. It is remarkable that he had such a large following among ordinary workers.

Moreover, anarchism—of his kind at least—is not a form of nihilism. It is not a purely negative philosophy. On the contrary, it is a positive philosophy with a history that can be traced back to nineteenth-century thinkers such as Proudhon and Kropotkin, and that is going through a strong revival at present. Anarchism is the philosophy that the state, private property, and all forms of authority are harmful and unnecessary. As Galleani himself put it, "We do not argue about whether property means greed or not, if masters are good or bad, if the State is paternal or despotic, if laws are just or unjust, if courts are fair or unfair, if the police are merciful or brutal. When we talk about property, State, masters, government, laws, courts and police, we say only that *we don't want any of them.*"[5]

These are not purely negative or nihilistic ideas. They spring from the hugely confident, optimistic—even utopian—belief that people can live together cooperatively without the need for property, the restraints of law, or coercive authority to maintain order. It is a hopeful and idealistic philosophy. At its basis is an enormously positive faith in human nature—the belief that people are basically good not evil, and that they do not need to be forced by law or authority to live and work together harmoniously: a voluntary cooperative community is possible. This is what Galleani and his comrades believed in and worked for. They called this "the idea," or even "the beautiful idea."

What is preventing such a community from being created, they believed, is capitalism. Capitalism exploits and oppresses people, and uses all the power of the state to do so. Galleani and his associates called themselves "communist anarchists." At the basis of the exploitation and oppression in current society are private property and the state. Like Marxist communists, they advocated the abolition of bourgeois or capitalist private property (i.e., the private ownership of the means of production). Production, they argued, should be organized collectively, for use and not for private profit.

However, they rejected what they regarded as the authoritarian side of Marxism: they questioned the Marxist belief that a socialist state would be required to create a communist society. People, they maintained, are capable of living together and organizing themselves by themselves, without needing to be forced or coerced; and they would do so spontaneously when the forces preventing this—private property and the state—are abolished.

The anarchism of Galleani and his associates took a rigorous and uncompromising form. In the first place, they advocated and practiced an "anti-organizational" form of anarchism that involved the radical rejection of hierarchy in all its forms. They repudiated every kind of political organization and party structure as oppressive and coercive, and they criticized trade unions on the same grounds. Recent writers have increasingly come to refer to them as "Galleanisti," but Galleani and his associates did not use this title. If they had to describe themselves collectively, they called themselves followers of "the idea." Their policies and activities were not imposed from on high, but decided by direct democracy at informal meetings, often at Sunday picnics held at the family farm. My mother remembered these gatherings well and enjoyed arguing about politics with the participants who came to them.

As well as being a prolific writer and speaker, Galleani also advocated "propaganda of the deed"—direct action against the state and the forces of oppression. To understand this one must see it in the context of the time. The political situation in Italy and in the United States at the end of the nineteenth century and in the early decades of the twentieth century was extremely volatile and violent. The police sided with employers and broke up strikes and demonstrations, often with brutal force. Workers and those who supported them were spied upon, assaulted, arrested, imprisoned, and even deported. Galleani and his associates believed that when they were attacked, as they constantly were, it was legitimate for them to fight back—they were not pacifists. They were also convinced that, in the tense and volatile conditions that then existed, a few insurrectionary acts would spark off spontaneous revolutionary risings of workers to overthrow the system.

In 1906, Galleani published a slim and plain-looking pamphlet with the innocuous sounding title, *La salute è in voi.*[6] It was in fact a practical bomb-making manual. In 1919 and 1920, there was a series of bombings in the US for which Galleani's comrades were prime suspects. It was not suggested that Galleani himself was directly involved, he had been deported by that time but he was regularly held to be a main advocate of violence and branded as the prime instigator of terrorism. For example, in a widely syndicated article under the banner headline "On the Trail of the Anarchist Bandits," William J. Flynn (Director of the Bureau of Investigation, 1919–1921) accuses "the Galleani reds" of numerous bomb outrages and claims, "The United States government has conclusive evidence of the truth of what I say."[7] In fact the government had no such evidence, although the Bureau of Investigation had worked very hard to find some, even sending agents to Italy after Galleani had been deported, but they eventually returned empty handed.[8]

Terrorism is again at the center of political attention, and Galleani is being cast once more in the role of one of its main advocates. Articles, scholarly books, and even novels portraying him in this way have proliferated in recent years. Perhaps the most egregious instance is the current English-language *Wikipedia* page on Galleani.[9] It gives no sense of his ideas or of what he stood for, but it contains a lengthy catalog of bombings throughout the USA starting in 1914 and stretching all the way to 1932, most of which have no conceivable connection with Galleani.

One popular writer recently even called him the "Osama Bin Laden of his time."[10] That is absurd. In contrast to recent Islamic terrorism, the bombings of 1919–20 (whoever was responsible for them) were not indiscriminate explosions in crowds. For the most part they were carefully targeted at individuals: at big businessmen and bankers like John D. Rockefeller and J. P. Morgan; at politicians responsible for waging war on working people and anarchists, such as Attorney General Palmer, responsible for the "Palmer Raids" and mass deportations.

Having such a prominent supposed terrorist in the family has made me aware of how false the popular stereotype of the terrorist is, in my grandfather's case at least. He was not a cold-blooded and hate-filled fanatic; he was a warm and devoted father and family man, loved and revered by his wife and children. He was not a twisted and ruthless extremist; he was an immensely cultured, educated, and thoughtful person, trusted and admired by his comrades and friends. He was not a narrow and callous nihilist; he was a visionary thinker with a beautiful idea of how human society could be—an idea that still resonates today.

There is no doubt that he advocated violent means when he thought them necessary. I do not seek to defend him for this. However, if one is to understand him one must see that he lived through extremely violent times, and it was clear to many of the working people and immigrants for whom he spoke that the main perpetrators of this violence were the police and the state. What happened to Galleani happened also to thousands of anarchists and other radicals: they were attacked, arrested, and deported without any legal process. Some resisted and fought back. Galleani was at the forefront of that fight as this book shows by telling the story of his remarkable life and explaining the enduring significance of his ideas.

Sean Sayers
Canterbury
October 2017

PART ONE

Insurgent in Italy

CHAPTER 1

From Law Student to Labor Organizer

On November 3, 1880, Luigi Galleani, not yet twenty years old, was among many who rushed to Milan to welcome Giuseppe Garibaldi during the inauguration of a monument to the fallen of the Battle of Mentana. There, in 1867, his red-shirted volunteers were defeated by French and papal troops in an attempt to wrest Rome from Vatican control. Galleani's republican sentiments were deep, as was his admiration for Garibaldi, who was known as the "Hero of Two Worlds" because of his military successes both in Latin America and Italy. The struggle against religion, which he considered to be the main factor in human oppression, was and always remained central in his imagination. Mentana was one of the most frequently used among his countless pseud-onyms in his future publishing activity, and it was the name he chose in 1909 for one of his daughters.

However, the impression he formed upon meeting Garibaldi was ambivalent. When he was introduced to the Hero of Two Worlds, he was disappointed to find him old and physically weak, unable to speak, almost a prisoner of his strict coreligionists, far from the charismatic leader who had ignited the hopes of several generations.[1] Disheartened by this brief visit, Galleani returned to Vercelli (where he had been born on August 12, 1861) and to his parents' home. His father, Clemente, an elementary school teacher, and his mother, Olimpia Bonino, were both originally from Monferrato. The family was descended from a branch of a noble French line, the Gens de Galliana, who around 950 AD had first settled in Ventimiglia, then Genoa.[2] Luigi was the second-born and had two brothers and one sister. Camillo and Carolina (called Lina) became teachers like their father, while the first-born, Alfonso, became a railroad worker and an active socialist involved in the trade union, as well as president of their Turin consumer cooperative.

In Vercelli, nineteen-year-old Luigi was then in his final year of high school at the Lagrange Institute. He was not a particularly distinguished pupil, but got good grades in humanities subjects. He enjoyed history and had a particular interest in Latin and Greek. In later years he frequently used the classical world as a point of cultural reference, and the aesthetic of the ancient world is often evident in his writings and speeches.

Photo of a young Luigi Galleani

The young man returning to Vercelli to finish his last months of high school was bold and intolerant of the Catholic and monarchist patriarchal family model. It was not so much the small-town environment that limited him, but rather the closed and conservative ideas that characterized it. He was a great admirer of Giuseppe Mazzini, whose steadfast character he adored, and he felt closest to Mazzini's followers: Giovanni Bovio, Matteo Imbriani, and Felice Cavallotti. He criticized the idea of God and the power of the Church no less than emperors and autocrats. In spring 1881 he welcomed, although with some apprehension, the news of the assassination of Alexander II, Czar of Russia.

In the autumn of that year he enrolled in the law school of the university in nearby Turin, but did not completely abandon Vercelli, where for some time he frequented the Democratic Association and where he worked with the local newspaper *L'Operaio* [The Worker]. A few years later, in his columns, he supported the cause of the women workers in the button factories, a hundred of whom went on strike against piecework during the summer of 1883. The uprising lasted only three days, but even so it was an unusual event in the city, and it did not escape the attention of the military police that assistance was being given to the workers by a young student, whose elegant attire stood out amidst the workers' coveralls. Galleani was accused of being among the instigators of the strike. He was charged in court but acquitted.

That summer another event took place in which he played a prominent role. In June, several troops stationed in the city, who were decidedly tipsy, first insulted passers-by without an obvious reason and then assaulted them with sabers. Galleani criticized them in the pages of *L'Operaio*, calling them "cowardly," and when he met an official on a main street in the city he argued openly with him. The tension rose to the point that Galleani challenged the official to a duel. At dawn they met outside the city and crossed sabers in the presence of their respective doctors and four witnesses. The adversary was soon rendered powerless and was wounded and bleeding when the police caught them. Dueling was a crime and the young Galleani was condemned to banishment from Vercelli for three months and went to live in Turin.[3]

Pulling out a saber was nothing new for him, and this was not the first duel he had engaged in. Indeed one of his well-known friends, the future star of the Turin court, Carlo Felice Roggeri, later defined his youthful posture as that of a "musketeer."[4] Only a month earlier, on an evening in May, he had been involved in an animated political discussion with a fellow law student, Carlo Costa, and the two, with not a little wine in them, had decided to resolve the quarrel in their own way. In the contest that followed, again at the first light of dawn in a forest near the Sesia River, Galleani had come off worse and was left injured. In the subsequent trial he was absolved. It was only years later that he critically reconsidered dueling as a way to resolve quarrels or defend wounded honor, and it was only then that he finally freed himself from the "chivalrous" cultural heritage of his youth, an influence that reached other young people from good families.

We don't know how he supported himself economically during his university years. It is likely that a relative supported him, but he also seemed to be employed occasionally as the secretary of a local notable. According to a police report, however, he was "almost entirely kept [by] women of ill repute" with whom he led an "immoral life."[5] Tall, with square shoulders, a clear and vibrant voice, and eyes that burned intensely, no doubt he was popular with women.

When he was in Turin, in addition to the university, he frequented republican circles and the Caffè Progresso, where he met some of the "pioneers" of Italian internationalism, including Luigi Giraud, Alfredo Mari, and Guglielmo Castellano.[6] Castellano, who had close ties to Enrico Bignami, editor of *La Plebe* [The Plebeian] of Lodi, had established a library with socialist texts and literature, of which Galleani made full use. Turin's radical circles—according to reports—were rather quiet during this period, but in the spring of 1882 two events stirred things up. In April, a socialist newspaper, *Proximus Tuus*, began publication. The Latin *proximus tuus*—"your neighbor"—refers to the exploited, the oppressed. The next month, the impetus provided by that periodical led to the foundation of the *Circolo operaio torinese* [Turin Workers' Circle], local chapter of the POI (*Partito operaio italiano* [Italian Workers' Party]).[7] Established a few months earlier by the initiative of the *Circolo operaio milanese* [Milan Workers' Circle], the POI proudly asserted its class identity and aimed to bring together all manual workers, regardless of trade differences. 1882 was also the year that the first elections with extended suffrage were held. Until then, only 2 percent of the population could vote. Legislative reforms by the Depretis government then widened the electoral base to 7 percent with a total of over two million voters. This was a sufficient percentage for leftist groups—including the POI—to put forward their own candidates; and they managed to get two deputies elected to parliament, Andrea Costa representing the socialists and Antonio Maffi for the radicals.

It was during this period, as his political ideas moved from republicanism to socialism, that Galleani decided to embrace the workers' cause. He made this decision in the first half of the 1880s. This was a decade of general economic crisis and unemployment, during which farmers' struggles grew more rapidly than those of workers, first in the North, in the Padana Valley, then in the South, especially in Sicily. He began to collaborate with the Turin-based periodical *Avanti!* [Forward!]. His involvement in the cause of the proletariat became so all-consuming that he decided to abandon his studies, despite having passed all his exams and prepared his degree thesis. He would not be a lawyer but an insurgent, in close contact with the exploited workers. "Law"—he later wrote—"does not live in declarations. It is law only when one can exercise it."[8] Field hands; factory workers; domestic, day, and piece-rate workers; women, children, the unemployed: his organizing and propaganda work soon included all of these. It was pioneering at a time when the strike weapon was just beginning to be used and when wage earners, without distinction of sex or age, were forced to work fifteen or sixteen hours a day in oppressive and dangerous conditions, at inhuman speeds and often without enough food to eat. It was to these oppressed people at the bottom of society that he felt closest, and they inspired him to act. In 1884, during a cholera epidemic that broke out in several Italian provinces, he helped the ill in Vercelli, while other anarchists, socialists, and republicans went to Naples, the epicenter of the outbreak.

CHAPTER II

La Boje!

In 1885, Galleani edited two issues of *La Boje!*, a newspaper he published in Vercelli on his own and for which he himself outlined the program:

> To help, [by providing] our support [which is as] poor as it is free, all those revolts whose purpose is the moral and economic emancipation of the workers, to achieve the fraternity of democracies within humanity, [so that] they will hasten, with the destruction of international barriers, the creation of the noble utopia of all humanitarians, from Pisacane to Blanqui.[1]

Carlo Pisacane and Louis Auguste Blanqui were among the highest exemplars of revolutionary action in the nineteenth century, and they indicated the path Galleani was following. Pisacane played a leading role in the "other Italian unification," the unification of the socialists and the federalists. Blanqui was

La Boje!'s masthead

a communist ahead of his time in Paris, the capital of all progressive movements. They were two pole stars in the struggle for
freedom, two models for the young Luigi.

  La Boje! was the rallying cry of the first mass agrarian strike
in Italy. It took place in June 1884 in Polesine and spread in subsequent months, eventually involving forty thousand workers in
the countryside of the Po Valley. For a long time, peasant misery
had been seething, exacerbated by the flood of the Adige in 1882,
the poor harvest of 1883, and depressed rice and wheat prices due
to new competition from Russia. This was the cry that Galleani
figuratively brought from the countryside of Ferrara and Emilia
Romagna-Lombardy across the Po to the countryside around
Vercelli, where field workers were equally subjected to low wages,
unending workdays, and the endemic spread of disease.

  La Boje! only lasted for two issues, but it was an important
step in Galleani's development as an activist. He wrote almost
all of it using imaginative pseudonyms (Brutus, Gracco, *La
Sentinella* [the Sentinel]). From its pages, he unequivocally
commemorated the Paris Commune, which had been bloodily
crushed; and he supported the demands of citizen workers, particularly the bakers, explaining that the owners profited by rob-
bing the workers of their health and their lives. He clarified that
"rebellion, resistance, strikes are the only means of resolving
the eternal battle between capital and labor." He disputed with
La Sesia (the name of a river in Lombardy), a liberal newspaper
from Vercelli, and with the monarchist *Savoia* from Novara. He
argued for the necessity of atheism and materialism against religion, and urged the young bourgeoisie to action alongside the
exploited workers.[2]

  The newspaper printed a few symbolic lines of encouragement from Andrea Costa, at the most bitter moment of the conflict between the possibilism of the revolutionary socialist party
guided by Costa, and the anti-electoral intransigence of anarchist
socialism. *La Boje!* did not openly side with parliamentarianism,
but it certainly did not consider necessary the open anarchist
polemic of other libertarian newspapers against the legalitarian
strategy advocated by Costa, the deputy from Emilia Romagna.

Even in the Turin area, ever since the foundation of *Proximus Tuus*, the socialist camp had been riven by tension between those who favored legalitarian means and an anarchist minority who steadfastly opposed them. Between these two factions, however, there was a majority who concentrated on practical social struggles and, as was the case in many other Italian contexts, strove for united action and possible coexistence between the parties.

The latter was the aim of *La Boje!* and then of *La Questione Sociale* [The Social Question] of Turin, a periodical of the local Socialist League, which was published between March 1885 and February 1886 and with which Galleani collaborated. One of the tasks he set out to accomplish, also thanks to the increasingly important role he played in the League and in the newspaper, was to smooth over these differences and shape as cohesive an organization as possible, one that would be capable of spreading fruitful propaganda and supporting struggles in the workplace, and taking fundamental steps toward the inevitable future social revolution.

La Questione Sociale sold texts by Filippo Turati, Carlo Cafiero, Errico Malatesta, and Peter Kropotkin, and published the latter's *Words of a Rebel* in installments. It circulated even outside of Piedmont and connected French socialists in their campaign against the erection of a monument in Paris to honor Napoleon. It was not hostile to Andrea Costa; rather it advertised Costa's regional lecture tour in 1885, and yet it also devoted a lot of space to anarchist positions and referred to Louise Michel and Elisée Reclus as model libertarian activists. In this paper, Galleani wrote both theoretical articles—repeating his anti-religious propaganda and arguments for the emancipating role of science— as well as pieces urging rebellion, in which he denounced the inhuman conditions that field workers were forced to endure in the Piedmont countryside.

Decimated by pellagra, weakened physically, suffering pain and blurred vision, thousands of these wretched workers dragged themselves to work in the fields, most of the time surviving on polenta, which had insufficient protein and vitamins.

Pellagra attacks only those who cultivate the earth and prin-
cipally the most wretched among them, meaning those
who live in the most squalid poverty and eat only vegetables, rye bread that has not been well cooked, or bread
made from rice or rotten corn, and who quench their thirst
with muddy water and acidic, weak wine [...]. Unlike cholera, which does not differentiate between rich and poor,
pellagra attacks only the latter; it is the privilege of the
lowest.[3]

He also reported on the grievances of the women workers in
the six button factories in Vercelli. As mentioned, two years earlier they had initiated a strike that ended with a trial against them
and arbitration on pay rates. The situation had not improved
much. Paid by the piece, they were unable to earn enough to live,
as the factory owners preferred to save on lighting and have them
work less, especially in the winter. Galleani urged them to rebel
and to assert their class autonomy, resolving the contradiction
by which the trade unions they belonged to included their own
bosses as honorary members.[4]

He also sent reports from other parts of Piedmont, such
as Casale Monferrato, where he denounced the inauspicious
obscurantism of the Catholic newspapers.[5] He typically roamed
far and wide through Piedmont, particularly in the provinces
of Vercelli, Biella, and Turin. More than his written words, his
physical presence played an increasingly incisive role in organizing the labor force. He delivered many lectures. His "broad
culture," "easy and elegant words," and "strong and resonant
voice," the police reported, enabled him to "worm his way into
the minds of the workers."[6] His activity organizing farmers and
workers was intended to radicalize and spread the economic
pleas of the proletariat and strengthen class solidarity between
different trades. He thus found himself in agreement with the
social positions of the workerists: pushing labor associations to
adopt the strategy of resistance alongside traditional mutualism
and to organize local federations of all revolutionary workers to
nurture the principle of workers' autonomy, according to which

the emancipation of the workers must be accomplished by the workers themselves.

At the same time, from the mid-1880s, he developed an understanding of anarchism. Thus, within the POI, he became the spokesperson for a minority trend opposed to electoral participation: a strategy that was used several times by the party at both a national and local level. Committed to these convictions, he nevertheless continued to act in favor of unity and opposed the most intransigent libertarians, who were jealously [or fiercely] protective of their own autonomy. His interest lay in concrete organizing work for social struggles, based more on class identity than on standard political positions or specific ideological tendencies. These views provided the basis for establishing the Circolo socialista Difesa del lavoro e della Lega dei lavoratori [Socialist Workers' League and Labor Defense Circle] of Vercelli in 1886, which he promoted. This occurred in parallel with developments in Turin where, that same year, the Lega mista dei figli del lavoro [Mixed League of the Children of Labor] was formed. Both groups brought together workers from different trades.

In the mid-1880s, Turin was a city with 250,000 inhabitants, fifty thousand of whom were workers (and one-fifth of these were metalworkers and mechanics). They suffered the effects of several bank failures. Economic crisis and unemployment affected thousands of wage earners, especially metalworkers and construction workers. During this period, a number of workers undertook the direct action propagandized by anarchists and workerists. In spring 1886, a thousand bricklayers played a leading role in an uprising that blocked work sites that, after the intervention of the forces of law and order, became an urban revolt. They managed to win more "human" working hours than before (eleven hours in the summer and nine in the winter) and wages that were a little higher. Their paper, which supported the uprising, was *Il Muratore* [The Bricklayer]. It was edited by the worker Pietro Fassio, with whom Galleani was in close contact.

CHAPTER III

The Redemption of Labor

The redemption of labor
for its toiling children shall be;
either to live from work
or to die fighting![1]

Thus goes "Il canto dei lavoratori" [Hymn of the Workers], written by Turati in March 1886 for the inauguration of the banner of the Lega dei figli del lavoro [League of the Children of Labor] of Milan.[2]

The POI, which adopted it as a hymn, was a growing organization in several parts of Northern Italy. In Piedmont, it could count on the Lega mista dei figli del lavoro in Turin, a strong chapter in Alessandria (which brought together several profession-specific chapters and one mixed chapter), and others in Casale Monferrato, Novara, Intra, Vercelli, Biella, and Bra.[3]

In summer 1886, the government responded by ordering its dissolution, arresting its leaders and suppressing the POI's publication, *Il Fascio Operaio* [The Worker's Fasces]. However this was not the end for the POI—only a setback. The next year a reorganization began in which Galleani played an active role, and that resulted in two congresses. In the first, in Pavia on September 18–19, 1887, he participated as a delegate of the Lega dei lavoratori [Workers' League] of Vercelli; but it was during the second congress, which took place a year later in Bologna, that his participation had a major impact. He was the delegate of *La Nuova Gazzetta Operaia* [The New Worker's Gazette] of Turin, an "independent and combative periodical" closely linked to the party. *La Nuova Gazzetta Operaia*, like the previous *Gazzetta Operaia*, brought together the usual themes of workerism, such as class

struggle and strikes, with specifically anarchist topics, abstentionism above all. It clearly revealed the approach of Galleani,
who could now be defined as a "workerist anarchist" or an "anarchist workerist."

Leading socialist figures were among the delegates at the
congress, including Costantino Lazzari, Giuseppe Croce, Alfredo
Casati, Osvaldo Pais, and Andrea Costa. Galleani proposed a
motion that called for the exclusion, for reasons of expediency,
of the press from the congress, with the exception of *La Nuova
Gazzetta Operaia* and *La Questione Sociale* of Florence, a motion
that was also represented by Galleani.[4] His motion was accepted,
unlike another, much more important motion for which he also
served as a spokesperson. This was intended to formalize opposition to participation in elections at any level. This motion was not
supported and he failed to get the party to agree to an abstentionist position. Nevertheless he avoided rifts or splits, respecting the
mandate of the groups and the anarchist newspapers of which he
was the delegate, and he thus again emphasized the need for harmony between different currents. This was a shared strategy that
was contested by other anarchist groups that continued to show
explicit mistrust of the POI. In addition to its possibilism in the
electoral field, they reproached it for the way it confined its support
to working-class struggles, instead of widening the front to include
the entire mass of the exploited, the "disaffected from all classes."[5]

Galleani's prestige was already such that he was able to
address these tensions fearlessly. He was the leading anarchist in
Piedmont and Liguria, and he did not shrink from intervening in
Lombardy. After returning from the congress, his strategy, agreed
upon with his closest comrades, remained clear: to strengthen the
unity of aims and actions between labor associations beyond individual currents, to participate actively in economic struggles, and
then to gamble this organized force on the path toward insurrection. He carried this out by means of frenetic activity as a speaker
and promoter of rebellion, which kept him constantly occupied.

Between 1887 and 1889, he embarked upon propa-
ganda tours in the cities and provinces of Biella, Vercelli, Asti,
Alessandria, and Turin, where he led a number of strikes. In

1888, he again organized protests of button makers in Vercelli as well as of local cotton workers; and in May that year, he led a fourteen-day strike in Turin by mechanics employed as file cutters. He also played an active role in the uprising of sand extractors. Turin was an increasingly working-class city with a concentration of metal industries and a vast textiles industry that made extensive use of nighttime labor and employed a majority of women and children. Pressured by harsh discipline, they were forced to work eleven to fourteen hours per day in unhealthy surroundings, where dust from the cotton and the dyes caused many cases of tuberculosis. The use of piece-work was common, with payment per meter. Periods of forced unemployment, even for several months, were frequent.[6] From spring until the early summer of 1889, the workers organized a number of strikes and demonstrations of unprecedented intensity against these conditions. Galleani led them and urged them on, radicalizing them and attempting to widen their sphere of action.

He was also behind the strike of leather goods workers that began on April 5 and set off a domino effect. The uprising soon extended to women textile workers and especially cotton workers, who were mostly young or very young. Starting in early June, two thousand cotton workers from both large and small plants—who looked upon Galleani as an important point of reference since he was a delegate of the Turin Regional Federation of the POI and editor of the *La Nuova Gazzetta Operaia*—came out on strike and poured into the streets. Galleani actively worked to further widen the strike to other sectors, which then happened. Other trades joined in, including again the mechanics who had protested the year before, as well as porters and bakers, making a total of several thousand workers. It was a very tense time. The street demonstrations were obstructed by the forces of order, including the cavalry, and arrests began in mid-June that finally defeated the protests. Some of the most prominent insurgents were detained, and Galleani, already a hero of the workers, was forced to leave the city.[7]

His departure meant the end of publication for *La Nuova Gazzetta Operaia* and deprived the anarchist movement of its main representative in the northeast, as well as its main connection with the POI. This also resulted in the Piedmont POI, without Galleani, strengthening its collaboration with democrats and radicals, and cooling its relations with libertarian groups.

But what was most significant was that, starting from this time, Galleani reconsidered a good part of his previous strategy of "entryism" in labor organizations and constructive intervention in the congresses of the POI. He began to make it a priority to strengthen collaboration between activists and specific anarchist groups in order to make abstentionist and revolutionary propaganda more effective among workers. Moreover, he began to develop a specific critique of the practices of formal organizations, primarily the congresses, whether workerist or socialist, and instead concentrated on practical organization of the truly revolutionary minorities who, in his opinion, could light the fuse and ignite the anger of the exploited.

Thus one can see the vision that would come to characterize his subsequent strategy for action. He did not yet impartially praise all acts of rebellion against the established order, individual or collective, which would later become part of his revolutionary outlook; but this was, as we shall see, a small matter. Between 1889 and 1890, Galleani was already close to positions that would later be called, in a way that created misunderstandings, "anti-organizational." We will return to this central issue later.

CHAPTER IV

From *Il Nuovo Combattiamo!* to *L'Attaque*

Returning temporarily to Vercelli in the summer of 1889, Galleani increasingly focused his theater of action in Liguria. From the time it was created in August 1888, he collaborated with *Il Nuovo Combattiamo!* [The New Let's Fight!] of Sampierdarena, the work of the young Eugenio Pellaco, typesetter and member of the local Circolo di studi sociali [Social Studies Circle]. The newspaper played an important role in connecting Ligurian and Piedmontese labor associations and circles, and it provided ideological clarity for anti-legalitarian and abstentionist currents, particularly against the republicans. In this it closely followed the policies of the Bakuninist International and openly refused political methods, seeing them as the practices of governments and contrary to the interests of workers. The weekly benefited from frequent contributions from Francesco Saverio Merlino. It published articles by Kropotkin, Elisée and Elie Reclus, Giovanni Rossi, Mikhail Bakunin, and Johann Most. It was also in contact with several Italian and French anarchist groups in Rome, Forlì, Livorno, Pisa, Paris, and elsewhere.[1]

Galleani collaborated with the newspaper as a correspondent from Vercelli, but he actually wrote very little. His main activity was lecturing and organizing. He and Pellaco had a close relationship built on trust and mutual support. Pellaco repeatedly went to Vercelli to make propaganda, while Galleani held meetings in the theaters of several Ligurian cities. His territorial range now also began to include Lombardy.

In 1889, he was the leading figure in a debate with legalitarian socialists at the Teatro Dal Verme of Milan, which left a profound impression on all listeners, friends and adversaries alike.[2]

At this time, the gap between socialists and anarchists was further widening, not only in Italy but also, and especially, across Europe. In September of that year there was an international anarchist congress in Paris intended as a response to two previous socialist congresses. One of these was a Marxist meeting, from which Merlino had been expelled, and that led to the establishment of the Second International. The other was a meeting of so-called "possibilists," mainly moderates, promoted by Paul Brousse, a former anarchist who had become one of the leading French socialists. The anarchist congress in Paris reasserted the intransigent and revolutionary character of socialism, in opposition to the social-democratic reformism of the two other kinds of socialism just mentioned, and marked a profound break with the latter.[3]

Back in Italy, the conflict within the labor movement was further deepened by the fact that representatives of democratic, socialist, and workerist views were increasingly deciding to participate in elections. This happened, for example, in the Turin municipal elections of autumn 1889 that were held under the new municipal and provincial law of December 30, 1888, which extended the right to vote to all male citizens aged twenty-one and older, who were able to read and write and who paid a minimum of five lira in municipal taxes.

Galleani no longer believed that an alliance with any of these forces was achievable. He continued to propagandize an abstentionist and insurrectionary position. In his eyes, criticism of the decline of socialism, which had turned to parliamentarianism, was corroborated by the political trajectory of European prime ministers such as Francesco Crispi, Neville Chamberlain, Léon Gambetta, and Georges Clemenceau, all former democrats who became prominent representatives of the ruling classes. This showed that the slippery slope of power led inevitably to betraying one's principles and joining the enemy camp.

This clear vision resonated powerfully with the exploited. Galleani's skills as an orator became a fundamental resource of the anarchist movement. His strong and clear voice, his compelling reasoning enhanced by a broad culture, and his polished eloquence brought the libertarian ideal to life.[4] The authorities were well aware of this. One of his lectures, which should have been held in September 1889 at the Ristori Theater in Sampierdarena, was prohibited by the police, a sign that the forces of order were clamping down on his activities.

Thus, in November 1889, just as voters were going to the ballot box, he was served with an arrest warrant by the investigating magistrate of Turin and was obliged to cross the border into France and spend several weeks in Nice.[5] There, just a few months earlier, Errico Malatesta had started a new newspaper, *L'Associazione* [The Association]. Its release had been advertised by *Il Nuovo Combattiamo!*, a sign of the close contact between the two periodicals. The strategy of *L'Associazione* agreed with Galleani's ideas and was consistent with his actions. He/it supported popular demands, even if partisan, in order to raise them to a revolutionary level through a form of organization that could reconcile the free initiatives of groups with a necessary unity in action. For this "reconciliation" to be possible, revolutionaries needed clear thinking and mutual coordination, supporting one another with strong group solidarity.

Malatesta's presence in Nice was only fleeting. He was immediately forced to take refuge in London to escape the police, and the two did not manage to meet. In early 1890, Galleani also left Nice, first going to Lyon, then to Chaumant in Haute-Marne, and then, after some further stops, to Paris. He earned a living through the most varied and humble trades. He got jobs as a porter, a woodcutter, even a barber. Finally in Paris, he worked in advertising and then as a secretary to Ettore Molinari, a chemist and political comrade.[6]

In Paris, there was a significant colony of Italian-speaking activists with whom Galleani was in close contact. They included Francesco Merlino, Paolo Schicchi, Galileo Palla, Augusto Norsa, and Amilcare Cipriani, a colonel of the Paris Commune who had moved to Paris in summer 1888 after a long period in prison.[7] March 1890 saw the arrival of Costa, from whom Galleani felt distant, despite Cipriani's unsuccessful attempts at mediation between the two. Long gone were the times when Galleani published one of Costa's letters in *La Boje!*

Also living in Paris was Vittorio Pini. He was facing trial for theft and attempted homicide. In court, after openly asserting the right of the weak to expropriate from the rich, he was condemned to twenty years of forced labor in Cajenna, where he was a prisoner with another supporter of expropriation, Clément Duval.[8] Both were activists who came to command Galleani's admiration. He wrote about them several times in subsequent years, and translated Duval's *Memorie Autobiografiche* [*Outrage: An Anarchist Memoir of the Penal Colony*]. This was published in two volumes in 1929 and became an essential work for Italian anarchists who had immigrated to the United States.

In Paris, Galleani frequented the cosmopolitan group that, since June 1888, had edited the periodical *L'Attaque. Organe socialiste révolutionnaire* [Attack: Revolutionary Socialist Organ] and then, from August 3, 1889, the *Organe hebdomadaire anarchiste* [Weekly Anarchist Organ]. This newspaper gave new blood to the subversive movement, printing courageous and open-minded articles that actively campaigned for abstentionism, inciting people toward a general strike and open insurrection, spreading and arguing for propaganda of the deed.

The newspaper received the encouragement of Elisée Reclus, and its collaborators included Cipriani, Louise Michel, and Jules Guesde. Among the editors were Lucien Weil, Sébastien Faure, Ernest Gegout, and Charles Malato, with whom Galleani kept in very close contact. Malato's writing in particular was given increasing prominence. The task Malato set his sights on— whether through the book-length manifesto *Philosophie de l'anarchie* [*Philosophy of Anarchy* (first edition 1888)], or through articles in *L'Attaque*—was to demonstrate to opponents that libertarians were not violent people with no objective, but had very clear ideals. These ideals, to which Galleani dedicated all of his energy, were explained as follows: free association between individuals and groups replacing the hierarchy of rulers; voluntary agreements instead of laws; universal well being and equality of roles in place of class hegemony; and a higher ethics in conformity with the natural order instead of the current viciously hypocritical morality. These were the components of anarchism. Libertarian activists were well aware that in all probability the revolution to come would not be anarchist, in the sense that it would not establish anarchy in the narrow sense, however it was necessary to aim for this as an antidote to social paralysis, even if only to make partial gains.[9]

Galleani was also among the members of an international circle—or group—of anarchist students, together with Merlino, Schicchi, and the Romanian Peraskiev Stojanov. The group published two manifestos written in several languages, and several thousand copies were distributed in Italy, France, and Switzerland. These manifestos branded class division, the wage system, and the representative system as obsolete. One manifesto was addressed to students and called upon them to do as the Russians had done and abandon their own narrow interests and side with the proletariat. It sought to inspire insurrection yet prevent it from creating tyranny, since its aim was the emancipation of the entire human race and not just of a single class. The other manifesto was addressed to soldiers to prepare them, when there was an insurrection, to burn barracks, banks, and government offices, to kill the agents of the state, and to give arms to the people.[10]

It is difficult to follow this phase of Galleani's life and activities in precise detail. In early 1890, he was arrested and locked up in the Mazas prison in Paris, just when the international anarchist movement was preparing for a May Day strike, which was seen by the Parisian activists as a favorable time to start a movement on a national scale. Just as *L'Attaque* announced a special ad hoc issue, of which one hundred thousand copies were to be printed, it had to interrupt publication. In April—when Malatesta was heading for the French capital—the police arrested Jean Grave, Paul Reclus, Merlino, and Malato, dealing a heavy blow to the movement. The Italian-language activists nevertheless urged the workers to arm themselves, take to the streets, and force the strike with violence, so as to win "and win forever."[11] But they succeeded in persuading only a very few, whose activities that day were limited to a few skirmishes and the seizure of a few shops.

Galleani was held in prison for four months without a trial, and finally released thanks to intervention by the socialist

Alexandre Millerand and the mediation of Cipriani. These two were linked by a certain affinity of ideas, as they were promoters of a political project that was under discussion for a Union of Latin Peoples against the feared danger of war between France and Italy. However, Galleani was forced to leave France. He was expelled with Luxembourg as his mandatory destination. But he decided instead to go via Switzerland.

CHAPTER V

With Reclus on Lake Geneva

He thus arrived in Geneva, which was a place of refuge for many former Communards. There he got settled by working as a laborer building a railroad line and formed friendships with François Dumartheray and Georges Herzig—both activists in the Jura Federation and founders, with Peter Kropotkin, of the newspaper *Le Révolté* [The Revolt] (Geneva, 1879)—and with Jacques Gross.

Gross was French by birth, but a long-time resident of Switzerland. He lived first in Boncourt, in Jura—where he worked as a salesperson for the Burrus tobacco factory—and then in Geneva. He became a friend without equal for Galleani. He was already a member of the Jura-based Federation of the International and an important channel for activists of different nationalities. He was in close contact with Max Nettlau, Elisée Reclus, and Kropotkin. Gross's activity showed the importance of solidarity as the main means of anarchist organization. He contributed greatly to sustaining the movement and meeting its needs. He supported comrades in prison and those who had been expelled from their own countries, including Galleani, who benefited from Gross's help over the years. Moreover, Gross was a bibliophile. He possessed "one of the most precious libraries of the anarchist movement" and played an important role in introducing Galleani to many political, scientific, and literary works.[1] Galleani was commissioned—for pay—to translate some of these, including *La morale anarchiste* [*Anarchist Morality*] by Peter Kropotkin and *Le suffrage universel et le problème de la souveraineté du peuple* [*Universal Suffrage and the Problem of the People's Sovereignty*] by Paul Brousse, from French to Italian, something that guaranteed him a steady salary.[2]

Moreover, Gross introduced Galleani to Elisée and Elie Reclus, who, during the summer of 1890, hosted him on the shores of Lake Geneva. The country house of the Reclus brothers was in fact a refuge for those persecuted by the police across half of Europe, not least of whom were a few Russian nihilists. Among others, here Galleani again met Stojanov, with whom he would collaborate closely during the early 1890s. He also met the Armenian Alexander Atabekian, born in 1868 in Shusha, in present-day Azerbaijan, who was then studying medicine in Geneva. During these years, Atabekian became an important propagandist in Russian and Armenian.

Galleani came to appreciate the deep knowledge, vast culture, and great humanity of Elisée Reclus, and he developed a great admiration for him. Thus he wrote upon the death of Elisée in 1905: "In Clarens, living with him for month after month, in the intimate fraternity of work, of ideals, of common hopes, we were able to appreciate his marvelous aptitude for work, his unsurpassed goodness, his heroic boldness, his infinite modesty."[3]

The respect between the two was mutual. Elisée Reclus offered Galleani the job of writing part of the monumental geographic research project that he was working on, *Nouvelle géographie universelle* [*Universal Geography*], which Hachette published in nineteen volumes in Paris between 1887 and 1894. Galleani accepted and, although his name did not appear among the work's official authors, he contributed to volume XVII, dedicated to Central America and environs, and he compiled statistics on Guatemala. Leafing through this book, which is adorned with numerous maps, some drawn by Paul Reclus, enables one to appreciate the solid Enlightenment-era foundation that guided its desire for the scientific investigation of the earth and of humanity. Countries and territories such as the West Indies; Mexico; Guatemala; Honduras; El Salvador; Nicaragua; Costa Rica; the Strait of Panama; Cuba; Jamaica; Santo Domingo; Port au Prince, Haiti; Puerto Rico; Guadalupe; Martinique; and Dominica are discussed, as well as everything, or almost everything, that concerns them: the land, its surface area, population density, its orography, rivers, subterranean rivers, seas and their depths, volcanoes, flora, fauna, climate; and even the populations (indigenous as well as colonial), their languages and history, demographics, monuments, government and administration, church and religion, property ownership, social conditions, the constitution, borders, trade, imports and exports, debt, methods of communication, telegraph lines, industries, and so on.

In 1890, Elisée Reclus was sixty years old and had had uncommon life experiences. Raised in a Protestant environment, he was a pupil of the geographer Charles Ritter at the University of Berlin. Since his youth he had traveled far and wide across Europe and the Americas and developed an anarchist understanding of the world, in which freedom was seen as a means of ensuring love, in the sense of the most complete solidarity between people. He published many scholarly articles in geography journals and several books, which made him well known in the academic world, including *La terre: descriptions des phénomènes de la vie du globe* [*The Earth: A Descriptive History of the Phenomena of the Life of the Globe*].

In 1871, the Commune was proclaimed in Paris, and Reclus played an active role in it. Upon its fall he was first locked up in prison, then put on trial and sentenced to deportation to New Caledonia, but his prestige as a scientist caused his punishment to be commuted to ten years in exile. Thus he ended up in Switzerland, where he developed ties with Bakunin and Kropotkin and became a leading activist in the International. Upon Bakunin's death in 1876 in Berne, Reclus delivered the funeral oration in his honor.

From his "refuge" in Clarens he began work on the *Nouvelle Géographie*, after which followed his final work, *L'homme et la terre* [*The Earth and Its Inhabitants*], 3,500 pages long. For Galleani, the association with Reclus marked a profoundly important stage in his development, and many Reclusian ideas recur in his writings and in his lectures. Reclus's philosophy was a philosophy of progress, in which violent revolutions perform the essential task of accelerating the evolutionary process already under way.

Elie Reclus (left) and Elisée Reclus (right)

The task of anarchists was to contribute to triggering these revolutions. This was why we see Reclus in active roles within the International from the time of its creation. He fervently supported general strikes, and he defended acts of rebellion, even if they involved violence, as the inevitable results of an unfair and hierarchical system. In an 1889 article, Reclus wrote:

> Against injustice we call for revolution. But justice is only a word, they tell us. What exists is the right of force! Well, even if that is true, we are no less revolutionaries because of it. Of these two propositions, one must be true: either justice is the human ideal in which case we demand it for all; or it is only force that governs society and therefore we will use force against our enemies. Either freedom of equals, or the law of retaliation.[4]

At the same time he was aware of the importance of the issue of education based on anti-authoritarian principles, a current of thought that contributed to, and that would later be fully developed by the Modern Schools of Francisco Ferrer y Guardia.

Deeply influenced by the Enlightenment, his trust in science and technology was unbounded, as it was in reason. "Human progress," he wrote, "essentially consists of finding the totality of interests and desires common to all people: it merges with solidarity."[5] Fulfillment for all men was anarchy. This existed not only in a future society based on free cooperation between people, it was manifest whenever human beings act in a libertarian and mutually supportive way. Thus, in the preface to Kropotkin's *La conquête du pain* [*The Conquest of Bread*], another text central to Galleani's development, Reclus wrote:

> Anarchist society has already for some time been going through a phase of rapid development. [Anarchist society] exists wherever free thought breaks the chains of dogma, wherever the genius of the researcher ignores the old formulas, wherever the human will manifests itself in independent action, wherever sincere men, rebelling against imposed discipline, spontaneously come together to teach one another mutually and to reconquer together, without masters, their lives and whatever is needed to fully satisfy their own needs. All this is anarchy.[6]

Reclus was a major reference point for geographers and a fundamental hub in the international anarchist network during the last three decades of the nineteenth century. He was in contact with dozens of scientists and activists all around the world. In this way, too, he provided a great source of enrichment and knowledge for Galleani.[7]

CHAPTER VI

Come, oh May

Luigi Galleani left Clarens in October 1890 to travel to Geneva. There, on November 11, on the city walls, a manifesto appeared in French, Italian, and Spanish in memory of the "martyrs of Chicago," printed in the Kuzman print shop. This print shop was a meeting place for activists living in Geneva, and was also frequented by Galleani. Its activity provides a revealing insight into the transnational character of the anarchist movement, which deserves a digression.

In the Kuzman print shop, in the following years and until the middle of the decade, Paraskev Stojanov printed, among other titles, Romanian translations of Malatesta's *Between Peasants* and *Vote What For?* (1891). Alexander Atabekian printed an Armenian translation of *Between Peasants* with his own introduction (1893), and Russian and Armenian versions of writings by Kropotkin, of whom he was a great admirer, as well as of Bakunin, Elisée Reclus, and Jean Grave.[1] Both Stojanov and Atabekian became leading figures of international anarchism.

As well as being the Bulgarian publisher of anarchist classics, Stojanov was an organizer of the Bulgarian libertarian movement and, in 1919, he was among the founders of the Faculty of Medicine of Sofia. He held its first chair of surgery and was later appointed director of the local university hospital. Atabekian played an active part in Armenian revolutionary movements against the Ottoman Empire. He made propaganda based on these texts, first among Armenian immigrants in Europe, and then in the Caucasus, Turkey, and Bulgaria. In 1895, he fiercely denounced the massacres of Armenians by the Turks and the acquiescence of the European states. From the end of the century, he settled in Iran and worked as a doctor. When the Russian Revolution broke out in 1917, he moved to Moscow where he set up a new print shop. He was very close to Kropotkin. He tended to him on his deathbed in January 1921 and helped to organize his funeral, which was the last public libertarian demonstration in Russia before the descent of totalitarian darkness.[2]

No wonder, then, that these anarchists of various nationalities in Switzerland intended to commemorate their comrades killed three years before on the other side of the Atlantic Ocean. On November 11, 1887, a number of anarchists from Chicago had been hanged following the so-called Haymarket affair. In that city, a workers' demonstration for the eight-hour-day had been broken up by the police, in reaction to which some unknown person had thrown a bomb at the police, killing one. Eight libertarian activists had been accused of this act: two of them were condemned to life in prison, one to fifteen years of imprisonment, five to capital punishment. On November 10, one of the five, Louis Lingg, took his own life. The other four— August Spies, Albert Parsons, Adolph Fischer, and George Engel—were hanged the next day. From that moment on, remembering those activists became a moral duty for libertarians around the world.[3]

The reader will not be surprised that Galleani was behind the manifesto commemorating the "Chicago martyrs" that appeared in Geneva on November 11. He was not alone. Several of his comrades, who had been expelled by police across Europe and then found refuge in Switzerland, helped him. Among them were two with whom he had had close ties in Paris: Lucien Weil and Stojanov. Also involved were Gennaro Petraroja, Paul Bernard, and Giuseppe Hiskia Rovigo (alias Morelli). At least that is what the Swiss authorities thought. The authorities were also convinced that the manifesto propagandized "the violent overthrow of the social order indicating that murder and other crimes or evils are suitable methods of reaching this goal." They ordered the expulsion of all its authors.[4]

Deported to Italy in December, Galleani was immediately arrested in Como "for issues to be governed by Italian law,"

according to *La Gazette de Lausanne* [The Lausanne Gazette]. He
was incarcerated in the city's prison, where he remained for one
month before being released under an amnesty.[5] In the meanwhile, between 1889 and 1890, the Italian government published
a new consolidated act on public security and a new penal code.
The act on public security sanctioned the principle that meetings or public gatherings could be dissolved in the event of "seditious proclamations or demonstrations" that constituted "crimes
against the powers of the State or against the heads of foreign
governments and their representatives." It thus further restricted
the room for political opponents, who were often constrained to
secrecy under threat of mandatory repatriation to their municipal-
ities of origin, receiving an official warning, and internal exile—
measures directly imposed by police commissioners and mayors.
The new Zanardelli code, though it abolished the death penalty,
was consonant with the Albertine statute in many respects, including limitation of the right of association. It prohibited armed associations, criminal conspiracy, and associations intended to create
political conspiracies, charges that were used extensively against
anarchists. Strikes were permitted if they remained peaceful, but
became a crime if elements of violence or threats were observed in
them, which resulted in a severe limitation on the right to strike.

As soon as he was released from prison, Galleani again
crossed the border from Italy to Switzerland—although the
expulsion order hung over him—to participate in the congress
establishing the Revolutionary Anarchist-Socialist Party, held
in Capolago in the Ticino Canton, from January 4–6, 1891. He
arrived when the meeting was almost over, but still in time to
make practical arrangements with other activists and to sign the
manifesto of the "Anarchists Abroad to Italian Workers," urging
direct action against parliamentarianism.

The congress formulated an important program and made
relevant strategic decisions. Some of the points discussed were
summarized and explained most clearly by Malatesta in a pamphlet entitled "La politica parlamentare nel movimento socialista"
["Parliamentary Politics in the Socialist Movement"], published
by *L'Associazione*'s print shop in London in October 1890.

In this brief text, Malatesta attacked universal suffrage in no uncertain terms, for granting parliamentarism supposed popular consent, and in doing so corrupting a segment of socialism and turning it bourgeois. This was not an easy position to advocate at a time when universal suffrage was generally seen as an undeniable political and social advance. Yet according to Malatesta, in countries where universal suffrage had been introduced, the conditions of workers were the same as in countries without it. This was because the vote was never actually free due to social and economic constraints and the threats and pandering of bosses and government agents. It was granted by the government only to deceive the voters into believing that they were free. In the same way, he argued clearly, it was false to claim that parliamentarism was good for purposes of propaganda, as the reformists did. This strategy was deeply damaging to the objective of human emancipation. Those who accepted parliamentarianism in fact ceased to be socialists: "already in truth such socialism is no longer anarchist socialism, which by its very nature is anti-parliamentary and revolutionary."[6] Once this principle was accepted, anarchists proposed their own alternative. The purpose of the library of *L'Associazione*, as we read in *La politica parlamentare nel movimento socialista*, was in fact:

> To advocate the creation of an international socialist-anarchist-revolutionary party—through organization by free agreement—with a program for action shared by all those who want violent revolution to defeat governments, dispossess owners, make all existing wealth available to everyone, and oppose the re-creation of authority and individual ownership [...]. Revolution, violent action of the masses, roused and moved by a conscious minority [...] is only a method for making progress, a violent and quick way, which occurs, spontaneously or provoked, when needs and ideas produced from a previous development can no longer be satisfied.[7]

Only this method could resolve the social question and establish the conditions for socialism. According to the "Capolago

Manifesto," it involved "The principle of struggle according to which the individualistic principle, by which every man seeks his own advantage without concern for others, thus exploiting and oppressing others, is replaced as a rule for human relationships by the principle of solidarity, according to which the good of each is the good of all, and the good of all is the good of each."[8]

We have here three ideas that form the basis of Galleani's actions, then and in the future. Uncompromising opposition to the socialist parliamentary neo-oligarchy that was guilty of betraying insurrectionary theory, an opposition by which the anarchists—as Malatesta had written in the aforementioned pamphlet—"reject delegation of power and appeal to free and direct action by all."[9] Revolution, understood as a conscious acceleration of the process of evolution. And anarchy as the triumph of the principle of solidarity and free cooperation among all men. This theme is thoroughly theorized in another work by Malatesta, *Anarchy*, also issued as a pamphlet during these years, which also maintained that there cannot be liberty without equality, meaning the satisfaction of everyone's material needs.[10]

This is why Galleani, at this time, was a champion of the newborn party, which he understood as a working union between activist groups opposed to legalitarianism and dedicated to insurrectionary uprisings. These were to be as well coordinated as possible, uncompromising toward reformists but willing to act with whomever accepted violent methods of social transformation. The party was to be an autonomous organization, based on regional federations, with technical coordination committees in various regions.

Among the things decided in Capolago was that Galleani would make propaganda tours in Northern and Central Italy in order to prepare the workers morally and materially, continuing the work he had been doing in the previous years. It was also agreed that the date of the first of May would be considered a revolutionary occasion to which the movement would dedicate all of its energy and about which it would not compromise. In their reports, the police emphasized Galleani's charisma and described him a leader in every respect: "he is always the mind that thinks, that advises, that organizes; his comrades are his limbs."[11] Indeed he dedicated himself furiously to propaganda, now with more focus on the unemployed in Liguria, Piedmont, and Lombardy. His presence was also requested in Tuscany, but the economic resources of the groups there were scarce, and for this reason, together with constant police surveillance, he had to limit his range of activity.

Nevertheless Galleani's activism was frenetic, even though only a few traces of it have been preserved in the archives. On February 18–19, 1891, he gave two lectures in Alessandria, in a venue on Via Verona. To circumvent the law, which expressly prohibited public meetings considered subversive, the organizers described the meeting as private. But it was not private: a packed crowd listened to him speak on the theme "Who we are and what we want." He urged the poor to expropriate the bourgeoisie and branded the socialists as mere theorists and cowards. These were not words only. The authorities considered him among the leading figures of the continuous "subversive uprising" that was then sweeping through the center of Piedmont.

It remained Galleani's priority to stay connected to Ligurian regions as well, so that the next day we find him in Genoa, where two hundred workers and unemployed people, including women and children, gathered to listen to his new lecture in the Lega della Resistenza hall. The police burst in and charged him under article 247 of the Zanardelli penal code.[12] On March 30, he participated in an assembly promoted by anarchist and socialist groups from Sampierdarena, at the same time as a regional convention of Mazzinian associations from Liguria was held in Genoa. The theme of both meetings was the anniversary of May 1. Galleani, in the presence of, among others, Pellaco and Pietro Gori, took the floor and, despite a police officer attempting to interrupt him several times, presented a motion, which was approved, encouraging all workers to stop work on May 1 as a sign of protest against capitalist exploitation.

Again, on April 12, 1891, at the request of Milanese anarchist activists, he participated in an international assembly on workers' rights held at the Cannobiana Theater of Milan, promoted by a large number of socialist and democratic associations from Italy, Germany, Spain, and France. His speech, delivered to a thousand workers, caused a sensation. He argued vigorously with the legalitarian socialists, and particularly with Gustave Rouanet, municipal councilor of Paris and director of the *Révue Socialiste* [Socialist Review]. To thunderous applause, he insisted on the people's right to obtain bread and education by any means and to enjoy the benefits of science. The workers, he added, are ready to act if forced to do so. After these words an inspector protested to the meeting chair, but the audience clamored and dissuaded the public forces from interrupting. Galleani went on to declare openly that workers do not want more laws, nor do they want to send any of their own to parliament, because once elected they grow weak. These words earned him a subpoena for inciting class hatred. Next he outlined policies for the anarchist groups of Lombardy, Piedmont, and Liguria. He proposed that workers should forcefully assert their rights during the May 1 demonstrations and create a day of struggle to take possession of all social wealth. The proposals were printed on slips of paper and distributed throughout the hall. From similar episodes one can see Galleani's central role in making anarchism an autonomous and distinct movement, separate from socialism.

May Day 1891 approached as anarchists intensified propaganda and practical preparations for what they hoped would be a day of revolt. Galleani was the main organizer in the Central-North region. Two of his old acquaintances—Cipriani and Schicchi—were taking care of the South. But the government of Di Rudinì (who replaced Crispi in February) took countermeasures. In April, it issued a circular that expressly prohibited any demonstrations in the streets on May 1, just as Crispi had done the year before; and in an attempt to prevent the expected uprising, cautioned and preemptively arrested a number of anarchists.

Large numbers of police officers and military police were mobilized in the most radical districts of the Genoa area, and unemployed people not originally from the area were sent into internal exile to their own hometowns to prevent disorder. Yet a greater number of workers, as compared to the previous year, abstained from work, while in many cities of the center and the North, demonstrations of hundreds, in some cases thousands of people took place, demonstrations that sometimes ended in incidents. In Rome, about two thousand people crowded into Piazza di Santa Croce in Gerusalemme. During the meeting Cipriani and Palla, among others, spoke. Clashes broke out between demonstrators and police and then transformed into a violent riot.

In Sampierdarena, several anarchist speakers, including one woman, held a meeting attended by many unemployed people of both sexes at the end of which scuffles occurred with the forces of order. Galleani spoke in Forlì in public. The movement paid for this mobilization with arrests and sentences, so that many of the most prominent activists decided to cover their tracks. Galleani also made himself scarce. In early June he was in Lugano, where many of his comrades had taken refuge. They included Malatesta, Merlino, and Emilio Covelli. During the early summer, however, the Swiss police burst into the house of another comrade with the same beliefs, Isaia Pacini, where they were staying. Unlike Malatesta, who was locked up in the local prison, Galleani was lucky to escape arrest because he was away from the house when the authorities arrived.[13]

CHAPTER VII

"The Helm Remains to be Built"

Remaining in Switzerland had become too dangerous for Galleani. In early July he was again back in Vercelli, even though relations with some members of his family had deteriorated due to his continual trials and tribulations with the authorities, which risked affecting his parents and siblings. He resumed contact with some of his closest comrades: Cipriani, Schicchi, Pacini, Antonio Gagliardi, and especially Jacques Gross, whose money was indispensable for his survival and his efforts to resume propaganda. Aware that his correspondence was in danger of being intercepted, he avoided the post and used smugglers. In this way, he asked Gross to do his best to free Malatesta—which finally happened in September—and this is how we must interpret the visit that Gross paid to Malatesta in the Lugano prison.[1]

Galleani decided to settle in Sampierdarena in autumn 1891. Two anarchist brothers, Angelo and Giovanni Tardito, found him work as an accountant at their factory, which produced tin boxes to store food. With a salary of three lira per day, it was an occupation that guaranteed him economic security and gave him freedom for his real work: that of a revolutionary. In Sampierdarena, he gave several public lectures. Thus, at a meeting in February 1892, he urged workers to take action for themselves against the established institutions without fearing prison. For putting forward such an explicit position, the authorities marked him out as one of the most dangerous anarchists in Northern Italy, active in the provinces of Biella, Novara, Alessandria, Turin, Milan, and Genoa.[2] In fact, his range of action was much larger. On February 26, reports indicated that he gave a lecture in Rimini, in which he encouraged the audience to "get hold of a rifle, a dagger, a revolver, by means of theft if you have no money."[3] He was aware that he was running great risks, but did not plan to letup on that account. The authorities, however, were intent on stopping him. In late March he was arrested in Alessandria, put on trial, and sentenced to three months in prison and a fine of 50 lira, again for violating Article 247, and particularly for having encouraged the unemployed to rebel in a public lecture.

Shut away in cell 29 of the Alessandria prison, he made propaganda in his own manner, reading aloud *The Mysteries of Paris* by Eugène Sue.[4] He wanted to work on several translations that Gross had commissioned from him, but the stationery provided was barely sufficient for correspondence. Even for correspondence, the new prison regulations introduced by Crispi in 1891, were particularly severe. Galleani was permitted to send letters only once a week, on Friday, a day that he impatiently anticipated even though what he wrote was scrutinized and censored by the prison authorities.

His correspondents during this period were Elisée Reclus and Gross, with whom he reminisced, not without sadness, about the days spent in Clarens, which had been some of the happiest of his life. From these heartfelt letters it is clear that his emotions and beliefs were completely open and unreserved. He felt true love toward his comrades. In a letter to Gross in the following year he confided, "I'll love you forever with all of my heart." And this corresponded to feelings of deep hatred toward his enemies.[5] Ettore Croce wrote about Galleani:

> He asserts the right to love and is loyal to friendships, to the point of sacrifice; he asserts the right to hate and exercises it with tenacity, for which he is rebuked by his own friends. A balanced temperament, an adamantine character, steadfast in his convictions and in his intentions, he hates compromising words and compromising consciences and feeble characters, and parliamentarianism.[6]

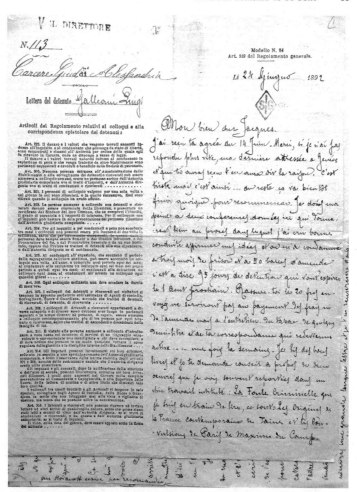

Letter to Gross from Galleani, sent from the Alessandria prison

He dedicated himself tirelessly to study, thanks to the books that Gross sent him. These included *Les origines de la France contemporaine* [*The Origins of Contemporary France*] by Hippolyte Taine in six volumes, and the texts of Jean-Marie Guyau, a philosopher whom he had begun to appreciate during his time in Clarens, until he became so enthralled as to make Guyau, as he wrote in a letter to Gross, his "inseparable friend."[7] He now dedicated himself in particular to the study of Guyau's *Esquisse d'une morale sans obligation ni sanction* [*A Sketch of Morality Independent of Obligation or Sanction*], a work that strongly influenced the libertarian world. Indeed, Kropotkin considered Guyau the founder of anarchist ethics, above all because Guyau's ethics did not seek to impose themselves.[8]

In this work, inspired by Charles Darwin and Herbert Spencer—two other essential references for Galleani—Guyau established, or rather re-established, a morality founded first and foremost on a form of free individual creation that could not be established by any social authority. As Kant had overcome heteronomous morality by affirming the autonomy of the moral agent, so Guyau now moved from autonomy to *anomie*, a principle according to which there were no universal moral imperatives. This did not mean that individual agents are devoid of any ethical sense; rather they were moved by a sort of "moral altruism" that impelled them to love others and act in solidarity with them: "all of our being is social. We must share our joys, we must share our pains."[9] Each person governs themselves morally according to a variety of beliefs and behaviors, the pluralism of which guarantees unity, which cannot be imposed by the constraining and sanctioning authority of society. Morality, in other words, does not come from external factors, but is "without either obligation or punishment," since it is based in the life of the individual. Thus Guyau writes, "A positive and scientific morality [...] gives the individual this sole command: develop your life in all directions, be an *individual* as rich as possible in intensive and extensive energy; therefore be as *social* and *sociable* as possible."[10]

This was to occur within a process of development, of a pressing drive toward progress characterized by the moral improvement of a humanity "on the march," ready for another transition.

> It is as if we are on the Leviathan, from which a wave has ripped away the helm and a blast of wind snapped the mast. It was lost in the ocean, like our earth in space. It thus roamed randomly, driven by the storm, like a large wreck loaded with men; and yet it arrived. Perhaps our earth,

perhaps humanity will also arrive at an unknown destination that they will have created on their own. No one directs
us, no eye sees for us; the helm was smashed long ago, or
rather we never had one and it remains to be built. This is a
large task, and it is our task.[11]

In Guyau's writing, and from the few newspapers received
from Gross that he was allowed to read, Galleani followed the
tumultuous events beyond the Alps, marked by Ravachol's
assassination attempt, which produced strong reverberations
in the French press. On May 1, 1891, scuffles were reported
between anarchists and police, and in Paris several activists had
been arrested and severely mistreated in the Clichy police station. Three months later, they were put on trial and sentenced
to several years in prison. In response to this, in March 1892,
two bombs exploded, one at the residence of the President of
the Court, and the other at the house of the Assistant District
Attorney. The material damage was enormous and several people were wounded, but there were no deaths. Ravachol and four
others were arrested. At his trial in late April, Ravachol was condemned to forced labor and then, two months later, to death for
several thefts carried out in previous years, which he argued were
justified. In that same time period, several bombs were also set
off in Spain that were attributed to anarchists, and similar events
took place in Switzerland and Belgium.

As soon as he was released from prison, on July 11, 1892,
Ravachol was guillotined. The event greatly upset Galleani, all the
more because the last words of the French activist, a true person-
ification of the desire to rebel, paid tribute to anarchy.[12] Another
ten days went by and, on July 23, on the other side of the Atlantic,
the anarchist Alexander Berkman shot and wounded the tycoon
of the Homestead Steel Company, Henry Clay Frick, considered
the person responsible for the death of twelve strikers by the
Pinkerton private police agency.[13]

CHAPTER VIII

Against Legalitarian Socialism

While anarchism launched the offensive in other places and at different levels, as shown by the not unconnected actions of Ravachol and Berkman, the whole of the Italian socialist world was preparing for a moment that would prove decisive. On August 14–15, 1892, the founding Congress of the Partito dei lavoratori italiani [Italian Workers' Party] was held, and it confirmed the final split between the socialists and anarchists. This split had been developing for a long time and reflected events beyond Italy's borders. 1889 saw the creation of the Second International and with it, particularly in Germany, France, and Great Britain, support for the view that revolution is not achieved through violent rupture: it could come about gradually and peacefully, through parliamentary and economic struggles.

In Italy, the previous national workers' congress, held in Milan in August 1891, had seen the victory of the current favorable to the labor legislation proposed by Turati and the defeat of an intransigent set of guidelines presented by Gori. Two weeks later, the international socialist congress held in Brussels decided to expel Merlino, delegate of the anarchists.

Galleani was there to represent the libertarians of Genoa. His sphere of action had focused for about a year on Liguria. In that region, he could count on a strong network of activists and wide popularity among the proletariat, particularly among the coal workers of the port of Genoa. These included the *camalli*— from the Arabic word *hammal*, those who labor with their shoulders—whose job was to carry loads from the ships' cargo holds to the warehouses. Edmondo De Amicis described their work as follows:

They unload [the coal baskets] into carts, and pass over moveable bridges: some horizontal, others inclined, some very steep. Just seeing them can make one dizzy. On these planks, barely wide enough for a man to pass, and as bendy as sword blades, the porters move almost running, carrying loads of more than one hundred kilograms, going up, going down, turning, jumping like tightrope walkers on tight cords, with straight chests, folded hats, and with attentive eyes; and as soon as their basket is unloaded, they run to load it again. One false step, a collision between someone coming and someone going, a lack of agreement on pace between two of them, which transmits a double impulse to the plank, one moment's distraction or a careless movement, and the man falls with his load into the sea—which is not the worst that can happen—or hits a boat or a chain, or a pier, and is torn to pieces or killed.[1]

In August 1892, the *camalli* came out on strike, and Galleani, with his pointed beard and floppy hat, actively participated in the uprising, and spoke at a meeting held at the Apollo Theater in Genoa. This was a sign of a more general fact: the most militant section of the working class in the Genoa area followed the anarchists, thanks to the work of Galleani and Pellaco.[2]

Thus Galleani did not lack the prestige and charisma to bring the message of the anarchists to the Genoa congress, where discussions were expected to be bitter. With him were Pellaco and Gori, whom Galleani had met personally at the congress at the Cannobiana theater in April 1891.[3]

In fact, Galleani had been hesitant to participate as he no longer had faith in joint congresses with socialists, but Gori convinced him to do so. Gori had not ruled out the idea that acting together with socialists was still possible. In the end, Galleani gave way to pressure and turned up at the Sivori Hall. It was he, more than anyone else, who resolutely expressed the arguments of the libertarians to the more than three hundred delegates, most of whom were opposed to the abstentionist strategy.

Students of labor movement history will be familiar with accounts of the first day's proceedings. The anarchists' obstructionism was clear from the very outset, thanks particularly to Pellaco, while the socialists, in response to the decrees of the Second International, subordinated economic struggle to a strategy of conquering power gradually, and sought to "modernize" the Party.[4] During discussion of the charter for the new party, which provided for participation in elections, Pellaco proposed that discussion be postponed until the next day, as several labor associations had not received a copy of the charter in time to evaluate it. To obviate this tactic, Antonio Maffi suggested proceeding to ratify the charter without the part concerning conduct during elections, and therefore postponing the discussion on that point. Turati yelled: "We don't want tyranny. Despots get out!" Clearly the anarchists had found the *casus belli* they were looking for and Galleani played a leading role. It was at this point, in fact, that he began his speech. He vigorously opposed Maffi's proposal and asked for the reason behind Turati's insult. This provoked uproar. Camillo Prampolini intervened, essentially asking the anarchists to separate their position from that of the socialists. Two subsequent interventions, by Gori and Turati respectively, did not change the already broken framework, and Turati then confirmed the need for separation.

The next day the separation was carried out. At the Society of Genoese Military Police there was a congress of those who accepted the electoral path, and they established the Partito dei Lavoratori Italiani. In 1893, this became the Partito Socialista dei Lavoratori Italiani [Italian Workers' Socialist Party] and, in 1895, the Partito socialista italiano [Italian Socialist Party]. The fundamental principles of its program were struggles in different trades and the conquest of political power through the electoral process. This now became a "duty of the party" and no longer a choice for individual chapters, as had been agreed in 1891 at the Milan Congress.[5] The legalitarians quickly managed to unite, but for the anarchists unity did not last long. The Partito Socialista Anarchico Rivoluzionario [Revolutionary Anarchist Socialist Party], created in Capolago, lacked direction. Its groups were crushed by repression and its best known activists were in prison or in exile. But the Partito dei Lavoratori Italiani now began a journey that made national history.

The anarchists and the workerists, followers of Casati's abstentionist line, continued with their work at the Sivori Hall, but they did not manage to reach a satisfactory agreement. Galleani—who in previous years had spent so much energy on united action with the POI—was against the formation of a structure uniting anarchists and "Casati-style" workerists. He was already convinced that the rigidity of formal organization, with its acronyms and congresses, mandates and resolutions, majorities and minorities, inevitably led to accepting the rules of representative democracy and, consequently, to possible entry into parliament: that is, to a betrayal of the revolutionary cause. He well knew, as the Ministry of the Interior noted, that "without an organization of comrades, nothing can be achieved," but he saw such organization as something exclusively practical, such as coordination between activists and anarchist groups to make propaganda more effective among the exploited, and revolutionary preparations that might find a decisive moment in a general strike.[6] We can therefore say that from the time of the Capolago Congress, he maintained the substance (the program) and discarded the form (the party). This, in my view, is how the "anti-organizational" label should be interpreted—a label that came to be used to define all of his future activities.

Moreover, since he had been schooled in the workers' and peasants' struggles of the early 1880s, he "naturally," so to speak, had a class-conscious and mass vision of revolutionary action, which must be the work of the workers themselves and not of a political avant-garde, no matter how enlightened. In contrast to other anarchists from the previous generation, his ideas were very different from the guerrilla-style *guerra per bande*, or "war by gangs," the strategy of the First Internationalists that, in Italy, had been grafted on to the remnants of Garibaldianism or Mazzini-style action by volunteers. What he sought to mobilize was action by an increasingly urbanized class employed in large enterprises such as factories and, in the case of Liguria where he was particularly active, the ports. He thus continued on the path he had been taking since the early 1880s: that of systematic participation in labor struggles. Indeed, this was the strategy that had been carried out by the majority of the anarchist movement and by a number of its best-known activists since the 1890s. Malatesta, for example, held similar views and gave greater value to labor struggles that made wide use of strikes, which both Malatesta and Galleani always understood in an instrumental manner, as a vehicle for insurrection.

Max Nettlau, who went to visit Galleani in Sampierdarena as soon as the split with the socialists took place, made an important observation on this issue. Galleani, he said,

> forged his first weapons in the industrial environment of the North that, in terms of government, was organized, presented all the industrial problems that directly concerned the workers. He had little or no contact with the central and Southern regions of Italy, where the old Garibaldians, who were internationalist, romantic, insurrectionary, and regarded the situation as still unstable, considered that a republican or anarchist or social uprising of the peasants was still forthcoming and rather than working among the laboring masses, had contact with individual activists.
>
> Galleani, although of a combative nature, was directly connected to the labor movement in the North [...]. So he was the most advanced of the advanced.[7]

The police did everything they could to thwart his activities. They monitored him closely, they intercepted his correspondence, and arrested activists who went to visit him, including two of his comrades from exile, Stojanov and Atabekian, who were consequently expelled from the country. They also followed him when he went for a dip in the sea in good weather.[8] In one of their reports, they wrote: "He is a very ardent advocate of that anti-social existence in which each person has a law of their own. According to him there should be no restrictions of any kind, collective and private property should be eliminated, family and morality should be abolished, each person should be free to think and act as they wish."[9]

Galleani received numerous invitations from anarchist groups to attend meetings and give lectures. Between the summer and fall of 1892, a long propaganda tour was planned in Northern and central Italy, with stops also in Rome and Naples, "in search of trials that will certainly not be lacking," as he wrote humorously to his usual correspondent Gross.[10] His presence was considered important since he was able to support the practical preparations of activists and effectively propagandize for abstentionism. In November, elections were to be held and he was called to speak in a number of constituencies with republican and socialist candidates, including Imbriani, Cavallotti, Costa, Maffi, and Valentino Armirotti. He went to San Remo, where Imbriani was running for the republicans, and Carrara, a constituency in which there was another republican candidate, Maffi. His meetings were often very turbulent. In Carrara, the local authorities prohibited him from speaking and threatened to disperse the meeting by force. Galleani spoke secretly in the woods of the Valenza Canal.[11]

His efforts were rewarded with some success. In Carrara, he wrote in a letter to Gross, "they are all uncompromising republicans or anarchists."[12] In Sampierdarena, which remained his operating base, the socialists accepted the abstentionist strategy advocated by the anarchists, and even in Alessandria his lecture unmasked the workers' candidates and was "extraordinary." It was a time of turmoil and great confidence, even if, in reality, the scarcity of resources available to the movement made it impossible for him to get to all the places where his presence was requested. "There's no way to stop the movement, which is very promising in Italy [...] *ça marche, ça ira!*"[13] he wrote to Gross.

In his rare moments of rest from giving speeches, he collaborated with the publications *Combattiamo!* (which came out from September to November 1890 to replace *Nuovo Combattiamo!*) and *Il Carbonaio* [The Coalman] (1892–1893) of Genoa, founded during the strike of the coal porters. He kept in contact by letter with Schicchi, Stojanov, and, of course, Gross, from whom he received, during this period, two works by Kropotkin, *Paroles d'un révolté* [*Words of a Rebel*] and *La conquête du pain*. These books helped to define Galleani's vision of anarchism and he described them as "our best propaganda works."[14] *Paroles d'un révolté*, a collection of writings that had appeared in *Le Révolté* between 1879 and 1882, painted a lurid picture of bourgeois society, marked by injustice, war, chronic economic crises, generalized exploitation; and, conversely, it showed the need for a new and more radical '48, a people's revolution to destroy all institutions of privilege, starting with nation states. These were sick from old age and already anachronistic. The people needed to expropriate the wealth from the hands of the few, so that all could enjoy it.

La conquête du pain, which Galleani regarded as a "superb" and "perfect" text, was published in articles in *La Révolte* [The Revolt] between 1886 and 1891, and was issued as a book in 1892.[15] It could be seen as a necessary complement to *Paroles*, one that elaborated many of these themes, and described in greater detail the nature and rationale of the anarchist society to come. Galleani repeatedly used the ideas expounded in this work in his speeches and articles. On his death in 1931, Luigi Fabbri wrote that he had made the Russian's ideas, as articulated in *La conquête* and *Le Révolté*, his own, making them even "more audacious."[16] Humanity, Kropotkin wrote in *La conquête*, possesses enormous wealth and a prodigious set of machines. If ownership was shared instead of private, there would be affluence for all. It was therefore necessary to take direct action and expropriate the bourgeoisie in order to return to the workers everything that, during the course of history, has been stolen from them, so that there would no longer be a single human being forced to sell their labor in order to live. This revolution was approaching and was inevitable. There were many signs and events to indicate that humanity was at the end of a historical era and ready to begin a new stage in which anarchist communism would be established. This would be a form of organization in harmony with the spontaneous and harmonious order of nature. It would not require government since it would be based on free agreement between people. Nor would it require private property; it would be capable of guaranteeing to each person everything that they need.

To Galleani, this theory of a forthcoming radical transformation of society seemed to be confirmed by the facts. All over Italy, new groups of the exploited were being organized, determined to act against and beyond the reformist socialists who, following the German social democrats, focused ever more narrowly on the efficacy of elections. 1893 was the year when *fasci* of workers developed.[17] In the months before May 1, the anarchists increased their agitation for a general strike and armed uprising. The *fasci*, which brought together mutual aid associations, resistance associations, cooperatives, and political groups, took on the characteristics of a mass movement of peasants. In many cases women and very young people played leading roles.

There was ferment throughout the country, but in Sicily, the uprising caused a social conflagration that seemed almost uncontainable. There, the anarchists—who had been in correspondence with Galleani for years—pushed the *fasci* towards open insurrection, and they were met with repression by the police and army that resulted in more than one hundred deaths. In Lunigiana, an area where Galleani had recently focused his propaganda, there was also a long series of struggles. Galleani criss-crossed the north of the country in an attempt to widen the influence of the *fasci*. We find him in the Genoa area, in Milan, Turin, Valsesia, Monferrat, and around Biella, where a large group of militants was active. There, he gave two lectures in March, during which he talked of inequality between social classes, hurled abuse against parliament and the king, and pressed those present to be ready for insurrection.

Hunted by the police, his life was tiring and difficult. Among his few consolations was his correspondence with Gross and reading books, particularly about history, which Gross continued to send to him. The police knew that he was playing a major role in Genoa and Sampierdarena and that he was keeping in contact with other parts of Italy, both in the north and elsewhere. In August 1893, after the Aigues Mortes massacre, which cost eight Italian workers their lives, the people took to the streets everywhere. There was an uprising in Genoa during which several tram cars belonging to a French company were burned. Throughout Liguria the situation was growing increasingly tense. Galleani and his comrades were hastening preparations for an insurrection that anticipated the involvement of the *fasci*, and that was planned for the end of the year.

In December, just when the anarchist groups of Carrara requested his presence in the city to support their propaganda, the authorities decided to arrest him as part of a much larger repressive operation. The third Crispi government, established in December 1893 following the Banca Romana scandal and the fall of the previous Giolitti government, declared a state of siege in Sicily. This led to the intervention of thirty thousand soldiers, the dissolution of the *fasci*, about two thousand arrests, and a large number of people being sent into internal exile. As a consequence and in solidarity with the island's people, the uprising, which continued for months in Lunigiana, took on the form of guerrilla warfare with bands in the mountains defeating the forces of order, severing their lines of communication, and pushing the population to armed revolt. Here, too, the government proclaimed a state of siege and requested the intervention of three thousand soldiers. Seven hundred arrests were made and five hundred people were sentenced. These included the anarchist Luigi Molinari, who had been invited to give two lectures in and around Carrara on December 25 and 26, 1893, instead of Galleani and was regarded as the main instigator of the revolt.[18]

Galleani, together with another thirty-four from Liguria and Piedmont (mostly young workers, many of whom were porters or dock workers), was charged with conspiracy to commit crimes "against the administration of justice, or public trust, or public safety, or good customs and family order or against people or property" (Article 248 of the Zanardelli penal code). According to the Genoa Police Headquarters it was a "very dangerous factional manipulation" stirred up by Galleani and "ready to rise up at the opportune moment."[19] The accused included Pellaco and Plinio Nomellini, a young painter who had already done some important paintings on the theme of labor. During the Brera

Triennial of 1891 he had the audacity to show the painting *Piazza Caricamento in Genoa,* in which the protagonists were indeed the *camalli* with their typical blue sweaters. Testifying in his defense was Telemaco Signorini, his famous colleague and former professor at the Accademia di Belle Arti of Florence, who praised his skill as a painter and predicted a glittering career for him. On May 22 the accused were brought in handcuffs from prison to the Court of Assizes in four police wagons. A crowd awaited them and applauded them, despite the presence of an impressive show of force, including a platoon of soldiers and a large number of military police under the orders of their respective lieutenants.[20]

Galleani was certainly the best-known of the accused. His sturdy physique, his chestnut beard and distinct bearing were, as always, his distinguishing traits.[21] The accused were defended by a board of attorneys, including Gori and Antonio Pellegrini. The former defended their ideas politically, the latter addressed legal issues. When interrogated, Galleani made a statement denouncing the court and asserting that it was inherently biased and had the purpose of defending the bourgeoisie. He declared himself to be a revolutionary anarchist who did not believe in legalitarian means, and he did so with an extraordinary fluency of words and phrases that impressed the reporters who were present. He then went on to maintain that the real wrongdoers were those presiding over the trial. This provoked the anger of the prosecutor, who stopped the proceedings and ordered the accused to be taken back to prison. This set off a scuffle between the accused, the attorneys, the military police, and the large audience of family members and sympathizers.

There was another session of the court on the afternoon of June 2. The hall overflowed with people as Gori took the floor with an impassioned speech in defense of the accused, who were locked up in cages and closely guarded by the military police with fixed bayonets. The trial was based on the work of police Commissioner Sironi (although by the time of the trial, he had been transferred from Genoa to Rome, still in the role of police commissioner). He made use of a number of police informants, whose identities he stated could not be revealed. Gori himself had previously been charged by Sironi for conspiracy to commit crimes but subsequently acquitted. Now he intended to defend his position.

He thus explained that the trial, prior to which the accused had spent several months in preventive detention, was a trial of ideas and intentions, a political tactic. The crime of the workers was wanting to improve their material conditions. These "noble offenders" were like Christ, "the red-shirted anarchist of eighteen centuries ago [...] the first to bring the good news to the poor and afflicted," and like Garibaldi, that other red shirt, "the outlaw, the offender," the anniversary of whose death was being observed that very day.[22] The socialist-anarchist model was the model of fraternity. Because "history moves inevitably from tyranny to liberty," it could not be prevented from developing.[23] Anarchists desired the abolition of the state and the government, and the extinction of the bourgeoisie as a class, but not the killing of the bourgeoisie as such.

Even so, it was difficult for the Court to ignore the echoes of the attacks of "Parisian bombers" such as Ravachol. Gori described these as "revenge against the cynical satiety of the wealthy classes," and took pains to characterize them as individual acts that did not implicate all those who called themselves anarchists. Nevertheless, he added, we must understand the "inferno of pain and poverty" from which the bombers came and how it made their hearts "overflow with hatred."[24]

Attention was also paid to Gori's relationship with the people he was defending, and, in particular, to a meeting at the station in Sampierdarena. What, for Gori, was nothing more than a "cutlet devoured together in the buffet of a station between the arrival and departure of a train" was depicted by the prosecutor rather as evidence of coordination between the anarchists of Lombardy, Piedmont, and Liguria.[25] Gori concluded by addressing the presiding judges as follows: "remember [...] these last simple words of mine: above your verdict is the verdict of history, above your court is the incorruptible court of the future." Thunderous applause followed, which the president of the court was unable to prevent.[26]

CHAPTER IX

In Prison

On June 8, the Court condemned some twenty of the accused to sentences of between six and sixteen months of imprisonment. Galleani's sentence was somewhat more severe: three years of imprisonment and two years of special surveillance. He was penalized more heavily both because of his reputation, and also for the courageous and scornful way he had conducted himself. Outside of the courtroom, the cordoned-off crowd formed a procession to accompany the police wagons to the prison. They sang "Il canto dei lavoratori" and shouted: "Long live the honest law breakers!" and "Viva Galleani!" "I'm going to prison for my principles," he replied. From the windows of the working-class districts, people waved handkerchiefs and hats, and during the next few days hundreds of posters inciting retaliation were put up.

Galleani entered prison during a time of open confrontation between anarchists and governments, with a number of dynamite attacks and other notable events. In February, Emile Henry, avenging Auguste Vaillant, bombed a café near Saint-Lazare Station in Paris, causing one death and numerous injuries. He was guillotined.[1] In response, the Parisian police headquarters were the target of a long series of attacks. When they were arrested, activists frequently used the courtroom for their own propaganda, making proud declarations that worsened their sentences but fired the imagination of rebels.

Galleani was among those who did most to commemorate them, exalting their actions and praising their moral integrity and abnegation, even to the point of sacrifice, as an example for all activists. On December 28, 1893, a few days after he entered the St. Andrea prison, one of his articles appeared in *Il Caffaro*

[Caffaro is a river in Northern Italy]. In it, he defended both Paulino Pallas, who, on September 24, had thrown two bombs into a military parade in Barcelona, killing General Arsenio Martínez Campos, and had been executed one week later, and also Vaillant, who on December 9, in Paris, had thrown a bomb into the Chamber of Deputies and, on February 5, had been guillotined to cries of "Long live anarchy!"

Another of his articles, for *L'Indipendente* [The Independent] of Genoa, led to the charge of inciting class hatred, but this ended in acquittal.[2] For some time, the Ministry of the Interior had noted that he "praises individual initiative."[3] And this was no mistake: indeed, he was already convinced that any act of revolt against authority, no matter how small or politically risky, could contribute toward social revolution.

From his cell, number 73, he immediately wrote to Gross, who supplied him with a new wardrobe, sheets, books, and French newspapers: *La Société Nouvelle* [The New Society], *Le Mercure de France* [Mercury of France], *La Revue Blanche* [The White Review], *La Revue Encyclopédique* [The Encyclopedic Review], and *Les Temps Noveaux* [The New Times]. He read books on English and French history, including *L'Histoire de France* [The History of France] by Jules Michelet, which had been translated into Italian by Giambattista Vico and served as the main work of historical reference for Elisée Reclus. And then Grave, Malato, Faure, Leo Tolstoy, Paul Verlaine, Gustave Flaubert, *Underground Russia* by Stepnjak (Sergej Kravčinskij), Multatuli (Eduard Douwes Dekker), biology books, and works on art by his beloved Guyau, Max Stirner, and Friedrich Nietzsche.

Nietzsche's *Thus Spake Zarathustra* left him deeply perplexed. The German philosopher, in Galleani's opinion, opposed the altruistic ethics that Guyau hoped for and, in the name of egoism, rejected the idea that a rich life is characterized by doing all one can for others. Every life, in Nietzsche's opinion, seeks to achieve its own will to power. These ideas were having an influence on some libertarian activists. Galleani, who had a deeply social and collective vision of the dynamics of liberation, denounced this philosophy several times during the next few years. He wrote: "No less sophistical is the tendency of those who, under the comfortable cloak of anarchist individualism, would welcome the idea of domination. They stretch Rabelais's aphorism: *fais ce que veux!* ... But the heralds of domination presume to practice individualism in the name of their *ego*, over the obedient, resigned, or inert *ego* of others."[4]

In addition to books and newspapers, Gross supported Galleani with money, as he did the families of other prisoners. Moreover, he provided news of Galleani's unhappy predicament to their mutual friends, Stojanov and Elisée Reclus. The latter expressed his great affection for Galleani, and began to write him and promised to act to help him.[5] Aside from his brother, Camillo, and sister, Carolina, with whom he wrote now and then, it was Gross, his *"bien cher Jacques,"* who gave him the most comfort. He made him forget the unhappy life he was leading for a few moments, when—in his words—his mind relived the world of the movement, his comrades, and the struggles of the past. Through Gross, he was able to stay in touch with Atabekian, Nettlau, Grave, Kropotkin, Luigi Bertoni, and Henri Roorda, and he corresponded directly with other activists including Reclus and Stojanov. He did so secretly, by bribing the guards to smuggle out the letters that he wrote on rice paper and, to receive incoming ones for him, so that he was regularly informed of events relating to the European political situation.

From the newspapers he learned, in mid-June, of the assassination attempt on Crispi by Paolo Lega—*Marat* to his comrades from Emilia Romagna—and only a week later of the murder of the president of the French Republic, Sadi Carnot, in Lyon—the work of an activist he knew well, Sante Caserio.[6]

In December the Court of Cassation confirmed his sentence. This news was not easy to accept, all the more so because conditions in detention were so severe. In the Crispi era, a series of stringent measures were enforced in prisons to control communication between prisoners, their dress, their use of tobacco, their conversations, et cetera. Those who did not obey the rules could be punished with isolation and the use of straitjackets and shackles on the arms and legs.

To cap it all, in February 1895, he learned that when his prison sentence was completed, he would be sent into internal exile. In July of the previous year, the Crispi government had introduced three exceptional laws, called "anti-anarchist" laws. One of which, no. 316 ("exceptional provisions for public safety") redefined the crimes that one could be condemned to internal exile for up to five years, extending this punishment to those put on trial for crimes against public order, those who "demonstrated the deliberate intention to commit acts against the social order" and membership in "associations against the social order," a category into which Galleani fell. As a result, from that date more than five hundred anarchists were arrested and sent into internal exile, first in Porto Ercole and on the island of San Nicola (Tremiti), then in Ponza, Ventotene, Ischia, Favignana, Pantelleria, Ustica, Lipari, and Lampedusa.[7]

For about three years, between 1894 and 1897, there was an almost complete interruption of the publication of libertarian periodicals in Italy. Crispi reaction affected the entire labor movement. In October 1894 the Crispi government decreed the dissolution of all labor organizations including the socialist party. Galleani, proud and smug, affirmed to the authorities that, as an anarchist, he did not recognize the State's right to judge his life and that once released he would resume his propaganda more vigorously than ever. The government's "exceptional laws," he protested, were promulgated seven months after his arrest, and were therefore being used against him retrospectively and hence illegally. In response, he was given the maximum sentence of five years of internal exile. However, he did not reproach himself for anything. He had acted with full consciousness of what he was doing, in line with his character and convictions.

During the election of May 1895, he agreed to be a candidate for parliament in the region of Turin and in the constituency of Vercelli. He did not believe that he would be elected; his intention was to use the occasion to arouse public opinion. He ran as what was known as a protest candidate, a means by which the parties of the left planned to rescue their most popular leaders from internal exile. If he was elected, the government would be forced to release him. This was not an uncommon tactic during this period. It had already been used in the mid-1880s to support Cipriani, held in the prison of Porto Longone with a sentence of twenty-five years. However, Malatesta had publicly renounced it since 1890.[8] Moreover, Galleani's use of it conflicted with his stance against parliamentarianism. It was also unsuccessful; he obtained only 372 preferences [votes] in Turin and 152 in Vercelli—not enough to be elected.[9]

This was not the last setback. For some time he had been worried about being transferred to another prison with an even more severe regime, which happened in the summer of 1895. He was moved to the prison in Parma, where the management prohibited writing and receiving books and newspapers, other than from relatives. To overcome this, he created a simple triangular system: Gross sent things to his brother Camillo, who in turn sent them to the prison.

During these years Camillo was also occasionally subjected to pressure and threats from the authorities due to his relationship with Luigi. Together with their sister Carolina, however, Camillo was among the relatives who stayed closest to Luigi during this difficult period of imprisonment. For some time Luigi had broken off relations with his other brother, Alfonso, who had been exiled in Switzerland for political reasons at the end of the 1890s. He had an even more difficult relationship with their father, who he describes as the "son of a soldier who has the cult of authority in his blood."[10]

Through Camillo he received works by Kropotkin, and also Stirner's *Ego and Its Own*, which, he thought, unlike Nietzsche, made "not only a virile call to revolt, but a categorical and sharp rejection [of the idea] that each can do to their fellow beings whatever they please."[11] He also continued to read *Le Libertaire* [The Libertarian], *La Société Nouvelle*, and *Les Temps Nouveaux*— his preferred periodical and one of the few anarchist sources of information available to him. From Stojanov (through Camillo) he was sent *La biologie* [Biology] by Charles Letourneau, which he read with great interest. Despite his reading, he now suffered from solitude more than in Genoa, as well as from health problems, particularly his eyes, for which he asked Stojanov for advice and remedies. He felt old and alone, yet he did not give in. He circulated propaganda pamphlets among the prisoners. His sole comfort was his correspondence, through which he learned about the major developments of the international movement. He confided in Gross that he was not surprised at the outcome of the International Socialist Congress in London (July 27–August 1, 1896) at which there were more than seven hundred delegates. In the course of it, there had been another major dispute between the socialists and anarchists, and the anarchists had been expelled from the meeting and decided to organize a series of public meetings separately in the city.

The prison administration, however, did not intend to tolerate his independent and rebellious character. When he slapped the director, accusing him of profiting from food and supplies intended for the prisoners, his situation got worse. He was constrained for days in a straitjacket, and held in isolation in a punishment cell.[12] This punishment was inflicted upon him a second time when a prison guard, bribed in Parma as they were in Genoa, was discovered taking out Galleani's letters and was fired.

He spent an entire month in an isolation cell. Finally, in October, his deportation to internal exile was ordered, although the anti-anarchist laws were officially no longer in force as of January 1, 1896, the date after which the government allowed— through amnesties—the gradual release of many detainees. On November 11, the anniversary of the martyrs of Chicago, he was escorted out of the prison in handcuffs. After a two week journey, he reached Pantelleria on November 30.

CHAPTER X

Internal Exile and the Question of Protest Candidates

Pantelleria is a black and steep volcanic island where rough seas often prevent boats from docking. A number of political prisoners and hundreds of common criminals were held there. Frequent fights broke out among them, linked often to gambling and loansharking.[1] Galleani was incarcerated in one of the shared dormitories of the Barbacane Castle, a terrible hell-hole, dark and sweltering hot, with dripping, damp walls. From its window, through the gratings, one could glimpse the Tunisian coast.[2] His bed consisted of two wooden planks, a straw mattress, and a blanket. These were the only possessions the administration allowed him apart from a scant allowance, enough to purchase some bread and beans. At first he was disheartened, but soon enough he befriended and identified with the other political prisoners, with whom he shared money and food.

The rules required that the prisoners were confined to their dormitories from 6:30 p.m. in the evening until 6:00 a.m. the following morning, when they were allowed out for the day. Outside, the island's people were poor, but they were receptive to anarchist principles, as a result of the activities of some comrades in previous years. Galleani could therefore quickly resume his propaganda work, which he particularly addressed to the young, among whom his ideas soon kindled interest and admiration.

This was probably the reason why, in early 1897, he was transferred to Favignana, another small island off the coast of Sicily, where about four hundred prisoners resided. It was described by the English-Italian patriot Jessie White as follows:

I saw decrepit old men, robust middle-aged men, others young, all of them unemployed, many drunk. I never before laid eyes on a mixture of human beings so disgusting, so despicable [...]. They are prisoners—a gentleman told me, who had kindly offered to show me around—the scourge of our island, which has been chosen as residence for these people, who are put ashore haphazardly, without discipline and without work [...]. The atmosphere is plague-ridden: the streets, clean every morning, soon become sewers.[3]

Galleani did not waste time and immediately dedicated himself to organizing the local tuff quarrymen, "dehumanized, hopeless, and unconscious slaves," who he soon succeeded in transforming into "rebels."[4] To try to stop his tireless attempts at organizing these workers, the Ministry of the Interior transferred him again, this time to the island of Ustica. He reached there in March and immediately established good relationships with the residents and terrible relationships with the guards. Through his contacts he received pamphlets and newspapers, and in addition to Gross he corresponded with, among others, Nettlau and the former Communard Jean-Louis Pindy.

During the elections of March 1897, just as had happened two years previously, several of his anarchist comrades, together with socialists and republicans, decided to nominate him as a parliamentary deputy in the third electoral constituency of Rome and the first constituency of Turin.[5] They organized public meetings in his support. One of these, on Ponte Garibaldi in Rome, although obstructed by the police, was an impressive event, with the crowd concluding the demonstration by shouting "Viva Galleani!"[6] The advisability of his protest candidacy provoked a lively debate in the labor alliance and, indeed, some bitter disputes. Several anarchists, including groups in Turin and Rome strongly influenced by Merlino, had begun to give credence to the potential of parliamentary political struggle, and they saw protest candidacies as a valid and necessary tactical expedient. Others remained strongly opposed to them because they considered them to involve a dangerous acceptance of electoral and legalitarian means.[7]

The issue of protest candidates also came up in the debate on abstentionism, which ran through the movement. It revived support for the view that anarchism and parliamentarianism mutually excluded one another; and that to resolve the "problem of freedom in a socialist society," the "anarchist solution" of consent was effective, rather than the "democratic" solution with majorities and minorities.[8] Malatesta clearly expressed this position, which was then followed by Galleani.

Malatesta, writing in the periodical *L'Agitazione* [Uprising] about the candidacy of "our friend Luigi Galleani" organized by activists in Rome and other parts of Italy, reiterated his disquiet about a strategy that he regarded as a "slippery slope where it is hard to keep one's footing." In contact with Galleani through Gross, Malatesta said he was sure that Galleani agreed with him because he knew that once elected, he would never go to Parliament except to "spit his contempt into the face of the deputies."[9] This was a clear warning to Galleani, on whom weighed the precedent from two years earlier and who now, instead, was adopting Malatesta's position. Thus he wrote a letter to the public "declaring he is for the anti-parliamentary struggle and will maintain this struggle to its final consequences," and asking for his candidacy to be withdrawn.[10] But in vain. He received 487 votes in the Turin I constituency and 263 votes in the Rome III constituency (making a total of 750). Again this was not enough for him to be elected.[11] Radicals, socialists, and republicans together obtained about 16 percent of votes out of a total of about 1,200,000. For the socialist party this round of voting was a success: they received 140,000 votes, sixty thousand more than in the elections two years earlier.

Immediately after Galleani received news of his election defeat in April, he was again transferred to Pantelleria, the next stop in what was becoming a continual transfer from one island to another. Not only had the protest candidacy proved useless, but bad luck also attended another attempt to liberate him undertaken by his family and a girlfriend from Turin who attempted to intercede with the help of a former Undersecretary of the Interior. The political climate was anything but favorable. That spring, the Di Rudinì government introduced legislation that actually restored the previous Crispi-era law on internal exile. The islands again filled up with political prisoners when anarchist Pietro Acciarito's attempt to stab Umberto I marked the end of any possible reconciliation.

Galleani had little faith in the outcome of his protest candidacy or in the informal attempt launched by his family, with which he had nothing to do. For some time he had been planning to escape from Pantelleria. To this end, he had activated his own contacts, starting with Gross and Elisée Reclus, who sent him maps of the sea channels around Sicily and Malta, with water depths and landing places along their coasts.[12] At Galleani's request, Reclus collected 700 francs from his European comrades, and sent them to Nicolò Converti, a veteran activist who had been living in Tunis for some time, so that he could procure a suitable boat. Gross then sent him the money to rent an isolated house with a bit of land around it, together with shoes, clothes, and other essential items.

It had actually been the struggles and protests of previous years that had ensured that, from 1895, the political prisoners on Pantelleria had the right to find their own lodgings. This arrangement, as well as being more comfortable, was indispensable for evading the constant surveillance of the guards at night (the best time for attempting an escape) as happened in the dormitories. Galleani's house, located on the top of a hill with a view of the sea, was about four kilometers from the residential area. It had three rooms. During the summer, two other exiles went there to live with him: Palla, his old friend, who had already attempted two escapes in vain from Porto Ercole and Favignana, and Emidio Recchioni, one of the editors of *L'Agitazione*. The terrace was made into a kitchen area and Recchioni was appreciated for his skills as a cook. He was the one who prepared their favorite dish: spaghetti with *lardo*, onions, and tomatoes from the large garden that surrounded the house.

Here Galleani could comfortably do what he was most proud of and passionate about: his work as a private teacher. He gave lessons in politics, sociology, sciences, and languages, usually in exchange for food (vegetables, rice, and eggs), to many of the island's children, including a sixteen-year-old named Andrea Salsedo.[13] Not only the children, but the island's inhabitants in general grew to like him. They knew him as "the professor" and greeted him warmly when he went down to town riding a mule.[14] His home became a place of sociability, study, and discussion. Gross was always sending newspapers, books, pamphlets (including "Socialisme en danger" ["Socialism in Danger"] by Domela Nieuwenhuis and Grave's "L'individu et la société" ["The Individual and Society"]). He did so by using the addresses of two local residents with whom the anarchists had close relations, Salvatore La Scola and Antonino Genovese.

The attention of the prisoners was being taken up by the insurrection in Crete (called Candia at that time) against the Ottoman Empire. News of it filled the front pages of popular newspapers and occupied the attention of many socialists and anarchists, including Cipriani.[15] Galleani expressed his desire to support the Greek rebels, believing that at such times of national struggle, good practical propaganda for anarchist principles could be created.

However, in July that summer, some terrible news arrived: the money collected by Reclus and sent to Converti had been lost, as had months of preparation for escape. Galleani needed to start again from the beginning, as it still remained his priority to return to the mainland and to his proper place.

Battles were raging in the world outside: on August 8, 1897, Michele Angiolillo, a typesetter and anarchist from Foggia, shot the president of the Spanish Council, Cánovas del Castillo, who had been guilty of violent repression using exceptional laws and massacres. Angiolillo's act was motivated by news such as this:

We have received horrible details of the torture of Spanish anarchists. It is like reading a grim tale of Torquemada's infamy, hearing similar horrors well into the nineteenth

century. The accused are brought into hearings atrociously
transformed, with their limbs broken, their nails pulled
off, flesh burned, genitals torn away. Before going in to the
hearing the accused are tortured again and threatened with
other more horrible torments if their statements before the
War Council are not pleasing to their oppressors.[16]

Angiolillo was "garroted" twenty days later, after openly
claiming responsibility for his own actions—another of the
fallen to commemorate.

CHAPTER XI

From Island to Island

On December 2, 1897, attempting to stop Galleani's propaganda activity among the inhabitants of Pantelleria, the authorities ordered another transfer, once more to Favignana. He stayed there a few months before being transferred, in May of the following year, again to Ustica, in what seemed to be an endless pilgrimage around these islands. Nevertheless he succeeded in reestablishing contact with Gross, Elisée Reclus, Stojanov, and Malatesta, and in receiving newspapers, books, and pamphlets, including some by Grave, Giuseppe Ciancabilla, and Elisée Reclus, and in staying up-to-date on current events through the publications of the international movement.[1]

1898 was a particularly incendiary year. In January, the popular neighborhoods of Ancona, where Malatesta's *L'Agitazione* was printed, rose up following an increase in bread prices. This was a sign of what was to come. In the following months, the insurgency expanded to all of Le Marche and to parts of the center and South of Italy, in both the countryside and the cities. Jacqueries, barricades, and attacks on government buildings followed until, in May, the rebellion spread to the North. In Milan, a state of siege was declared and hundreds of workers were mercilessly fired upon in the Piazza del Duomo. The slaughter of the people, ordered by the executive authorities, went hand in hand with legislative measures. In April, the Pelloux government approved a bill by Di Rudinì to restore internal exile, which had previously been suspended. Thus between 1898 and 1899 numerous anarchists were again banished to the islands, including almost all of the movement's leading figures. The libertarian press, which, in the two-year period from 1896–1897, had shown signs of being reborn, was again silenced with the arrest of the editorial staff of *L'Agitazione* and interruption of the publication of Messina's *L'Avvenire Sociale* [The Social Future] from May 1898 until October 1899.

The unexpected explosion of popular rage on the one hand, and the government's violent repressive action on the other, strengthened Galleani's belief in the possibility of revolution in Italy. During this period, he believed, the anarchists needed to proceed cautiously, resurrecting the "'48er" methods of organization, which were clandestine and conspiratorial.

He confided in Roberto D'Angiò, his comrade in internal exile who hailed from the same town as Angiolillo, about his fear of being deported to the Bay of Assab on the Red Sea. This was an area under Italian rule where the government, during its last clampdown on public order, had created a new prison location and where several dozen prisoners from Ustica and other islands had been transferred.[2] In August of 1898, he was transferred instead back to Pantelleria for health reasons. He arrived there after an eight-day journey, via the prison of Palermo and the "small and horrendous" prison of Trapani.[3]

Returning to Pantelleria was a relief for him. Here, he would at last be able to recover from stomach problems that, he knew, were caused by the impurity of the water in Favignana and Ustica. Pantelleria, by contrast, boasted of excellent spring water that had provided him with relief during his previous stay. Moreover, on the island he was able to return to his own house and to his work as a teacher. In the autumn, he and Recchioni were transferred to the Velcimursà contrada, near the port, and to a more spacious dwelling given by the father of one of the children Galleani had taught since the early days of his forced stay.

In autumn 1899, he met a neighbor, thirty-one-year-old Maria Rallo. It was love at first sight, a *coup de foudre* for both of them. Later he recalled their early, furtive nighttime meetings in a letter to his friend Gross: "We were under the surveillance of ferocious guards [...]. She was beautiful and kind and we loved each other despite [this] terrible surveillance [...]. I love her with all of my strength."[4]

Luigi left his girlfriend, who had stayed behind on the mainland, and Maria left her second husband, Dante Tessiere, a sailor from Pisa whom she had married three years before and with whom, just a year earlier, she had a daughter, named Ilia. Maria also had another child, Salvatore, a ten-year-old boy, from her first husband, Giuseppe Errera. Maria had married him when she was not yet twenty years old but he had died only four years after their marriage. Luigi and Maria remained together throughout the years to come. In addition to Salvatore and Ilia, who was always treated as the daughter of them both, they eventually had more children: Cossyra (the ancient name of Pantelleria), Olimpio, Balilla (named after the young protagonist of the anti-Hapsburg insurrection in Genoa in 1746), and Mentana.

Their house welcomed many visitors. Increasingly it became a place for discussions, readings, and meetings, as the anarchist colony grew, with dozens of activists spending longer or shorter periods of time on the island. Galleani had also become friendly with the municipal secretary assigned to the post office, Vincenzino Lo Pinto. Lo Pinto and a merchant named Girolamo Valenza agreed to receive books and pamphlets, concealed within other non-threatening publications, for Galleani at their own addresses. Galleani himself also used a steamship with an obliging captain to send and receive mail. In short, he had the trust of several residents of the island, some of whom shared his ideas, and tried and true methods of communication with the outside world.

During this period, he studied Spanish, English, and German grammar. And he paid particular attention to articles by Kropotkin, which were later collected together in *Mutual Aid: A Factor of Evolution*. He considered these articles to be of great importance and worthy of rapid publication in an Italian version. He circulated them clandestinely among the prisoners and islanders and he did the same with a number of pamphlets Grave sent him, including "Between Peasants" by Malatesta, "La loi et l'autorité" ["Law and Authority"] by Kropotkin, and "Les déclarations d'Etiévant" ["Etiévant's Statements"] and "La genèse de l'idée de temps" ["The Genesis of the Idea of Time"] by Guyau.

On the mainland, meanwhile, the campaign for amnesty and the abolition of internal exile continued. Andrea Costa supported the cause in Parliament while outside a succession of protests took place, as anarchists published various periodicals and single issues on the subject.[5] Despite the attempts by some groups to form a joint campaign, what divided the anarchists from the Socialist Party, sometimes bitterly, was now more than ever the issue of protest candidates. The socialists wanted to continue to use this tactic to free prisoners who were already almost all anarchists. Galleani, however, was now firmly convinced of the errors of this method, and engaged in a fierce dispute via letters with libertarians willing to be candidates in order to be released.

In early 1899, socialist deputy Oddino Morgari, Galleani's old acquaintance from his time in Turin, arrived in Pantelleria on a parliamentary investigation to survey the willingness of anarchists to be candidates. They divided into two factions, one in favor and one opposed. During one of his lectures on the socialist program, Galleani spoke and articulated the course of action to his comrades, making it clear that anarchists should no longer have anything to do with the legalitarian socialists. Protest candidacies, he argued, constituted a strategy that only appeared to be useful. They were in fact ineffective and damaging. They did not achieve their objectives and weakened the fighting spirit and commitment to action. He no longer had any intention of being a candidate, even if it truly meant release.

In the middle of this dispute, the socialist Ferri called the anarchists politically "dead." So I Morti [The Dead] became the title of the single issue of a journal that Galleani put together with other comrades on Pantelleria, Ponza, Ventotene, and Lampedusa in answer to the socialists. It was printed in Ancona on November 2, 1898, and immediately confiscated by the public prosecutor of the city.

The article on the front page was signed by Galleani. It bore the title "Manet immota fides!" [The faith remains unchanged!] It was hard-hitting and impressed those comrades who shared his views.[6] It criticized the few anarchist activists who, in the recent past, had shown appreciation for the obstructionist

The single issue of *I Morti*

parliamentary tactics of the Socialist Party and who in two cases—"two weak temperaments," as he called them—had publicly repudiated their own anarchist beliefs to avoid further legal troubles after being released from internal exile. And he added: "If we must leave here bowing down to a flag that is not our own, if release is subject to a deal, if we must leave these rocks counting, among our days, a single day that we must be ashamed of, if we must return reduced, crippled, deserters, after having burned the incense of deceitful adoration to the idols that we repudiate ... it is better to stay!"[7]

Galleani wanted to use other methods to return to be with his comrades, all the more so because, after five years of internal exile, another two years of special surveillance awaited him. Weeks after the failure of his planned attempt at escape, he began organizing another attempt. He could count on the support of a trusted network of activists based in Geneva, Brussels, London, New York, Malta, and Paterson. These included Gross, Reclus, and Emidio Recchioni, who had been released from internal exile and taken refuge in London. There, he in turn received the support of Kropotkin, Nettlau, Varlaam Cherkezov, and others to collect the necessary money, several hundred francs. Gross managed to send this to Galleani by setting up a fake trade in *passito* wine with Valenza.

Going by sea was no easy task, especially after April 1899 when Malatesta had been able to escape from Lampedusa. The Ministry of the Interior had intensified its surveillance, and the escape attempt had to be postponed several times. But in February 1900, at last, Galleani set sail in a boat captained by the father of one of his students.

Maria, five months pregnant, remained on the island. The plan was for her to join him later, with the help of an anarchist from Messina, Giuseppe Prestandrea. But Prestandrea instead proved to be her persecutor. After inviting her to his house, he locked her in and raped her repeatedly. She was liberated through the action of other activists who broke into the house, and Prestandrea was publicly banned from participating in the anarchist movement.[8]

INTERLUDE
On the Other Side of the Mediterranean

CHAPTER XII

In Egypt

Galleani escaped toward the end of his sentence. In just a few months more he would have been released. However, he knew that once released and returned to the mainland, he would have been put under surveillance and subjected to a regime of conditional freedom, which would have made it almost impossible for him to carry out his own political activity. For this reason, as Malatesta had done, he preferred to escape and find refuge abroad, where he would have more room to maneuver.

On March 4, 1900, the authorities conducted an investigation into his escape and suspected he had taken refuge in Alexandria, Egypt. They were not mistaken. In fact, from Pantelleria he had landed in Susa, Tunisia, and from there he used a false passport to rush to Malta and then to Alexandria, the first steps on a new transnational path that his activism took for the next twenty years.[1] As soon as he arrived in the Egyptian city, he looked for employment, but without success. Initially, with the assistance of several former Italian internationalists, he thought he had found an opportunity to work as a watchman at the Aswan Dam, which was just beginning to be built, but nothing came of it. Then another job opportunity, this time as director of livestock disinfestation services in Zagazig, an area between Cairo and Ismailia, also evaporated.[2]

Yet he had an immediate need for money: he wanted to bring Maria and the children to Alexandria. In the meanwhile, they had set sail from Lampedusa. Maria told her relatives on Pantelleria that she needed to go to Tunis to enroll Salvatore in school. She left with Salvatore and Ilia never to return. For a while, she settled in Monastir, a small Arab village on the Tunisian coast, which was inhabited mostly by Bedouins, where she waited to be reunited with Luigi. Thanks to the generosity of Gross and some activists based in Alexandria, Luigi managed to scrape together the necessary funds to guarantee the survival of Maria and her children in Monastir and to cover the cost of the trip to Alexandria. In mid-May he went to Tunisia. From there, the four traveled to Alexandria, to settle down in a modest house where Maria, almost at the end of her pregnancy, was able to get some much-needed rest.

Once the family was reunited, Galleani's idea was to spend a few years in Egypt, a country with a certain level of anarchist activity. The libertarian presence in the area dated back to the 1870s, when the first Italian internationalists moved there to avoid the repression that followed the Bakuninist uprisings of 1874 and the Matese uprisings three years later. In 1898, an event captured the attention of the world's press. Thirteen Italian anarchists who lived in Egypt were arrested and accused of plotting an assassination attempt on the life of Kaiser Wilhelm II of Germany, who was visiting Istanbul and Jerusalem. The event had a particular resonance because, during the subsequent trial, the anarchists managed to reveal the role played by an undercover agent, who was then sentenced to several years in prison. Apart from that, the libertarians had tried to maintain constant propaganda activity and they played leading roles in organizing the local labor movement, so that, by late 1899, several activists were directly involved in promoting the first major strike of tobacco workers in Cairo.

When Galleani arrived, the most militant Italian activists included Icilio Parrini, from Livorno, previously among the founders of a section of the International in Alexandria in 1876, and Pietro Vasai, from Florence. Galleani immediately entertained the idea of starting a weekly periodical. He had a title in mind—*Verso la Libertà* [Toward Liberty]—and an approach. *Verso la Libertà* was to be ambitious, and somewhat similar to *L'Humanité Nouvelle* [New Humanity], a theoretical journal to which the cream of the international revolutionary intelligentsia contributed, "but a little more aggressive." With Gross's help he wanted to ensure the regular collaboration of Elisée Reclus, Augustin Hamon, Bernarde Lazare, Cherkezov, and Nettlau. Elisée Reclus, to whom Galleani confided his plans, encouraged him and promised his own collaboration together with that of his brother Élie.[3]

The necessary funding was missing, as too was the likely and indispensable collaboration of Gross, who was busy at this time establishing the bilingual periodical *Le Réveil-Il Risveglio* [Reawakening]. This was a journal that would play an important role in the international revolutionary movement for fifty years. Its first issue was published in Geneva on July 7, 1900, thanks to the joint efforts of Gross (who signed his newspaper articles as "Jean qui marche"), Eugène Steiger, Herzig—another of Galleani's old acquaintances—and Bertoni, an activist whom Galleani was fond of and had always thought highly of, and with whom he continued to maintain close ties.[4]

Lack of money was a pressing problem for Galleani and his family, and it was further aggravated after the birth of Cossyra (middle name Libertà) on June 6, 1900, and the onset of serious health problems. In early summer, Luigi began to suffer from persistent fevers. Confined to bed, he woke at night with his mouth full of blood and was unable to consume any kind of food apart from a few sips of milk. He had malaria. Treatment with massive doses of quinine, up to two grams a day, left him severely exhausted. It intensified old stomach problems and caused damage to his sight. After three months of treatment the malaria was eradicated, but for a long time he remained so weak he could not walk, and he also suffered from heart problems. To make matters worse Maria, after giving birth, also suffered from serious health problems and was hospitalized. "We are in a mess up to our necks. We have nothing, nothing, nothing," he wrote with a cry of pain in a letter to his friend Gross. Soon they no longer had the money needed to pay for Cossyra's nurse, and lacked food and clothing. Despite the persistent help of other activists living there, they were forced to go into debt and sell personal possessions.[5]

Even so, in addition to Cossyra's birth, there was more news to lift their spirits. On July 29, 1900, in Monza, Gaetano Bresci shot King Umberto I of Italy, killing him and putting an end to an era marked by repression and slaughter on the streets. The most famous massacre took place in May 1898 in Milan, and

Umberto I had pinned military honors on the chest of General Bava Beccaris, who had ordered the slaughter of the people. Now, Galleani wrote, justice had been done. Bresci, an anarchist from Prato who had immigrated to Paterson, served as a herald for numerous popular discontents. With his gesture, he succeeded in liberating the country from increasing militarism, like that of Luigi Pelloux. He gave birth to a new phase in Italian history, in which the ruling classes had to grant relatively greater recognition to popular demands.[6]

Following Bresci's act, Galleani was arrested and the Italian authorities, through their consulate in Cairo, requested his extradition. His arrest triggered a sudden protest from the substantial Italian-language anarchist colony, which was echoed in the local press. The Egyptian government rejected the request for extradition and, through an *ad hoc* amnesty, decided to release him.

Having recovered from malaria with difficulty, he got a temporary job at a legal firm and thus a minimum of financial security. The idea of the periodical had faded but he nevertheless succeeded in contributing decisively to the birth of two significant libertarian initiatives: the free popular universities of Alexandria and Cairo. In early 1901, he promoted several meetings at the Italian Masonic Lodge of Alexandria during which the first concrete decisions to establish these universities were made. For reasons of political expediency and in line with the thinking of Elisée Reclus and Gross, both of whom were Masons, he intended to create an institution that was not exclusively anarchist, but open to the progressive world in general, over which anarchist content and methods could exert a certain influence.[7] To this end, and with the help of Elisée Reclus, he also involved the Alexandria Geographic Society through its president, Abbate Pasha. He took on the role of president of the temporary committee and drafter of the bylaws. D'Angiò, another anarchist and a former comrade from internal exile who had also come to Egypt, served as secretary.

In early May, a General Assembly at the Alcazar Theater, with about 150 people in attendance, approved the Constitution of the Free Popular University of Alexandria and elected the first committee of twenty members. The anarchists were represented in a good number, but there were other representatives from various political schools and different geographic origins: Italians, Greeks, Germans, French, Armenians, and Egyptians. Socially, the majority of them were manual laborers, but representatives of the well-heeled classes were not missing. Galleani did not sit on the committee, but there were other well-known anarchists who did, including Vasai, Francesco Cini, and the Lebanese Jew, Joseph Rosenthal. The University was inaugurated on May 26, 1901, with a public meeting at the Zizinia Theater. In front of a numerous audience of Egyptian and foreign resident workers, several inaugural speeches were given in French, Greek, and Arabic.

The University was supported through voluntary subscriptions and founded on the principles of independence and autonomy from state and religious authorities. Its objective was established in an Article of the bylaws: "to promote the diffusion of literary and scientific culture among the popular classes" by means of independent, modern, and free education in several languages. This path was considered fundamental to emancipate the working population from the double yoke of religion and nationalism, and to raise them up morally.

An intense photographic portrait of Luigi Galleani

This initiative, which followed similar experiments started in France and in Italy, was successful. In the first few weeks, three hundred students of both sexes enrolled. Female students were present in good numbers and there were several lectures on the subject of women's rights. Every evening except Sundays, well-known teachers who worked voluntarily gave classes, mostly in French, Italian, and Arabic. Subjects included natural history, anatomy and physiology, chemistry and physics, law, languages, Greek, Italian, Arabic, French, German, and English literature, and topics such as the theory of evolution, hygiene and first aid, workers' rights, and the strike as a tool. Musical and theater performances were organized and a well-stocked library was open during the evening, an initiative that made the headquarters on Mahmud Pasha Al-Falaki Street a popular meeting place for local progressives.[8]

Meanwhile Galleani moved to Cairo. There he provided the necessary stimulus to start another free popular university, for which he was the spokesperson among workers and for the public. In Cairo, he benefited from the support of Parrini and the local anarchist community, in addition to the union of tobacco industry workers, fresh from a major and victorious strike the previous February, to which several anarchist activists had contributed. The University was established publicly on June 9 in a civic theater. According to the tactic already tested in Alexandria, a generally progressive committee guided it, in which a good number of Italian anarchists participated. The committee made use of the support of the Masonic Lodge of the Nile, the local Geographic Society (with support obtained by Galleani from Elisée Reclus) and was sustained by branches of workers, Egyptian as well as Italian, Greek, Armenian, and Jewish, residing in Cairo.[9]

Attention to pedagogical issues became a constant for Galleani. He was convinced, like many in the anarchist movement, that self-education that avoided state and religious interference was a fundamental element in guaranteeing workers, and the oppressed in general, a degree of freedom from the ruling powers. Similar to how several of the most important anarchist activists were dedicated to the subject, including Elisée Reclus and Kropotkin, who signed an "Anarchist European Manifesto for the Foundation of Free Schools" issued in Paris in 1896, Galleani continuously dedicated energy to help initiate educational institutions in the form of free (or "modern," as they were later called) universities and schools throughout the course of his activism.

Partially satisfied with the political results achieved in Egypt, particularly the foundation of the two universities, he nevertheless understood that his time in North Africa was coming to an end, primarily for material reasons. He was unable to guarantee economic stability for his own family in Egypt.

CHAPTER XIII

On the Move Again

Yet, where could he go, if Italy was still effectively off-limits? When Galleani was in Pantelleria, he had thought it was time to move as far away from Europe as possible. He had asked Elisée Reclus to contact Kropotkin in order to determine the feasibility of moving to Australia, but nothing came of it. Then, once he had landed in Egypt, he changed his thinking and considered staying in Brussels, where Elisée Reclus himself had moved some time ago. Yet even this turned out to be unfeasible.[1]

The Americas remained. The South American anarchist scene did not appeal to him and he had no intention of collaborating with Gori—then active in Argentina—with whom he found he had a certain incompatibility of character.[2] There were two things that made him hesitate about the United States, where Gross urged him to go. The cold climate, which was not ideal for the precarious condition of his and Maria's health, and the fact that the Italian-language movement was experiencing a deep division between two currents: organizationalists and anti-organizationalists.

The former believed in adhering to a definite program and to fixed structures for groups and federations of groups; the latter refused to keep to a program and were in favor of "free initiatives," leaving as much autonomy and independence as possible to the individual and to groups that associated spontaneously, either temporarily or for an agreed purpose. Two leading spokespersons drove forward these two visions: Malatesta and Giuseppe Ciancabilla. Both resided in Paterson at the end of the nineteenth century.

Ciancabilla had formerly been a socialist activist and editor of *Avanti!*. He was shifting toward anarchist views. He had moved to Paterson in autumn 1898 and taken over the editorship of the weekly *La Questione Sociale*, marking it with his own increasingly anti-organizational ideas. These ideas were soon criticized by the Diritto all'esistenza [Right to Existence] group that was responsible for the newspaper, and which depended on the activism of, among others, Catalan typesetter Pedro Esteve, a companion of Malatesta who sided with the pro-organizational line.

The dispute intensified in 1899. It drew in a growing number of activists in and outside Paterson, and reverberated in the paper. As a matter of principle, the newspaper should have provided space for both organizationalists and anti-organizationalists, but that proved difficult to achieve because of the amount of friction. Malatesta, a known organizationalist, was then called on to resolve the issue. After repeated requests, he agreed to settle in Paterson during the summer of that year. A few weeks after his arrival, the Diritto all'esistenza group excluded Ciancabilla from the editorial staff and appointed Malatesta in his place. Ciancabilla then founded another periodical, *L'Aurora* [Dawn], which was first printed in Paterson, then in nearby West Hoboken, and finally in the mining centers of Yohoghany (Pennsylvania), and Spring Valley (Illinois). A few days before the first issue of *L'Aurora* came out, the tension reached a point of no return. During a meeting in West Hoboken, the anarchist Domenico Pazzaglia shot Malatesta, injuring him in the leg before being disarmed by another activist, Gaetano Bresci, who a little later became infamous for assassinating King Umberto I in Monza.

Although the opposite has often been stated by historians, Galleani was certainly closer to the political positions of Malatesta than to those of Ciancabilla, of whom he had a rather poor personal opinion.[3] However, he did not side explicitly with either party on the issue, and would later informally accuse both parties of having uselessly wasted time and money on a sterile internal dispute. He defined himself neither as an organizationalist nor as an anti-organizationalist, but as an anarchist "without adjectives."[4] In fact, his position did not coincide with either current. On the one hand, he still agreed with the substance of the "old socialist-anarchist-revolutionary program" released by the

Capolago congress of 1891. He also believed that it was necessary to leverage the masses of the exploited, the only group who were capable of making a victorious uprising and achieving social revolution. This aspect was fundamental for the organizationalists but was also supported by the anti-organizationalists, particularly in the issues of *L'Aurora* that Ciancabilla published in Spring Valley.

What Galleani did not agree with, however, was the initiative of US-based organizationalists to create a federation bringing together various Italian anarchist groups in the United States. Although he believed that association between activists was indispensable, he did not think that fixed connections between groups (in the form of correspondence committees) were useful, nor formal congresses with many delegates and motions, nor permanent political delegates. Finally, he argued that any act of rebellion, even if individual, against the established order was justified, and he believed that the phase of destroying the current social order was essential, themes present in Ciancabilla's work to a greater extent than in Malatesta's.

At the age of forty Galleani already had two decades of experience as an activist in a labor movement whose crosscurrents he knew through and through. Over time, his own independence of thought had matured, and he proudly asserted it. Once he was sure that Ciancabilla had definitely transferred his propaganda activities away from Paterson, and with Malatesta having left for London, in spring 1901, he finally accepted the invitation of the *Diritto all'esistenza* group: they would pay for a one-way ticket to Paterson for the whole family.

Before getting to the United States, Galleani decided to pass through England. It was essential to reach agreement with Malatesta in person. Thus on August 3, 1901, with a regular passport, Luigi, Maria, and the three children left from Port Said on a steamer that stopped at Naples and Genoa, before finally landing in Southampton.

In London, historically a place of refuge and a meeting point for revolutionaries, Galleani met, not only Malatesta but also Kropotkin and other activists, including Recchioni, who had collected the money in the English capital to finance his escape from Pantelleria. He also reunited with Petraroja and Pacini, old acquaintances from his time in Switzerland. Malatesta, together with the other activists, was organizing the creation of a popular university that was to begin operation the next year, and Galleani's advice was useful for him.[5] In turn, Malatesta offered Galleani the necessary reassurances concerning the work awaiting him in Paterson, both from a political and from a material point of view. The activists in New Jersey were capable of supporting propaganda in an efficient manner and guaranteeing him the conditions necessary so that he could dedicate himself exclusively to editing the paper and to speaking tours.

The police informer Ennio Bellelli, alias Virgilio, who had infiltrated the London anarchists, considered Galleani to be a "great speaker" and an "outstanding journalist." He described him as "one of Malatesta's best lieutenants," and emphasized the harmony between their ideas. Aside from the differences in definitions between the two, discussed earlier, what Bellelli surmised was substantially correct. Galleani effectively went to the United States with the full agreement of Malatesta, to continue the work that Malatesta had done during his time as editor of *La Questione Sociale,* and in a very different manner than Ciancabilla and *L'Aurora.*[6]

He was still in London, waiting to set sail, when on September 6, in Buffalo, the Polish anarchist Leon Czolgosz, a twenty-eight-year old admirer of Emma Goldman and Gaetano Bresci, killed President William McKinley, a symbol of stars-and-stripes imperialism following the United States's bloody victory against the Philippine independence movement. It was a sensational event that filled the pages of newspapers around the world and risked triggering a wave of intolerance against the entire anarchist movement. Although many activists undoubtedly applauded an act they considered heroic, others distanced themselves from it, judging it mistaken from an ethical and political point of view, as did Luigi Fabbri in the pages of *L'Agitazione* in Rome. This article provoked anger among the London anarchists. Tellingly, it was Malatesta who responded by publishing

❧ STATISTICA DEI REGICIDI ❧
dal 1801 al 1907

Data	Sovrani o capi di Stato	Stato	Esito	Autore	Nazionalita'
1801	Paolo II	Russia	F.	Congiurati	Russi
1809	Napoleone Imperat.	Francia	I.	Stapps	Tedesco
1832	Ferdinando V	Ungheria	id.	Reindel	id.
1835	Luigi Filippo	Francia	id.	Fieschi	Còrso-francese
1836	id.	id.	id.	Alibaud	Francese
1836	Id.	id.	id.	Monier	id.
1840	id.	id.	id.	Darnès	id.
1846	id.	id.	id.	Lecaut	id.
1846	id.	id.	id.	Henri	id.
1840	Regina Vittoria	Inghilterra	id.	Oxford	Inglese
1842	id.	id.	id.	Francis	id.
1844	Fed. Guglielmo IV	Prussia	id.	Tischeck	Tedesco
1848	Fran. V di Modena	Modena	id.	Rizzati	Italiano
1849	Principe di Prussia	Prussia	id.	——	Tedesco
1850	Fed. Guglielmo IV	id.	id.	Sefelage	id.
1852	Regina Isabella	Spagna	id.	Marinos	Spagnuolo
1852	Napoleone Presid.	Francia	id.	Congiurati	Francesi
1852	Regina Vittoria	Inghilterra	id.	Un ufficiale	Inglese
1853	Francesco Giuseppe	Austria	id.	Libenyi	Ungherese
1854	Carlo III di Parma	Parma	F.	Ignoto	Italiano
1855	Napoleone III	Francia	I.	Pianori	id.
1855	id.	id.	id.	Bellemare	Francese
1856	Regina Isabella	Spagna	id.	Fuontes	Spagnuolo
1856	Ferdinando II	Napoli	id.	A. Milano	Italiano
1858	Napoleone III	Francia	id.	Orsini	id.
1861	Guglielmo re	Prussia	id.	Oscar Beckers	Tedesco
1861	Regina Amelia	Grecia	id.	Drosios	Greco
1865	Pres. Lincoln	Stati Uniti	F.	Booth	Americano
1866	Alessandro II	Russia	I.	Karakosoff	Russo
1867	id.	id.	id.	Berenzeski	Polacco Russo
1868	Michele	Serbia	F.	Radavanavich	Slavo
1869	Vicerè d'Egitto	Egitto	I.	——	Egiziano
1869	Napoleone III	Francia	id.	Congiurati	Francesi
1872	Regina Vittoria	Inghilterra	id.	O'Connor	Irlandese
1872	Amedeo di Savoia	Spagna	id.	Pastor y Fernon	Spagnuolo
1872	Pres. Balta	Perù	F.	Insorti	Peruviani
1872	Lord Mayo. Vicerè	India	id.	——	Indiano
1872	Pres. Belivia	Bolivia	id.	La Fayè	Boliviano
1875	Pres. Garcia Moreno	Equatore	id.	Insorti	Equatoriani
1876	Abdul-Azis Sultano	Turchia	id.	Musulmani	Turchi
1877	Pres. Gill	Paraguay	id.	Insorti	Indigeni
1878	Guglielmo I	Germania	I.	Hodel	Tedesco
1878	id.	id.	id.	Nobiling	id.
1878	Alfonso XII	Spagna	id.	Oxliva y Moncasi	Spagnuolo
1878	Umberto I	Italia	id.	Passannate	Italiano
1879	Alessandro II	Russia	id.	Solovieff	Russo
1879	Milano	Serbia	id.	——	Serbo
1879	Alessandro II	Russia	id.	Nihilisti	Russi
1879	Re e Regina	Spagna	id.	Otero	Spagnuolo
1880	Alessandro II	Russia	id.	Nihilisti	Russi
1881	id.	id.	F.	id.	id.
1881	Pres Garfield	Stati Uniti	id.	Guiteau	Illinese orig. f.se
1882	Francesco Giuseppe	Austria	I.	Oberdanck	Italiano
1882	Regina Vittoria	Inghilterra	id.	Maclean	Scozzese
1888	Alessandro III	Russia	id.	Nihilisti	Russi
1893	Guglielmo I	Prussia	id.	——	Tedesco
1894	Pres. Carnot	Francia	F.	Caserio	Italiano
1895	Regina	Corea	id.	——	Coreani
1896	Nassir-ed-Din	Persia	id.	Mollak Reza	Persiano
1896	Faure	Francia	I.	François	Francese
1897	Umberto I	Italia	id.	Acciarito	Italiano
1897	Faure	Francia	id.	Gallet	Francese
1898	Imp.ce Elisabetta	Austria	F.	Luccheni	Italiano
1898	Giorgio II	Grecia	I.	Carditzi	Greco
1898	Pres. Moraes Barros	Brasile	id.	Bispo de Mello	Brasiliano
1899	Milano	Serbia	id.	Knezevick	Serbo
1900	Principe di Galles	Inghilterra	id.	Sipido	Belga
1900	Umberto I	Italia	F.	Bresci	Italiano
1900	Muzzafer-Ed-Din	Persia	I.	Salson	Francese
1900	Guglielmo II	Germania	id.	Ichuapka	Ted. orig. Polac.
1900	Pres. Alfaro	Equatore	id.	——	Equatoriano
1901	Pres. Mac Kinley	Stati Uniti	F.	Czolgosz	Polacco
1902	Leopoldo II	Belgio	I.	Rubino	Italiano
1903	Re e Regina	Serbia	F.	Congiurati	Serbi
1905	Loubet, Alfonso XIII	Francia, Spagna	I.	——	
1906	Re e Regina	Spagna	id.	Moral	Spagnuolo

N.B. La lettera F. significa Felice, ossia che l'atto è riuscito; la lettera I. significa Infelice, ossia che l'atto non è riuscito.

Regicide statistics from *Cronaca Sovversiva*

"Arrestiamoci sulla china: a proposito dell'attentato di Buffalo" [Let's Stop Going Down this Slippery Slope: Concerning the Buffalo Attack], an article in which he publicly denounced the position taken by the Roman periodical and affirmed the necessity of feelings of hatred against the oppressor and the practical realization of what had been propagandized in words.[7]

Galleani, who personally participated in internal discussions within the movement and agreed with Malatesta, mentioned several times during the coming years how important Czolgosz's act had been, stressing his courage and consistency, and making him an example of the importance of acts of rebellion, even if done by individuals.

Two weeks after McKinley's murder, Galleani departed for the United States. For security reasons he traveled alone, leaving Maria and the children temporarily behind in London, where they were supported economically by Malatesta and other comrades.

PART TWO

The Most Dangerous Anarchist in America

CHAPTER XIV

The Revolt of the Dyers

The postmark should tell you the weather is stormy [...]. Once again I've been outlawed. The general strike of dyers and textile workers, prepared by fruitful revolutionary propaganda, exploded powerfully on June 18, despite schemes to thwart it (calls for calm from Italian socialists and unionists of the Socialist Labor Party). The general strike was unanimously proclaimed in two general meetings at Turn Hall and Haledon Park. MacQueen and I led the demonstration to stop work in factories where people were still working, and to expel scabs from those factories, where for a month they had received room and board in the dye works without leaving, during either the day or at night. We forced all of the factories to close, driving out the scabs—going around all of the factories from 8:00 in the morning until 6:00 at night—and destroying the dye works of Gaede and Bamford, where the police attacked us. The police were warded off everywhere by revolver shots from our angry little Neapolitans. We had numerous losses from the Sinnon dye works, where cops armed with Winchesters seriously injured about twenty comrades. Now the strike is going to end, seven owners have agreed, the others resist but they will agree too.

The bourgeoisie and the city authorities are furious, they want our heads and the application of new laws against anarchists, fifteen years in prison and a two thousand dollar fine. They're hunting for us everywhere. MacQueen, the English comrade, fell into their hands and bail will cost 250 francs, which he'll find.

For me it'll be more difficult, because they consider me the person responsible for the movement and the riots, particularly as several thousand Italians took part in the demonstration. Luckily I have escaped and I can wait in the hope that the brutal impulsiveness of the moment will fade somewhat over time and with the changing conditions [...]. A revolver shot [from an agent] went through my left cheek and damaged the skin on my head a little, but there is no danger of complications, in two weeks it'll be alright. It's not yet my turn...

In early July 1902, Galleani took clandestine refuge in Montreal, escaping the police. From there he wrote the above letter to Gross, recounting what had happened in Paterson a few weeks earlier without mincing his words.[1]

The first days of his residence in the United States could not have been more eventful. He came ashore on October 10, 1901, to settle in Paterson. His immediate objective was to rebuild psychologically an environment still torn apart by political disagreement, as well as the deep personal conflict between Malatesta and Ciancabilla. This was not an easy task and, as he later recalled, it would consume a great portion of his energy during his first three years in America.

Paterson is not far from New York City. It was a center for silk production, a sector that had undergone major expansion in the 1890s, coming to employ about twelve thousand textile workers and dyers, plus several thousands more in nearby towns. Among these workers, Italians—both men and women—were numerous, drawn from textile districts in the provinces of Biella and Como, as well as from the South of Italy.[2] Those from Biella and Como were mostly textile workers, the Southerners more often than not were employed in the dye works doing poorly paid and arduous work. In the city, Italian-language anarchists had a solid presence and, as previously mentioned, it was from Paterson that Bresci left to assassinate Umberto I.

On October 16, without any time to get settled in, Galleani, after an introduction by Pedro Esteve, gave his first lecture to a packed hall on Straight Street in Paterson, on the topic of "The anarchist idea and political parties." Several days later, his arrival was celebrated at the Colombo Restaurant in New York. He was introduced by a brief speech by Luigi Rafuzzi and recalled with emotion the past few years and the figures of Schicchi, Palla, Recchioni, and Malatesta. He then traced two courses of action for the future of the Italian-language movement in the United States: seek harmony between groups, and never bow your head to the reaction that will inevitably follow any act of revolt. His presence provoked "enthusiasm, affection, a reawakening" among the rows of activists and immediately inspired renewed activity, involving even women.[3] Already, from the first weeks, he paid particular attention to the emancipation of women and the family, with several impromptu articles and lectures, even outside of Paterson. Soon, groups made up only of women activists appeared, first in New York and then in other places as well.[4]

His talents as a speaker immediately ignited enthusiasm. Several US-based groups began collecting money to support Galleani's wider propaganda tours, which lasted for several months. These activities were a major feature of his life in the coming years. His range of action gradually extended until it reached the most remote corners of the country. Some comrades organized a "miles" book, a type of permanent subscription that allowed him to travel throughout the United States. Repeated tours from North to South and East to West represented a fundamental element around which the Italian movement organized.

Social studies circles were often formed wherever he spoke. In a letter to Gross in 1910, he wrote: "I always go around like a spinning top." He had just returned from several weeks spent in Illinois, Missouri, and Kansas and was about to leave again for the states of Washington, Oregon, and California.[5] Influenced by the rhetoric of republican speakers he had listened to as a young man, such as Bovio, Cavallotti, Imbriani, and Edoardo Pantano, his speeches were marked by rigorous argument, by a "perfect and elegant literary form, [with a] rich, but precise language," and they were magnetic.[6] Some years later a comrade described the profound impression that his words left upon listeners as follows:

His colossal stature, severe and penetrating gaze, broad
and noble gestures, voice supple through all inflections,
fascinated and commanded the respect of the most hesitant
listener [...]. His eloquence [...] engulfed the audience like a
storm [...]. There was no resistance. As if in a film, human
events and institutions thought to be age-old tottered on
their pedestals [...]. A lecture by Galleani, although in a foreign land, was an event and the Italians, who had hastened
from everywhere, were left entranced, shaken, enraptured.[7]

Meetings could last from two to four hours in the frequent
event of a debate with socialists or representatives from other
schools of thought (including prelates). They were reasoned and
multidisciplinary narratives, which addressed with clear logic
numerous themes, including poverty and its causes; emancipation and revolution; scientific socialism and utopian socialism;
religious lies; the fraud of parliamentarianism; anarchism and
science; anarchists and what they want; achieving happiness;
the Paris Commune; the universe and God; why we are slaves;
democracy and anarchy; the origins of religions, their nature and
their effects; et cetera. Hundreds of people attended, more than
had come in previous years to listen to Malatesta or Ciancabilla.

In addition to public meetings, individual propaganda was
also important. Such propaganda included private meetings by
which Galleani intended to establish close relationships with
activists in different places, which thus became points of reference and trust for Cronaca Sovversiva. "Wherever he goes," wrote
comrades from Milford, "warm discussions light up around him.
Persistent objections, doubts that have tormented our souls for
months and months, unravel before him."[8]

CHAPTER XV

La Questione Sociale

In addition to his speaking activities, Galleani dedicated himself with total abnegation to working on *La Questione Sociale*. The first issue he edited came out on October 26, 1901. The newspaper was immediately more aggressive than the previous issues edited by Esteve. It urged workers to action and soon became a point of reference and connection for many US groups, which often sent in notices and reports. Galleani was able to promote individual activists and groups, to whose activities he gave credit and space, thus bringing to life the words of Étienne de La Boétie, which had appeared from the first issue of the paper: "decide to serve no longer and you will be free." Every reader must have known that their own conditions of exploitation were similar to those of millions of others on earth. Hence the pages of the newspaper gave considerable attention to international events and carried reports of labor struggles in Europe, as well as resistance to tsarism in Russia.

At the same time, the newspaper acquired greater theoretical depth than it had under Esteve's management. In addition to original articles by Galleani, it published others by Elisée Reclus, Kropotkin, and Lev Mechnikov, as well as excerpts from Guyau and republications of Proudhon. Passages from Kropotkin's *Mutual Aid: A Factor of Evolution* were published in Italian. This text was published in English and was partially translated into French. It was a fundamental theoretical point of reference for Galleani's anarchism.

Through these authors, Galleani intended to give his readers tools for understanding, nurturing rather than imposing a subversive view of the world. Self-education, in this sense, was a central feature. Hence his propaganda for the establishment of a popular university in New York, and the regular column, "Biblioteca anarchica" [Anarchist Library], in which he provided short summaries of texts that were fundamental to his vision of the world.

These are worth describing. All seven works by Guyau published at that time, among which *Esquisse d'une morale sans obligation ni sanction* stood out as "the most splendid work on ethics of the [nineteenth] century." Also *L'irréligion de l'avenir* [*The Nonreligion of the Future*], and *Man Versus the State* by Spencer were "stupendous pages in defense of the individual," which, although they were written in defense of the bourgeois individual—he maintained—could also be used against this restricted vision. *Les assemblées parlantes. Critique du government représentatif* [Speaking Assemblies: Critique of Representative Government] by Emile Leverdays, a critique of universal suffrage and the parliamentary system. *Mélanges philosophiques* [Philosophical Miscellany] by Denis Diderot on "religion, love, materialism." *Critique sociale* [Social Critique] by Blanqui. The magazines *L'Università Popolare* [Popular University] by Luigi Molinari, *Les Temps Nouveax*, the libertarian periodical for children *Jean-Pierre*, and *Les primitifs* [Primitive Folk] by Elie Reclus, "a study of many primitive people and a ruthless indictment against our so-called civilization and against capitalist atrocities."[1]

A characteristic of Galleani's editorial work was his severe and untiring critique of the activity of socialists. Italians were the main targets, both those in Italy and immigrants in the United States. The latter were represented by Giacinto Menotti Serrati, who was to become a leading figure of maximalism, and who at that time edited *Il Proletario* [The Proletariat], the mouthpiece of the Italian socialists in North America. Galleani had a first debate with Serrati on May 2, 1902, at the Socialist Labor Party Hall in Barre, Vermont. He then made Serrati the subject of a fierce critical campaign in the years to come. Galleani believed representatives of the Italian Socialist Party, who identified either with the current led by Turati or the more radical current of Arturo Labriola and Enrico Ferri, had two unpardonable faults. First, they deceived the workers, asserting that their parliamentary action had moved the Italian government in a liberal direction, when instead it was known that every small improvement was obtained only through direct action. Second, since they made only timid protests or performed sterile obstructionist maneuvers in Parliament, they validated the actions of a state whose essence, contrary to what they affirmed, had not changed and that was guilty of repeated massacres of people, as demonstrated by the cases of Berra (Emilia-Romagna), Candela (Apulia), and Giarratana (Sicily). Thus they diverted the large mass of workers who, instead of taking to the streets to demand justice in their own names, delegated their complaints to them with the illusion of being able to improve the wretched conditions they were forced into.[2]

His judgment of the government of Giovanni Giolitti, who he described as "a crook and a recidivist Jesuit [...], a jackal," remained completely negative in the years to come. He judged advances in social legislation and civil liberties (such as freedom of assembly) promoted by the government in the first years of the century to be useless and illusory. Without touching the regime of private ownership or the monopoly of the means of production and exchange, the rights Giolitti authorized could only be illusory and destined to vanish according to the whims of future governments.[3]

In autumn 1901, Maria and the children joined Galleani in Paterson. The family seemed finally able to get some stability, which was no small matter because Maria was again pregnant. The new child born in January 1902 was named Olimpio with the middle name Eliseo, a clear reference to Galleani's friend Elisée Reclus.

However, 1902 was not a tranquil year. In February, a fire burned a good part of Paterson and damaged the newspaper's offices, sending the library and printing materials up in smoke. To make things worse, this was later followed by a flood. The mood among textile workers, though, was increasingly heating up.

Galleani, as we will see, was directly responsible. He was a born insurgent and was at his best at the side of manual workers. To this group, understood in the widest sense, he addressed a large part of his propaganda. It was no accident that he began his experience as an editor of *La Questione Sociale* with a front-page article on the eventful strike of five thousand tobacco workers that broke out in October 1901 in Tampa, Florida, where many anarchists were active.[4] Max Nettlau explained Galleani's abilities, relating them to his previous activity in Italy, as follows: "He was directly connected to the labor movement in Northern Italy, and this explains how he found himself in the milieu of the Italian labor movement in America, where various industrial centers constituted a magnification of the labor environment in Northern Italy, which he knew very well."[5]

CHAPTER XVI

Strike!

Beginning in early 1902, Galleani held several meetings of dye workers, paying particular attention to those who spoke Italian. These men and women were forced to work in "despicable sheds or underground halls with no air and no light, [with] the suffocating stench of acids," often suffering from "arthritis" and "chlorosis." Now they were rising up and demanding an increase in their wages, which were lower than those paid in other American states.[1] In mid-April they went on strike. At that point the main aim of Galleani and other anarchists was to extend the mobilization to other textile workers, and to transform it into a general strike of all textile plants.

The general strike, understood in a revolutionary way, was, for Galleani, the practical means to begin expropriating the wealth of owners for the benefit of all, and thus to launch the revolutionary process. He agreed with the Marxist theory that wage increases were inexorably destined to be eroded by the progressive increase in the cost of living. He did not believe that the proletariat could make real gains as long as the means of production remained in the hands of the capitalists. Yet every dispute about wages and working conditions was worth undertaking. Partial struggles were useful for preparing the ground for a general revolutionary strike understood "not [as] folded arms, but [as] expropriation, battle, destruction of the institutions of privilege."[2]

He therefore urged the dye workers to make their union into a tool to radicalize the protest, while, from the pages of *La Questione Sociale,* he attempted to overcome divisions between branches of industry by connecting their struggle with the miners' strike in Pennsylvania.[3]

In the early 1900s, workers in the United States were going through a gradual process of unionization, although the percentage of workers belonging to unions was still relatively low: about twenty percent, or two million workers. Unions, Galleani wrote, could be a valid tool for creating the general revolutionary strike. Anarchists should encourage activity and militancy among union members, promoting strikes and rebellion.[4] He said, "All demonstrations of solidarity can open the door for achievements that, even without anarchist labels, prepare minds in an anarchist way against any abuse of power by the authorities, the owners, the bosses."[5]

However unions must be autonomous from institutions, decentralized, and apolitical, bringing together workers apart from specific party allegiances and according to their class interests. This meant they must shake off the reformist and bureaucratic attitudes that endangered their revolutionary potential.

About three years before, in the columns of *La Questione Sociale*, Malatesta had encouraged comrades to participate in all labor struggles and had warned against the bureaucratic degeneration of the union movement: "Therefore the first task of anarchists within workers' societies is to rip the members out of their passivity, excite their initiative, and see to it that they live and battle with the active endeavors of all, and thereby come to understand the uselessness and harm done by presidents and committees with authoritarian assignments and lavish stipends, and eliminate them."[6]

There was another idea, dear to Galleani, that Malatesta too had propagandized ever since the time of *L'Associazione*: that intervening in the world of labor was not an end in itself, but only a means for creating as wide a strike as possible, capable of changing into insurrection. Now, with the publication in London of the bilingual periodical *Lo Sciopero Generale* [The General Strike], Malatesta was more determined to maintain this: "During a general strike the people should not take to the streets without being ready to shoot the soldiers the bourgeoisie will use to resist them."[7] The strike, therefore, must be "armed": "Revolutionaries should arm themselves so that they are ready to make the revolution whenever the opportunity arises. Non-revolutionary workers should arm themselves as well, if only to avoid being beaten like so many sheep."[8]

In full agreement with these words, in meeting after meeting, in Paterson and in the surrounding areas, Galleani forged ahead and the strike widened. It followed the example of what happened in Barcelona the previous February when the uprising moved beyond mere demands, and managed to lead to "partial and immediate expropriations."[9] As regards arms—light arms at least—the anarchist groups of the entire area were already well equipped.

From early June, *La Questione Sociale* published several issues in Italian, German, and English aimed at dye and textile workers of different nationalities. Meetings were often held in three languages, thanks to the intervention, alongside Galleani, of the Englishman William MacQueen, editor of the newspaper *Liberty* and Rudolf Grosmann, spokesman of German-language anarchists in New York.[10]

On June 17, 1902, during a crowded meeting held by the Dye Workers Union at Turn Hall in Paterson, a general strike was proclaimed. Eight weeks earlier, a relatively small nucleus of Italian workers from the dye works had started the uprising. Now the strike involved about fifteen thousand workers, including dye and textile workers from the city and surrounding areas, of whom two-thirds were Italian.[11]

The day after, Galleani was at Saals Park in Haledon, a few miles from Paterson. According to reports, between three- and eight thousand workers were present.

> After a few brief speeches Galleani takes the floor, the crowd calling for him; he jumps on top of the speakers' table. The onlookers get excited, yell, raise their arms, throw their hats, handkerchiefs, newspapers, and canes into the air, then all of a sudden they grow silent as he begins speaking in a clear, vigorous manner. With large gestures he speaks in Italian, but English, French, and German speaking workers are also listening to him. He says: "A mob

La Questione Sociale

Periodico Socialista-Anarchico

Entered at the Post-Office at Paterson, N. J., as second-class matter.

Per lettere, comunicazioni, ecc., dirigersi alle
QUESTIONE SOCIALE
Box 1639,
PATERSON, New-Jersey, U.S.A.

Abbonamenti
Anno . . . . .
Semestre . . .
Trimestre . . .
Estero spese . . .
Numero Separato 5 Soldi.
Gli abbonamenti si pagano anticipati.

ANNO VIII.   PATERSON, N. J., SABATO 24 MAGGIO 1902.   NUOVA SERIE. No. 137.

La settimana di sangue

...... Je dis que la société n'est pas à l'aise ayant sur elle ces fantômes Que leur rire est terrible entre tous les symptômes

Et qu'il faut trembler, tant qu'on n'aura pû guerir

Cette facilité sinistre de mourir.

V. HUGO.

Resterà nella storia, illuminata di sinistri bagliori, a richiamare sul regime, che fu vergogna del secolo nostra aver tollerato, la maledizione dei nipoti più lontani.

Se essa non segnasse che il 22 ed il 28 Maggio del 1871 che un periodo particolarmente bieco di reazione od inaudito ed ineffabile di carneficina e di strage — quale dopo la San Bartolomeo non avevan visto gli occhi del mondo — come di tutte le vergogne, di tutti i dolori avrebbe anche dei suoi ultimi echi ragione il tempo, maestro oblioso di postume riabilitazioni.

Essa ha ben più preciso e più educativo contenuto.

Noi abbiamo accennato nel nostro numero del 18 Marzo quale appaia, man mano che gli si sbebbiano d'attorno i veli pudibondi, le ipocrisie interessate e le ripurazioni d'orpello, il significato politico e sociale del movimento comunalista e come sia vano ormai volerlo contenere entro i discreti confini d'un patriottico disgusto o d'un'amorfa agitazione disperata.

Il movimento comunalista del 1871 che senza frasi e senza spavalderia aveva messo alla porta l'autorità centrale, deposto il governo del 4 Settembre rincantucciato a Versailles, fronteggiato il nemico in armi che stringeva d'assedio Parigi, il moto comunalista fu soprattutto reazione contro il regime borghese, contro la menzogna parlamentare che lo caratterizza, contro l'autorità dello Stato che lo riassume.

Quando fosse arduo o temerario desumerlo dalla storia documentata dal periodo brevissimo che corre dal 18 Marzo al 22 Maggio 1871, tale carattere apparirebbe evidente dalla natura e dalla rabbia della repressione.

Mentre la Comune brancolava tra i giudizii scipiti e grotteschi dei Comitati di salute pubblica con cui i suoi parlamentari ritentavano sottrarsi alle responsabilità gravi del-

l'ora; mentre nella dichiarazione del 16 Maggio la minoranza anarchica rivendicandole per intero, distingueva tra la sua condotta rivoluzionaria e quella dittatoriale ed autoritaria della maggioranza, Thiers, a cui gli sciacalli del patriottismo morboso e schiaffeggiato, le iene della sacristia, i beccai del militarismo in ribasso chiedevano l'ora e l'occasione della rivincita che non sapevano credere nè dare alla frontiera dell'Est e gli intimavano sens'altro di dimettersi, Thiers rispondeva, nell'assemblea versagliese dell'11 Maggio: Accordatemi ancora otto giorni ed ogni pericolo sarà sparito!

Dieci giorni dopo Parigi era invasa, i massacri cominciarono e proseguirono con un accanimento ed una ferocia tali che il nuovo salvatore della Francia il piccolo e crocioso Thiers oscurò ben presto la fama dei beccai di Giugno e degli assassini del 2 Dicembre.

Lo spirito del governo repubblicano è ben riflesso nel seguente articolo della Gazzetta Ufficiale di Versailles, la quale preoccupandosi della malsana pietà e mollezza dei giudici a cui gli insorti eranbbero stati deferiti e ribelandosi alle dichiarazioni fatte alla tribuna perchè non fosse fatto torto al regolare e normale corso della legge, si chiedeva:

"Non è periccoloso affidare cotesti assassini ai giudici ordinarii, colti, plevi di erudizione, 'noti all'estero, e capaci forse di larghi sentimenti umani?

"Fate quello che ogni popolo

energico e grande farebbe in simili casi:

"NESSUN PRIGIONIERO.

"Se nel mucchio vi sarà un galantuomo vero voi lo troverete, in qual bulicame di delinquenti un galantuomo è distinto dalla propria aureola."

"Accordate ai bravi soldati la libertà di vendicare i loro compagni facendo sul luogo e NELLA RABBIA DELL'AZIONE quello che a sangue freddo non farebbero più domani: FUOCO!

Avverte a proposito il compagno Lefranca nel suo "Etude sur le mouvement communiste" che per trovare qualcosa di simile bisogna risalire al XIII secolo, all'assedio di Bézier e che la feroce borghese sorpassa di cento cubiti l'odio religioso e fanatico dei Castelnau e dei Montmorency.

E Gallifet, l'immondo marchese de

Gallifet, investito di pieni poteri, esercitò sui parigini e con particolare coraggio sulle donne, sui vecchi e sui bambini la vendetta dei fug-giaschi vili di 8e lan, delle terribili paure pretesche, dell'odio borghese illividito e pazzo.

Le fucilazioni in massa durarono tutta la settimana a Satory, alla rampe, Lobau, al Pere Lachaise. Le mitragliere risuonarono durante le sette giorni nei più eccentrici quartieri di Parigi, mietendo tra la rivoluzionaria del proletariato quarantamila vittime tra cui infinito il numero delle donne e dei fanciulli.

E damine borghesi accompagnate degli ufficiali che avevan salvato le lacche fuggendo a rompicollo dinanzi ai prussiani, percuotevano dell'ombrellino nel volto le madri del popolo dirette al supplizio; le vecchie marchese sopravissute ai lupanari dell'impero, imbellettate e

ritinte di rispettabile bigottismo predicevano in pubblico che occorreva ad evitare le rivoluzioni nuove, uccidere le donne ed i bimbi dei comunardi (!). I figli di lupi diventano lupi.

La settimana di sangue è gravida di ammaestramenti severi. Essa ci avverte che durante i periodi rivoluzionarii ogni sentimentalismo tra cattolico e cicisbeo deve essere rapidamente soffocato, che tutto quanto tende a far degenerare in adattamenti parlamentari l'energia rivoluzionaria è tradimento, che i borghesi tornati all'imperio vi si scaldano colle stragi esemplari senza dar quartiere neppure ai bimbi inconsci perchè i figli di lupi diventano lupi.

Bisogna ricordarsene domani, in cui germogliata dai morti del maggio, maturate nell'aspra vigilia dei ribellioni periodiche e progressive dovranno le aspirazioni del proletariato, sulle rovine della borghesia disfatta, raccogliere il frutto della abnegazione e del sacrificio.

22 Maggio 1901

Se avevano d'se hanno ancora paura lo s'ha.

Per questo lo strozzarono che la un anno nella grigia e silenziosa cella di Portolongone, per questo oggi i sagaci della polizia repubblicana ne insegnano la campagna ed i timidi senza tregua e senza quartiere.

Gli è che vivo par sotto la volta cupa dell'ergastolo, pur tra i vincoli i forzati dei reg'i neppi gli tar-ribili ancora come un arcangelo dell'alboato triste della gelera aggiungeva gagliarde vibrazioni all've della sua ultima libera parole:

"Ho sentito il capo della Stato perchè egli era, a mio avviso, responsabile di tutte le ultime politiche e magnistanti del sistema che egli incarnava e difende."

Era la minaccia perenne la quale dagli scogli dell'Elba fingolava im-placabile la poltronerir parassitaria d'ovvegone che spossata la vita del paese bianco nella vedette asce.

A di virra generazione feroce d'idioti ceerebro soffrono ogni vece di rivolta in una serta di draconiano complotti o sentire di pietà buona volta i vostri vostri impieghi e convulsi di fame o di ribellione.

Per questo se rimasto or fa un anno nella grigia e silenziosa cella di Portolongone.

Per questo la rabbia dei birri insegue ancora di maledizioni silenziosi i venti dei suoi ammaestamenti la compagna ed i timidi senza tregua e senza quartiere.

Ma sulla tomba abbandonata alle ortiche ed al maledizioni ufficiali i venti dei suoi raccolgono il voto e le aspirazioni, i fremiti ed il senso del martirio o la diffusione, sentono senza di perdizione nuova di ribellione, dalla azzurra incantatore dal mare lupeo fine alle abrupte scogliere calabresi, fine alle affigurimmi conche sicilliane, più nelle miniere, lungo le spiagge, nei cantieri, per le officine semani di lavoro o di malediioni, pei campi fioruiti di spighe e di tirolia preparadovri le fatali rimarcoioni della vita, le scaturale la-crime di i lavoratori, o germono gloriose della libera germogliata sulla terra d'un mondo di cui GAETANO BRESCI affretto la caduta.

Per questo lo strozzarono che la un anno nella grigia e silenziosa cella di Portolongone.

Per questo la rabbia dei birri ne insegue ancora di un non momento prende fittutto il culto e la gratitudine dei ribelli, dei fieri, dei generosi, della
QUESTIONE SOCIALE.

thirsty for gold and blood, has been exploiting you for too long, comrades. They have the wealth and the luxury. You have poverty and shame. The more they bleed you dry the more they fill their coffers. With that money your bosses will collect other fortunes, and if necessary, as always happens, buy the consciences of the wretches whose job it is to slit your throats. Will you let them slit your throats?" A shiver runs down everyone's spine. "Look at your women: they were beautiful and healthy. The work the owners have condemned them to has made them pale, emaciated, anemic. Look at your children: you dream of watching them grow up beautiful, affectionate, intelligent: the factory ruins them. Look at yourselves. Were you not full of hope when you left your country, tired of medieval tyranny? And now in this place of so-called progress you are similarly subjugated to a tyranny no less fierce. Comrades! Rise up! Answer the legal violence of capital with the human violence of revolt!"[12]

Once these words were pronounced, a noisy and partially armed procession left the park and headed, resolutely, toward the town's dye works. Galleani was at the head with a cane in one hand and a revolver in his pocket. The aim was to stop production, even in plants where scabs continued to work.

They ignited the greatest uprising that Paterson had ever seen, as the public prosecutor affirmed in the subsequent trial. Several dye works were stoned, occupied by the crowd, and in some cases burned down. Barricades went up around the city. The police were attacked with clubs and pistol shots and responded in turn: several workers were injured, including some women.[13] The next day, the mayor of Paterson suspended the Chief of Police for failing to stop the rioters, and took on the duties of public safety himself. More police officers were sent. Squads of firefighters and a regiment of the Newark militia were mobilized to protect the streets and factories. But the strike spread even to neighboring suburbs, and there was disorder in Passaic, Sandy Hill, Hudson County, and West Hoboken. Workers stoned the few factories that remained open and were dispersed by police and firefighters with water cannons. The only factory still open in Paterson on June 20, Lockwood & Hurd, decided to close after workers threatened to blow it up with dynamite.

The action continued solidly everywhere for a week. It concluded only at the end of the month when there was a general wage increase, and one dead and many injured among the workers. Immediately the authorities searched the houses and properties of Italian rebels, believing that those responsible for what had happened were from the Diritto all'esistenza group. They hunted for Galleani in particular, considering him to be one of the main instigators of the uprising, together with MacQueen and Grosmann. They were convinced that they were still hiding somewhere in Paterson, but could not find them.[14] Maria endured repeated pressure from the police, but did not utter a word.

CHAPTER XVII

A Spaniard in Montreal

By the morning of June 20, realizing that the situation was becoming dangerous, Galleani vanished. He went to Philadelphia, and then he secretly crossed the border into Canada and settled in Montreal. A few days after his arrival he wrote to Gross: "My children stayed with their mother in Paterson. I've been here for three days and I detest this city [...]. I'd like to leave, but to where? I need to wait until at least October. I wait for ... my star, meaning a job in a Havana cigar factory."[1]

In the Canadian city, he was hosted by a local community of Spanish anarchists, and passed himself off as a Spaniard. Meanwhile, the authorities were hunting for him throughout New Jersey. They put a bounty on his head that increased week after week from $400 up to $5,000—an enormous sum.[2]

That September, the trial began with only MacQueen and Grosmann on the bench of the accused. The following month, they were each sentenced to five years in prison and a fine of $1,500. Galleani remained at large, all the more so because New Jersey law did not allow trials *in absentia*. If he had appeared in court he would have been liable to the maximum sentence of up to twenty-six years in prison and $8,000 in fines.[3] As he explained in a letter to Gross: "My case is particularly serious, since the Italians stood out in the attacks on the factories and the police, and since I was among them, and participated in and spoke at all of the meetings of the strikers, almost every day for eight weeks—even at some meetings after the warrant for my arrest had been issued. They're furious."[4]

Thus he remained secretly in Montreal, in continuous contact with Maria and the children, who "beautiful, strong, and

intelligent [...] are beginning to understand pain [and] will be rebels," he wrote.[5] To Maria, who was supported by the local anarchist community, he also sent a good part of the allowance of
nine dollars a week that he had been receiving from the *Diritto
all'esistenza* group since he started editing *La Questione Sociale*.
During all of this upheaval, he had not ceased to dedicate himself
to the periodical, and continued to edit it with verve and care,
despite his distance from it and all the other difficulties.

In the columns of the paper, he violently attacked Serrati,
who was guilty of assisting the authorities in their work, and
publicly accused him of responsibility for the violence in
Paterson and the consequent police reaction. Fearless, he was
convinced that the actions taken in Paterson were right, and that
it was necessary to continue on the path of permanent rebellion
and armed revolt. *La Questione Sociale* therefore "welcomed" the
announcement of the publication in London of the periodical *La
Rivoluzione Sociale* [The Social Revolution]. With this newspaper,
Malatesta and his comrades further sharpened their self-crit-
icism of the strategy that could be traced back to *L'Agitazione*,
edited by Malatesta himself in Ancona between 1897 and 1898.
This strategy would have led the anarchist movement to concen-
trate exclusively on propaganda for workers without dedicating
the necessary energy to practical (meaning military) preparation
for insurrection. He said, "We believe that it is necessary to take
an active part in the labor movement, but without allowing oneself to be absorbed, without compromising with its conservative
and reactionary aspects, and always remembering that it cannot
be anything but a means for making propaganda and bringing
together the forces of revolution."[6]

"Take an active part in the labor movement" meant, for *La
Rivoluzione Sociale*, "not accepting roles [in unions] and remaining simple members, active, vigilant, always ready to seize the
occasion to spread the idea of emancipation, to provoke an act of
rebellion."[7]

On the other hand, "bringing together the forces of revolution" also implied material preparation for armed insurrection,
since "improved weapons requires one to provide oneself with

the means capable of resisting [them]."[8] These positions were the same as those that Galleani had been propagandizing for some time.

In late September, he found work in a cigar factory, where several Spanish-speaking anarchist activists were employed. He worked for up to eleven hours a day for a few dollars a week. His job was that of the *despadillador*, which involved removing the rib (*despadillado*) from tobacco leaves with a special thimble. He also continued to work for the newspaper iñ the few hours that remained, but now the *Diritto all'esistenza* group backed him up with an editor on the spot, Esteve, who was also the typesetter for the newspaper. With his factory wages he managed to arrange for Maria and the children to join him in Montreal in December 1902.

Given this situation, the *Circolo di studi sociali* of Barre, a city in Vermont not far from Montreal, suggested that the movement should transfer *La Questione Sociale* to there, with Galleani's agreement. The idea was for Galleani to cross the border and direct the newspaper from Barre, a place considered to be safer than New Jersey, where he was a wanted man, and where, during the course of 1902, new, more restrictive laws were passed on freedom of expression, aimed to strike at the most radical fringes.[9] The idea of the transfer was widely discussed among various groups in the United States, even in the newspaper's columns. Overall, most activists were not in favor of the idea. They argued it was useful to keep a publication in Paterson to maintain continuity of propaganda activity on the ground. Thus an idea began to grow in the following few months that would lead to the birth of *Cronaca Sovversiva* [Subversive Chronicle]—the idea of a sister publication of *La Questione Sociale*, a new newspaper to be based in Barre and edited by Galleani. To follow through with this idea, in early 1903, he decided to quit as editor of the Paterson paper and move to Vermont with the whole of his family.[10]

Among the Quarry Workers of Vermont

At the beginning of the twentieth century, Barre was a town of just over ten thousand inhabitants, including 2,500 immigrants, mostly employed in various aspects of the granite quarrying and processing industry. Among these, there were many Italians, most of them from Carrara or Varese. The former were known for their anarchist views, the latter were primarily socialists. They worked together with people of other nationalities, particularly the large number of Scots, most of whom came originally from the Aberdeen area.

A particular set of events had determined the migration route from Carrara to Barre.[1] Since the 1880s, a small nucleus of sculptors and stonecutters had accepted job offers from the Vermont Marble Company and decided to leave Carrara and cross the ocean. Others joined them in subsequent years, including some who came to escape the continuing repression following the 1894 insurrection known as the "Lunigiana uprising." Galleani had participated in those events, working to connect anarchist groups and to boost the movement in Liguria and Northern Italy. He now encountered some of these workers in America. There were not only marble workers—mostly stonecutters—from Tuscany, but also the direct descendants from many different industries of the oppressed people of the Po Valley, who had been the target of his intense propaganda in the 1880s.

At the time of Galleani's arrival, the entire area of the Green Mountains, of which Barre is the main town, was dotted with mines where granite with a low iron content was extracted. This granite remained white over time, even when exposed to bad weather. Next to the mines were often large sawmills, factories, and workshops of different types containing lathes, supporting frames, polishing machines, and lifting cranes. About two thousand workers of Italian origin contributed to the development of this flourishing industry. They were proud of their work, and aware of their rights. Most were members of the local chapter of the Granite Cutters National Union, founded in 1886. In 1900, the Union had over one thousand members, mostly Scottish and Italian.

In addition to Barre, where they lived in the Northern part of the city, the Italians had settled in Rutland, West Rutland, Proctor, Williamstown, Northfield, and Montpelier, the state capital of Vermont. They had brought with them the customs and habits of their native land. Rice, polenta, pasta, wine, and grappa were never missing from their kitchens. Every house had a garden next to it, and several immigrants had opened shops with Italian products. They were strongly politicized. In 1895, they hosted several lectures by Gori, after which a club was founded in order to "promote and maintain friendly and fraternal relationships among its members, reawaken and cultivate within these members feelings of social and worker solidarity, and educate them through lectures, discussions, recreational readings, and study concerning the social question."[2]

Since then, anarchist ideas had spread through the Italian colony. In 1898, Emma Goldman visited the club to give some public lectures, and the next year Malatesta came and held five meetings and several debates with the socialist Dino Rondani.

Men and women from Carrara and its surroundings had long formed a particularly cohesive community. They were well suited to host Galleani and Maria and their children, who joined him after a few months. He remained in Barre just short of ten years, first at 92 Pleasant Street and then in a country house outside the town center. He lived modestly and received a salary for his work as editor of *Cronaca Sovversiva* equivalent to that of a local laborer. One of the few pastimes he indulged in was hunting.

The people from Carrara welcomed him and guaranteed his safety and the means necessary for a productive stay in the city.

Although pending legal charges in New Jersey did not apply in the state of Vermont, the risk of extradition was always present. Thus he took many precautions, including going out into the street only during the evenings and passing himself off under the name of G. Pimpino.

It was with this name that he directed, and for a large part wrote, *Cronaca Sovversiva*, a weekly that for almost twenty years (1903–1919) served as a fundamental tool for the Italian-language anarchist movement in the United States.[3] The audience for *Cronaca's* propaganda were Italian-language working communities, primarily those in the United States and Italy, but soon also in South America, Australia, Canada, North Africa, and various European countries, where copies were also sent.[4]

The first issue of the new "anarchist weekly of revolutionary propaganda," as its subtitle proclaimed, appeared on June 6, 1903. It had an initial weekly run of three thousand copies and was printed with the equipment already used by the periodical *Aurora*. Its circulation increased to five thousand over the years, and reached up to ten thousand for special issues. With it, Galleani succeeded in achieving the goal that unavoidable circumstances had prevented him from achieving with *La Questione Sociale*. He created a newspaper that brought together groups and activists scattered across the land, and acted as a propulsive force for an incisive and, at the same time, plural movement, founded on the autonomy of local groups. In other words, he succeeded in making the best use of a strategy Malatesta had already successfully pursued in various phases of his activism, which can be summarized as follows: "The creation of a base of support represented by a newspaper and the construction, through its distribution, of a network of activists capable of expanding and strengthening all forms of propaganda and organizing activity."[5]

The movement that was created with *Cronaca* certainly revolved around Galleani. It could not be separated from him. He was a "leader" with huge influence over his comrades and, at times, over large groups of workers. His presence was essential for written and oral propaganda, and, using his charisma, he was able to maintain unity among groups and places often marked by a centrifugal tendency. In other words, Galleani and his news-paper performed the function of strengthening understanding and association between groups and circles. This was a form of "organization," that was all too dependent on Galleani's own per-sonality, a fact that Malatesta himself came to identify and criti-cize as an indisputable limit for a movement that intended to be anti-authoritarian.[6]

From its early years, *Cronaca Sovversiva* distinguished itself by being able to combine theoretical analysis with expressions of rebellion, even if only partial. Its editors wrote: "Our task [is] to adapt actions to words," to give life to a "new consciousness" and a "new morality."[7] It provided four pages of reflection and "battle," therefore, carefully presented both stylistically and typo-graphically. Particular attention was paid to graphics that were often updated, starting with the masthead. There was no inter-ruption to its weekly appearance, no periods of rest.

A strong and well-organized system, based upon the publica-tion, also became evident, capable of creating and following long-term plans. Proof of this were the numerous inserts and special issues; the capacity for editorial management during Galleani's frequent periods of absence; the ownership of its own printing machines and acquisition of new ones in the event of damage or fire, as occurred in January 1905; and the fact that intimidation from the police and postal authorities was countered by enlarg-ing the format, as happened in 1908.[8]

Galleani was assisted in editing the newspaper mainly by Giovanni Balloni Fruzzetti, a stonecutter who arrived in Barre from Carrara in the early 1890s, with whom Galleani was close and whose address he often used to receive correspondence. He was also helped by Antonio Cavalazzi (alias Ursus or Lo zio Virgilio), a twenty-five-year-old barber from Lugo, near Ravenna, who had recently been in internal exile for his political activity. He was the one who initially managed the enterprise. Although he earned the trust of a large part of the movement in Barre, over the years there were no shortage of quarrels about financial matters that were less than precise and transparent, and these gave rise to a dispute that also involved Galleani.[9] Nevertheless, it was Cavalazzi who replaced Galleani as editor-in-chief during his long propaganda tours.

Already in the first issue of the newspaper, notice was given of a "raffle." One might imagine that this was a minor event. The frequency with which these raffles were held, however, reveals two important things: self-financing as a guarantee of autonomy and the no less important aspect of sociability. Raffles, with prizes such as gold or silver watches, rifles, pistols, books, paintings, or bicycles, were in fact one of the many tools activists used to support the newspaper, to organize practical affairs, and to keep together. In this way, they created "a world of their own" within the American capitalist world—with its own ideals and its own cultural codes.[10] Their saying "anarchists do not wait for Anarchy to live; they act today," was proclaimed in the newspaper. This expression outlined how the society of the future was foreshadowed in the present. The society of the future would be perfectible, since "in anarchy life will not be easier, but fuller."[11] To help them to live immediately "in anarchy," meaning autonomously, the movement arranged, again through raffles and fundraisers, assistance for comrades who were sick, in need, or bereaved, and it conducted a constant campaign against "the pirates," the city shop keepers.

In Barre, when the weather was good, it was customary to go on weekends "to the woods," to Thousand Wood, in the countryside near the city. There, a stage had been built by activists where meetings were held, and musical and theater performances put on. The movement had its own amateur dramatic societies and groups such as the Transatlantic Band and the Stone Cutters Band. There were dances, running races for children, and games such as target shooting, tug of war, ball games, and many other events. This was also a favorite spot for frequent picnics in which fried fish, ice cream, and homemade beer was abundant, and in which activists participated with their families, friends, and supporters.

It was not unusual for the police to try to intimidate participants or directly intervene to confiscate weapons and alcoholic drinks, the production of which was prohibited in some cities of the state, but which the movement consumed abundantly. In summer 1905, the police charged into the middle of a picnic in Thousand Wood, enraging those present, including many women who fought them. Galleani also paid a price for this. He was arrested, and released only after the payment of a heavy fine.[12]

Celebrations outdoors or in halls in the city, such as Barre's Pavilion Hall, were held from time to time in this radical community. There were fruit and flower festivals, and masked balls, for which costumes were created to represent many themes, even including injured workers, the victorious Russian revolution, and the nightmare of capitalism.

Between meetings—which were often held twice a week— and other activities related to their politics, celebrations, concerts, and excursions into the countryside, time off work was spent mostly within the community that spoke the same language and shared the same ideas. This was particularly true of the men, but also, to a lesser extent, of the women as well. In the context of Italian immigration to the United States, gender issues were a cultural problem, but women took part actively in the movement's life and, over the years, wrote several articles in *Cronaca Sovversiva* to demonstrate that the presumed superiority of men has no rational basis and was only the result of a "desire for domination."[13] The prime objective for women was therefore to emancipate themselves from relations of economic and moral dependence, which kept them subordinate to men, and to free themselves from servile work, low wages, and poor education.[14]

Education was also a field that the Italian-language anarchist community of Barre wished to manage for itself. To hasten the social revolution, the first step was to reawaken consciousness through self-education and propaganda. If radical transformation in relations of ownership and the abolition of the state were indispensable for human emancipation, it was equally important that every exploited person combated the thoughtlessness so widely prevalent among the people. A "revolution within themselves" through self-education was to be performed at once. This was an indispensable condition for their volition to be able to modify the surrounding world.[15] Thus reading of works available for loan at the library of the local *Circolo di studi sociali* was encouraged, particularly those by Malatesta, Kropotkin, Most, Grave, Gori, Faure, Esteve, Reclus, Cafiero, Domenico Zavattero, and Paul Delesalle.[16]

Galleani's enduring commitment to the creation of rational or modern schools had the same ends. Since 1903, in Barre, he was active in an evening school for drawing, directed by an organizing committee which included Carlo Abate, who also contributed graphics for the newspaper.[17] The editors closely followed the work in Europe of the libertarian educationist, Francisco Ferrer y Guardia, for rational education and promoted the creation of modern schools in other parts of the United States. From 1910 to 1920 about twenty such schools sprung up, in New York, Philadelphia, Chicago, Seattle, and other places. Their main objective was to liberate the minds of the young from the ideas taught by Catholic and evangelical schools, which restricted free choice in every area of life starting with love and free time, and also from the influence of state schools and bourgeois pedagogy—"Children belong to themselves," not to the family or the State.[18] "They should be liberated not only from religious beliefs but also from the harmful influence of the idea of the homeland, which was used to propagate nonvalues of violence, brutality, and militarism."[19] In contrast, education that focused on history, geography, and the sciences, as well as physical fitness and the sport of shooting, would make children "strong and trained for life and the Social Revolution." This went hand in hand with celebrations and games dedicated exclusively to children.[20]

In summer 1909, Francisco Ferrer was arrested by the Spanish authorities and accused of being one of the instigators of the revolt of the Catalan people against mandatory conscription and military intervention in Morocco, which was called the *semana trágica*. That October 13, he was executed by firing squad at the Montjuich Fort in Barcelona. The news was received by Italian anarchists in the United States with shock and anger. From that time on, references to the work of Ferrer were a constant in Galleani's publications, including special issues of *Cronaca Sovversiva*.[21]

CHAPTER XIX

Cronaca Sovversiva

Ut redeat miseris, abeat fortuna superbis ("that fortune may leave the proud, and return to the wretched"). This quote from Horace, used previously by Jean-Paul Marat in *L'Ami du Peuple* [The Friend of the People], appeared from the first issue under the *Cronaca Sovversiva*'s masthead. It was typical of the classical references used by Galleani in his writing and speeches. The reference to Marat was a tribute to the French Revolution, an event that founded the modern age and created a wave of emancipation that the anarchists, in his view, had the task of completing.

France, with its repeated revolutionary achievements from 1789 to the Paris Commune of 1871, and its influential thinkers, was the pole star of revolution for *Cronaca*. Hence the prominence given to the Commune and its bloody repression, through special issues and inserts to mark anniversaries, and the use of quotations, not only from Marat, but also from Proudhon, Déjacque, Considérant, de Mably, Rousseau, and Blanqui. They presented "the most splendid example of abnegation, firmness, and heroism."[1] Continuing on from what had already been advocated by *La Questione Sociale*, the primary task of the new newspaper was to urge activists to abandon "passive Buddhist contemplation." It asked them to contribute, personally, both in compiling and supporting the newspaper, and in renewed and more energetic daily work of propaganda and action.[2]

The program was clearly written by Galleani. The first issue to tackle was "the glaring inequality of economic conditions" by which "we, the great laboring majority, are at the mercy of a handful of parasites," with the result that "thinking," "studying," and "acting" are "privileges" for the few, while "the low caste" remains unaware.

> Ideas of freedom [belong to] a few free minds [while] respect for ownership, trust in the State, reverence for laws and bourgeois morality have hardy roots in nearly the entire proletariat [...]. We are, at the same time, victims of and complicit with all the lies, all the tyranny: god [...], country [...], democracy. Progress and evolution have challenged the Church, the State, family morality, class, laws and statutes, but the workers have greeted ideas of progress and emancipation with indifference.[3]

In the course of history, people were first emancipated from God, then from the king (thus the centrality of the French Revolution); now it was time for them to abolish class and state privileges and build anarchist communism:

> Communism because, as everyone must contribute to social production, each should benefit according to their own needs [...] anarchy because we do not want any yoke of authority, feeling that we are capable of governing ourselves by ourselves [...].
>
> Government is the set of individuals who, delegated or not, gather in their hands the sum of social forces and impose their will upon everyone, under the pretext of providing public services and general security. In a harmonious society, based on solidarity and the greatest possible satisfaction of the needs of all, in a society in which the sound advancement of public affairs is the condition for the sound advancement of each person's private affairs, with no lords to protect or masses to keep in check, there is no reason for government to exist.[4]

Both the means and the ends of subversive activity were an equal, non-hierarchical association capable of guaranteeing individual autonomy. This autonomy was something very different from the individualism of Stirner, and even more of Nietzsche.[5] Despite appreciating several aspects of Stirner's thought, Galleani was nevertheless convinced that Stirner was wrong to "spiritualize" the individual, and to delineate a metaphysics of the Ego, that Nietzsche then further absolutized as the sole paradigm for modern man. According to Galleani, by contrast, man was a social animal whose freedom was achieved only in relationship with other men, in accordance with Bakunin's teachings. "What we understand as individualism is the tendency of modern man to free himself from the overwhelmingly oppressive protection of the State, or rather, from the social order that it represents."[6]

This concept was shared by a broad section of the anarchist movement. In Italy, it was best expressed by a series of articles by Armando Borghi in *L'Aurora* of Ravenna, reprinted in a 1907 volume under the title, *Del nostro e dell'altrui individualismo* [Of Our and Other's Individualism]. Borghi, as Leda Rafanelli wrote in the preface, showed on the one hand "the degeneration of the anarchist idea in the organizational current" and, on the other hand, "the exaggeration of Stirnerian egoism." Stirnerian individualists, or "innovators," Borghi maintained, "see nothing outside of their own ego with all of its instinct, moral and material needs, unrestrained tendencies, without worrying about other egos moving around them." This was why, he wrote, it was necessary to draw a clear line of distinction from them.[7]

Galleani agreed with this position and advocated the value of association, of which he had a particular understanding. To be an anarchist, organization must be based on free consent and not on a hierarchical order, and it must thus reject any formally defined structures. In his way of seeing things, the recent history of organizations in the European labor movement, through the formalization of gradually more restrictive and bureaucratic structures, had finally come to affirm parliamentarianism as their preeminent strategy for action. This history showed that "delegation and centralization [are] in effect: parliamentarianism and government" and that the "schism" between socialists and anarchists was not only a given, but could be "liberating," and

Cronaca Sovversiva on the Paris Commune.

help to clear false revolutionaries out of the camp.[8] Here he took on the task of warning all libertarians who seemed to be retracing the regression of the socialists.

One of the subjects Galleani criticized was anarchist congresses that involved delegates and resolutions. He believed that it was impossible to "anarchically delegate to another person one's own thought, one's own energy, one's own will." Every activist should only participate in congresses in person and not as a representative of others. He was extremely suspicious of congress resolutions, understood as instruments of "coercion" of a minority by a majority.[9] The only useful and positive congresses were those that remained consultative meetings, and provided an occasion for activists to meet and work together.[10] Opposition to congresses with delegates and resolutions was considered central by *Cronaca Sovversiva*, and gave rise to debates with other libertarians active in the United States. *La Questione Sociale* was an object of criticism. Its editor, Esteve, argued for the view, shared by a part of the movement active in Paterson, that it was essential to coordinate anarchist activity systematically through regular congresses attended by delegates of various groups, and by resolutions to standardize action across different areas.

Given these premises, it was not surprising that refuting the parliamentary strategy occupied part of the editorial energy of *Cronaca*. It considered "legalitarian" socialists truly to be enemies of the exploited, as they had abandoned all notions of abolishing the State. State and anarchy were diametrically opposed notions. Anarchy certainly could not be achieved through a socialist state.[11] At every level and in every way, this new type of socialist accepted government roles, doing "exactly what all governments in the past have always done and what ... future governments will do."[12] Against the "ambition" of parliamentary socialists, which they considered to be "the latest and hidden form of bourgeois tyranny," their criticism was bitter and incessant. This was the subject of two biting columns sarcastically entitled "Mandateli lassù!" [Send Them Up!] (meaning to parliament) and "Facce di bronzo" [Those with the Nerve].[13] Both revealed the corruption of, and betrayal by, representatives of the international labor movement who decided to embrace the parliamentary strategy, including quite a few former anarchists. Against them, the newspaper referred several times to the only union necessary, that which unites all proletarians "from below" to transform radically the existing state of affairs without relying on either political or trade union leaders.

Apart from socialism, the newspaper also criticized collectivism, which it contrasted with anarchist communism. It rejected the collectivist solution because paying people according to the quantity of work they performed ("to each according to their contribution") and therefore allowing there to be wage differences between workers meant allowing the state to continue. However, the state's regulatory function would no longer be required in a communist economy, where everyone would have the right to what they needed independently of the amount of work they performed ("to each according to their need"). It should therefore come as no surprise that the socialists, who supported the collectivist idea, aimed for the conquest of state power, unlike the anarchists who, as communists in economics, worked for the distribution of this power. In a society in which everything belongs to everyone, Galleani maintained, shared ownership would eliminate the production of excess (barracks, prisons, military arsenals, etc.) to focus on what was useful, transforming work into an occasion of celebration and joy.

These theoretical divergences sometimes threatened normal collaborative relationships between the two political camps. Specific events added fuel to the fire. In Vermont, relationships were already damaged at the beginning of the twentieth century. Events that started on December 28, 1900, ignited the conflict. In Montpelier, ten Italian anarchists were arrested on suspicion of having participated in an attempt to murder the Barre police captain, Patrick Brown, who had been injured by gunshots a few nights earlier. The socialists criticized an act that they considered reckless and moreover unsuccessful. Some of them collaborated with the police and identified several possible suspects. From then on disputes and mutual physical attacks followed. The situation further worsened with the arrival of Serrati as editor of New

York's *Il Proletario* (February 1902) and with Galleani's arrival at *Cronaca Sovversiva*.

In moving to the United States, Galleani and Serrati both aimed to give new energy to their respective movements. Serrati created an Italian Socialist Federation, supporting the Socialist Labor Party, which Galleani considered a rival, if not indeed an enemy. The two factions battled during the strike of the dyers and textile workers in and around Paterson. The anarchists worked to transform the strike into an uprising, while the socialists opposed this strategy, which they considered adventurist. The situation finally deteriorated on October 3, 1903, when the anarchist Elia Corti was killed by the socialist Alessandro Garretti at the Socialist Labor Party Hall in Barre on the very evening when Serrati was to give a lecture on "methods of socialist struggle."

At that point, Galleani repeated the accusation previously made against Serrati by *La Questione Sociale*: that Serrati had identified him during public meetings as the person responsible for the Paterson uprising. And he piled it on with two additional, very serious accusations: that Serrati had revealed his presence in Barre through the pages of *Il Proletario*; and that he was morally responsible for Corti's murder due to the continuous campaign of defamation he had waged against anarchists.[14]

Serrati thus became a "villain," "pusillanimous," a "provocateur," a "reptile," and a "Pagnacca" (the name of a well-known spy) in *Cronaca Sovversiva*, and the dispute extended to other parts of the United States. In *Il Proletario, Cronaca Sovversiva* was called *Cloaca Sovversiva* [Subversive Sewer] or *Cornacchia Sovversiva* [Subversive Gossip]; and while some socialists branded the anarchists thieves, counterfeiters, and assassins, the anarchists called the socialists traitors, sellouts, and racketeers.[15] The dispute crossed the ocean and followed Serrati wherever he went. Copies of two manifestos against him, entitled *Giacinto Menotti Serrati spia e assassino* [Giacinto Menotti Serrati Spy and Assassin] and *Cose a posto e farabutti alla gogna* [Setting the Record Straight and Scoundrels in the Pillory] were sent far and wide. After he was forced to return to Europe in 1904, Serrati became active in the Swiss workers' movement, and the libertarians of Lausanne, instigated by Galleani, gave the press a violent manifesto denouncing his behavior, and protested during his public appearances.[16]

However, Galleani's fears that Serrati's 1903 revelations of his identity and whereabouts would lead to his arrest were realized about three years later. On December 30, 1906, the police burst into his house while he was sitting down for lunch with Maria and the children. They arrested him and took him to the Montpelier prison before extraditing him to New Jersey to stand trial for the events of June 1902. During the next few days, anarchist groups, particularly those in Paterson and from *La Questione Sociale*, organized numerous protest meetings and, through fundraisers, concerts, and other events, collected the enormous sum of seven thousand dollars, which they used to pay the bail necessary to obtain his provisional release.[17] After another two weeks of prison, and after visits by Maria and about one hundred of his comrades, Galleani was freed to await his trial. His release was celebrated with numerous meetings in Paterson and in Barre, places where he appeared with other speakers, including Alexander Berkman and Emma Goldman.[18]

He had to answer six charges in the Paterson Court of Assizes concerning the damage and destruction of three dye works, the wounding of police officer Charles Robinson by a revolver shot and journalist Harry Harris of the *Morning Call* (who had been photographing the demonstrators during the uprising), and finally the usual charge of incitement to rebellion. He risked a maximum of twenty-two years in prison and seventeen thousand dollars in fines. Yet, thanks to financial support from the entire movement, he was able to provide the thirty seven thousand dollars needed to pay two particularly skilled lawyers. They assured him that they were capable of getting the charges reduced or dropped.

The trial began in April and was followed closely by several American newspapers. When the time came for his testimony, Galleani refused to swear on the Bible, stating that he did not believe in God. The judge then denied him the right to speak. The entire court was stunned, and so was the press. *The Call* described it as an act of integrity and courage. When the time came for the verdict, the jury was not able to reach the unanimous decision necessary for sentencing. Seven jurors were for acquittal, five judged him guilty. The court refused to order a new trial. The charges were dropped and the bail money was returned. For Galleani it was a triumphant victory over the judges and over Serrati.[19]

CHAPTER XX

The End of Anarchism?

Galleani's increasing criticism of the socialists was aimed primarily at their legalitarian and parliamentary strategy. In the early years of the 1900s, Galleani had played a leading role in the ongoing debates on this subject. He regarded the path taken by Merlino as paradigmatic. Formerly Merlino had been an internationalist with Malatesta, then a comrade in ideas and action of Galleani himself, but he had finally ended up embracing the parliamentary strategy. In an interview with Cesare Sobrito of *La Stampa* at the 1907 anarchist congress in Rome, Merlino, speaking as a former anarchist, said that he was convinced that the anarchist movement had been so torn apart by internal debates between those for and against organization that it was destined to end. The best anarchist ideas had already been absorbed by socialism, while the others—the utopian ones—were no longer of value. The interview was titled "The End of Anarchism."

Galleani added a question mark to this title for a series of ten articles that were published between August 1907 and January 1908, and judged brilliant by Malatesta. In them, he refuted Merlino's position, which he described as a "hybrid and ambiguous dream of parliamentary anarchist-socialism."[1] He argued that the internal conflicts within anarchism were "an inevitable crisis of development ... they are evidence of vitality, of energy and progress." Anarchism, as a doctrine and movement, had more reason than ever to exist. It had never before had such strength and influence. *"Far from being moribund, it lives, it develops and it goes forward."*[2] Against a world characterized by growing standardization and uniformity, and against reformism and parliamentary or "domesticated" socialism that attempted to sugarcoat the bitter pill of man's exploitation of man, he exalted spontaneity and pluralism, autonomy and independence, self-determination and direct action. Today, as yesterday, there was no other possible solution to the persistent social question except to overthrow the old order violently and establish a new one.

> Instead of the mere passive and polite resistance so fervently recommended by the socialists, the anarchists prefer boycott, sabotage, and, for the sake of struggle itself, immediate attempts at partial expropriation, individual rebellion and insurrection—actions which usually reap so much socialist horror and cursing, but which exert the most spirited influence over the masses and resolve themselves in a moral advantage of the highest order.[3]

His words had for some time garnered prestige within the international anarchist movement. It was not by chance that, in 1906—in disguise—he went to Europe and visited Paris, Brussels, and London to gauge first-hand the possibilities of insurrectionary agitation in the old continent. The year before, in Russia, a general strike in St. Petersburg had developed into a revolution and established the conditions for the election of the Duma (representative assembly). This showed that revolution was possible, and instilled new energy into subversiveness. Galleani had always followed the struggle against Tsarist authoritarianism with particular interest. In the pages of *Cronaca Sovversiva*, he expressed his support for the continuous tremors that rocked the autocracy: "Nicholas II will not die in his bed."[4]

This explains Galleani's decision to cross the ocean in secret. We have no details of his trip, except that he met with Elisée Reclus. No doubt he had been following developments within the labor movement. In 1906, there was an important series of congresses—in Amiens, Limoges, Liverpool, Mannheim, Rome, and Milan—that was fundamental for the policies of unions and socialist parties in several countries.[5] The Congress of the Confédération générale du travail [CGT, General Labor Confederation], which met in Amiens in the fall of 1906, voted almost unanimously for the Charter of Amiens confirming its adherence to revolutionary syndicalism, and to political neutrality, decentralization, anti-parliamentarianism, and direct action. Although this appeared to be an undeniable result of anarchist thinking, in Galleani's eyes there was an innate risk in it. This had been obvious for some time in the ideas of those, such as the "*cégétistes*" anarchists (meaning, those in the CGT), including Émile Pouget and Pierre Monatte, who aimed to go beyond anarchism and recognize the exclusive and self-sufficient role of syndicalism. In other words, he feared that anarchy, the idea of the highest form of emancipation in every field, would be absorbed and thus distorted by revolutionary syndicalism, which he viewed as only one particular method for human emancipation.

His position was shared by several Italian and other activists, including Malatesta, who was still in London. Through Malatesta, this divergence took on an important public significance in 1907, during the international anarchist congress in Amsterdam. This was what he said at the congress:

> The conclusion which Monatte reaches is that syndicalism is a necessary and sufficient means of social revolution. In other words, Monatte declared that syndicalism is enough in itself, and thus, in my opinion, a radically false doctrine [...]. Today, just as yesterday, I want anarchists to enter the labor movement [...]. I want [...] absolutely neutral unions [...]. In the union, we must remain anarchists, with all of the strength and in the full meaning of the term.[6]

This reflected an analysis Malatesta had been developing since the beginning of the century and that for some time had also characterized Galleani's thought.[7] To corroborate his own theories, Malatesta used as an example the situation of the labor movement in the United States and the increasingly unfruitful role of the unions, another theme dear to Galleani:

> I need not look for proof further than the example offered by the North American syndicates. Having shown

themselves radically revolutionary when they were still weak, these syndicates have become, as they grew stronger, and richer, merely conservative organizations ... General rule: the anarchist who accepts [a role as] a permanent and paid union official is lost to propaganda, lost to anarchism![8]

Galleani's judgment of unions also grew harsher over the years. Although, at the beginning of his time at *La Questione Sociale*, he collaborated closely with the Italian Dye Workers' Union in Paterson, in subsequent years his criticism of the unions increased exponentially. In the early days of *Cronaca Sovversiva* he agreed with the strategy of joining unions, while publicly expressing awareness of the high risk of being absorbed by a mechanism alien to anarchism. From the middle of the decade, however, he began to take the view that it was better to act outside of unions, together with all workers prepared to act in an autonomous manner. Unions were seen as a primitive expression of solidarity, which could instead be achieved outside of formal constraints. They became synonymous with corruption, weakness, and the disciplining of workers. He considered their leaders to be "fakers," capable of anesthetizing the struggle, and their mediation as arbitrators between capital and labor nothing more than a "fraud."[9]

The situation changed somewhat with the founding of the Industrial Workers of the World (IWW) in 1905. *Cronaca Sovversiva* immediately expressed a degree of distrust toward the new union, and Galleani described Daniel De Leon and Eugene Debs, the leaders of the Socialist Labor Party and Socialist Party of America, and both supporters of the IWW, as "political adventurers [whom] we never for a moment trusted." Yet the newspaper could not deny "the enthusiasm with which many from the libertarian side, and not all of them naive, accept and support them."[10]

This did not happen by chance. The IWW was born from the combination of anarchist syndicalism among recent European immigrants and the American proletariat. Characterized by anarchist principles of direct action and the decentralization of local groups in which formal organization was often absent, the IWW gave priority to practical experimentation in struggle, rather than ideological rigidity. This was greeted with some skepticism by activists who, like Galleani, were fearful that anarchist principles would be compromised, but it garnered the enthusiasm of those who were willing to create networks of unaffiliated workers. It was not by chance that several anarchists contributed to founding the IWW and that many groups, including those in Paterson and Spring Valley, endorsed the new union from the beginning, attracted by a milieu that fostered the spirit of solidarity in support of worker resistance. Many libertarians saw that the IWW intended to free itself from divisions dictated by trade and nationality.

The American Federation of Labor (AFL) defended only the upper reaches of the workers' hierarchy, occupied by Anglo-Saxons and Germans, and used strikes only when contracts expired and not as a means to create solidarity between different trades. The IWW, by contrast, strove to organize the labor force starting with the least qualified, in order to engage in processes of social conflict within increasingly large, concentrated, and mechanized industrial contexts, with a large number of unskilled (non-specialized) workers, many of whom were Italian. This was the case in the steelworks and mines, where many readers of Cronaca Sovversiva also worked. Thus the IWW came into conflict with AFL-affiliated unions, which, faced with the excessive power of employers, accepted increasingly restrictive demands made on workers and regressed in a conservative and bureaucratic direction. They were also discredited by several cases of corruption.[11] The IWW carried out struggles through meetings, demonstrations, and pickets, and often refused to sign agreements or contracts, which were replaced by continual disputes, as in the case of the great strikes of 1907.

In Barre, the anarchist groups preferred to maintain their own autonomy. Yet an understanding was reached with the local chapter of the union, founded by Spanish and Portuguese workers in 1905, so that the symbol of the IWW appeared on the back page of the newspaper next to the wording "Cronaca Sovversiva print shop" and remained there for several years.

Born during a decade of extraordinary class conflict, bitter disputes, and terrible tragedies—such as the thousands of miners who died due to failures to respect elementary safety standards—*Cronaca Sovversiva* distinguished itself by being a newspaper entirely internal to labor struggles, and therefore at odds with the IWW and other union organizations.[12] In addition to the stonecutters and quarry workers of Barre, others involved in correspondence and ad hoc campaigns, fundraising and other solidarity actions connected with the paper, included the textile workers and bricklayers of New York; the woodworkers, carpenters, barbers, and tailors of Chicago and Detroit; the port workers, railroad workers, and tram drivers of Philadelphia; workers in the stocking industry of New York and Lynn; the tobacco industry workers of Philadelphia and Tampa; iron and steel workers, and miners.

These miners included many active anarchists, such as Giovanni Scussel and Emilio Coda, both of whom were linked to *Cronaca Sovversiva* from the start of publication. They were involved in some bitter disputes. They were often repressed by militias directly paid for by the mining corporations. They fought to defend their wages and for the eight-hour working day from Arizona to Pennsylvania, Michigan to West Virginia, and Colorado to Utah.

In the latter two states, Galleani closely followed the struggles of 1903–1905. He traveled to Cripple Creek and other hot spots under the pseudonym Carlo Rofuggi and urged an armed general strike. There was a fierce battle in which the employer's Mine Owners Association organized thirty thousand armed men into the Citizen's Alliance. They used cannons against the strikers who were led by William "Big Bill" Haywood and Charles Moyer, and who themselves used dynamite. To try to break the resistance, the authorities declared martial law. In Cripple Creek, they imprisoned several groups of strikers in actual concentration camps, and ordered deportations. The dispute concluded with a victory for the strikers and the success of the Western Federation of Miners, which had forty thousand members in 1905, as compared to twenty-five thousand four years earlier.[13] In February

1906, when Haywood and Moyer were arrested together with the other leader, George Pettibone, a large united protest movement arose in support of the three, in which *Cronaca Sovversiva* also participated, showing appreciation for their work. It succeeded in convincing the IWW to declare a general strike to liberate them.

The IWW became explicitly "apolitical" in 1908. It embraced the view that it should free itself from electoral ideas and from any party support, and in particular from the influence of De Leon, who was expelled. Convergence with anarchists thus increased further, and the anarchists participated very actively in a new series of struggles and strikes, first in the eastern and then in the western United States. Within this dynamic, however, Galleani continued to express his own distinction. The IWW wanted to seize industrial power not to destroy the government, but rather to create a new, exclusively economic and democratic body. The alliance between anarchists and the IWW therefore had to be restricted to particular aspects of the labor struggle and specifically to the strike, understood primarily as a method of destruction and expropriation.

In activities in support of their demands, Italian workers encountered and benefited from the work of Carlo Tresca, a charismatic insurgent and powerful orator. He arrived in the United States in 1904. He was initially the editor of *Il Proletario*, organ of the Italian Socialist Federation of North America, and then from 1906, first of *La Voce del Popolo* [Voice of the People] and then *La Plebe* [The Plebian] (1907–1909). He was a "freelance revolutionary," an anarcho-syndicalist—as he defined himself—who collaborated closely with the IWW. He was a man who managed to win a great deal of trust among Italian workers regardless of their political affinities. In the second decade of the century, he played a leading role at important moments in the struggle in the United States, from Lawrence (1912) and Paterson (1913) to the Mesabi Iron Range (1916).

He gave voice to these struggles in two new newspapers, *L'Avvenire* [The Future] and, from 1917, *Il Martello* [The Hammer], a crucial publication for expressing "the other face" of Italian libertarian activity in the United States. This newspaper maintained an anarcho-syndicalist perspective until it closed in 1943 following Tresca's assassination. It devoted space to many battles on worksites and against American capitalism, and also against the "*prominenti*" (the Italian elite who had immigrated to America), against fascism in Italy and in the United States, and against Francoist Spain.

The relationship between *Cronaca Sovversiva* and Tresca was initially one of collaboration and solidarity. On several occasions Tresca served as a bridge-builder between *Cronaca Sovversiva* and the IWW, and in turn he received concrete support from Italian anarchists when he found himself in difficulty. However, this relationship of mutual support evolved into rivalry in the second decade of the century following differences of opinion on both theoretical and practical issues. Disagreements grew about the role of union organization in the labor struggle. This was deemed central by Tresca but often judged to be damaging by Galleani. In addition, on several occasions, such as in Lawrence in 1912, Italian anarchists accused Tresca of being dependent on the overly compliant strategy of the IWW. This contrast revealed a wider ideological dispute in the search for ideological hegemony within Italian-language subversive circles. This got worse over the coming decades. After Galleani returned to Italy, several anarchist groups, loyal to his ideas, created propaganda that strengthened aspects of them, above all aversion to syndicalism and alliance with other forces of the left.[14]

CHAPTER XXI

La salute è in voi!

Within this bitter class conflict, the central theme of *Cronaca Sovversiva* was the need to improve strategies for action, with the awareness that one cannot "confront troops with stones," and that revolution required material preparation.[1] As Galleani stressed: "The triumph of proletarian emancipation will only be celebrated on the ruins of all the bastions of the bourgeoisie: destruction is necessary!"[2]

Precisely in order to improve the techniques of destruction, in February 1906, the first notice appeared for a pamphlet entitled "La salute è in voi!" [Health Is In You!]. This "typographical jewel," costing 25 cents, had a red cover featuring a portrait of Ravachol, the very incarnation of iconoclastic revolt, with a guillotine behind him and a rising sun in the background. The following verses appeared as an epigraph:

From Conselice to Santa Susanna you
have seen
the painful passion and the horrendous torment
of defenseless law.[3]

You cursed, you wept
reaping
prison, poverty, pity.

Blasphemy is fruitless, it beautifies weeping,
Listen!
History warns you, Science teaches you,
it murmurs to you from the bloody earth

the death rattle of the fathers:
Between the iron of the spades and the flames of the stake
god triumphs.
From conspiracies, from martyrdom, from battles
the homeland leaps free and undivided.
On the ruins of the Bastille,
Two worlds crushed with iron and fire,
they will build your bosses fortune and glory

History opens the way for you, gives you science, weapons
From unavenged tombs, those dead from pellagra and
grapeshot,
the fathers
entrust your with their vendetta.
Dare!
From audacious revolts
redemption will sprout.

The pamphlet recalled previous publications such as Johann Most's *Science of Revolutionary Warfare*. It made use of Ettore Molinari's technical knowledge, and contained "simple, practical, impeccably scientific and experimental formulas" to create explosive devices.[4] Undoubtedly the most publicized among the many publications released by the *Circolo di studi sociali*, it was highly recommended by *Cronaca Sovversiva*: "To us, it seems that this [pamphlet] by anonymous publishing comrades is a precious work of opportunity, strategy, and reasoning. Why do we constantly cry out to the proletariat: rebel! rise up! destroy! if we do not know how to give them the means of revolt, insurrection, and destruction?"[5]

For some time Galleani had urged readers to "dynamite" the US authorities, starting with the observation that "dynamite is found everywhere in North America at fifteen cents a pound."[6] More generally, in previous years, he had never stopped propagandizing the extensive use of arms, the tools needed for the masses to be able to create as widespread an insurrection as possible. Since the beginning of the publication of *Cronaca Sovversiva*, he had focused attention on the necessity of destroying the current

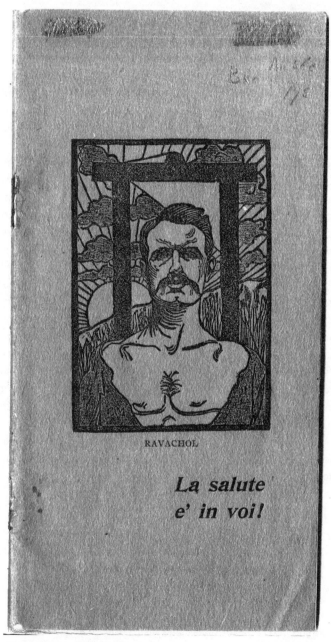

The cover of *La salute è in voi!*

order. An "immense, fierce period of destruction and demolition" was the "unavoidable condition to reconstruct" social life on a new basis, he wrote, adding: "Let us destroy all causes of our discontents: laws, armies, *sgherri*, courts, prisons, churches, brothels, parliaments: the privileges of private ownership, borders, and countries [...], the family based on selfishness."[7]

This emphasis was not universally shared by the anarchist movement. Malatesta, for example, was convinced that social life could not be interrupted, and therefore destruction had to go hand in hand with the creation of a new social order. He thought it unwise to think that "reconstruction" could be left to future generations, as Galleani seemed to predict. However, beyond different nuances and perceptions, the two agreed that the subject of destruction could not be ignored, and that it was an indispensable factor for turning general strikes into occasions for armed insurrection, instead of mere moments of retribution. This issue emerged during the international anarchist congress in Amsterdam in 1907. Malatesta's approach strongly influenced the conference. In his speech, he explained: "And now let's come to the general strike. For me, I accept the principle that I have been disseminating for years. The general strike has always seemed to me an excellent means for initiating social revolution. However we must take care not to fall into the unfortunate illusion that with the general strike, armed insurrection becomes superfluous."[8]

Thus the idea of insurrection reemerged in opposition to the syndicalist position, and was confirmed forcefully in the final motion:

> Anarchists consider the syndicalist movement and the general strike as powerful revolutionary means, but not as a replacement for revolution [...]. The anarchists think that destruction of capitalist and authoritarian society can occur only through armed insurrection and violent expropriation, and that the use of the more or less general strike and the syndicalist movement should not make us forget more direct means of struggle against the military force of governments.[9]

La salute è in voi! aimed precisely to improve these means of struggle, and was put to use several times in the 1910s in social conflicts across the United States.

CHAPTER XXII

A Little Bit of Theory

We have already described how great an ideological influence Elisée Reclus was on Galleani. He owed to Reclus his organicist vision of man and nature and of the mutuality between evolution and revolution, according to which the latter's task was to accelerate and complete the processes inherent in the former.[1] As Galleani said in a lecture: "Revolution is a complex phenomenon created in society when a long series of predisposing causes— economic disadvantage, political servitude, the heightened and intolerant consciousness of the proletariat—receives the impact of violent, determining causes."[2]

In Galleani's interpretation of Reclus's ideas, which pervaded his lectures and articles, the "inescapable law of progress" may be accelerated by acts of revolt, whether individual or collective: "rebellious upheavals" which *Cronaca Sovversiva* had the task of "provoking."[3] This was why the many "avengers" or "people who took justice into their own hands," activists who were distinguished by their audacity, played a doubly important role. They forged the spirit of revolt, giving shape to a strong subversive identity, and they accelerated the wider dynamics of social emancipation.

Cronaca Sovversiva featured articles, as well as news, portraits, postcards, lectures, and initiatives that recalled, among others, Pisacane—considered a precursor of the libertarian movement—Cgolgosz, the "martyrs of Chicago," Bresci (whose daughters were financially supported for two decades by Italian anarchists living in the United States), Angiolillo, Caserio, Ravachol, Henry, Vaillant, Lega, Sof'ja Perovskaja, Luigi Luccheni, Ivan Kaljaev, Théodule Meunier, August Reinsdorf,

Miguel Artal, Giovanni Passannante, Matteo Morral, Egor Sazonov, Denjiro Kotoku, Sugano Kanno, Simón Radowitzky, Stepan Kalturin, Antonio D'Alba, Antoine Cyvoct, Manuel Pardiñas, Claude Etiévant, Auguste Faugoux, Benoît Chevenet, Charles Gallo, Giuseppe Scarlatti, Aleko Skinas, and others. It is difficult to name all who were acknowledged, as the editors intended to save the "forgotten" from oblivion, including several Russian "terrorists." The word "terrorist" had an entirely positive meaning, as terrorism was considered to be an "effective battle weapon."[4] Even expropriators were by and large appreciated, including Pini and Duval, "among the first, after Gallo, who took responsibility for their actions, arguing for the right of expropriation."[5] Some of these writings were included in the book *Faccia a faccia col nemico* [Face to Face with the Enemy] published in 1914 by the Gruppo autonomo [Autonomous Group] of Boston.[6]

The means used for these acts of revolt were necessarily violent. "Violence, the law of extreme defense and supreme power, will respond to violence. This is not a wish, it is a prediction that does not mislead and does not deceive. Against violence, violence!"[7] This was a view that Galleani spread by both speech and writing, in a constant and particularly intense manner when repression increased: "Far from repudiating individual and collective violence, we recognize its necessity and we claim the right [of violence] before and against the social order born from fraud and violence that prospers and rules through fraud and violence."[8]

Alongside Reclus, Kropotkin was certainly the other "great" figure whose thought had a strong influence on the newspaper. After the first excerpts from *Mutual Aid* appeared in *La Questione Sociale*, its re-release was continued in *Cronaca Sovversiva*, which also provided space for the Russian's subsequent work, *Fields, Factories and Workshops*.[9] From Kropotkin's theories, Galleani adopted the idea that solidarity was of central importance to revolutionary action, and an essential factor for achieving full freedom.

Kropotkin became interested in the phenomenon of mutual aid among animal species when reading Darwin's *On the Origin of Species* and *The Descent of Man* and when, in the early 1880s, he had the opportunity to hear the lectures of zoologist Karl Fedorovich Kessler. Kessler had developed some suggestions from Darwin, going further into the phenomenon he called the law of mutual aid, which went together with the law of mutual struggle.[10] Kropotkin clearly believed Darwin had the enormous merit of introducing the scientific principle of the evolution of species, which refuted the Mosaic creation tradition. But Kropotkin also stressed that Darwin, particularly in *The Descent of Man*, had used the idea of the "struggle for existence" in a broad sense, to include both adversarial relations between living beings and their mutual dependence. What Kropotkin opposed was the vulgarization of Darwin's thought that led to a restricted and erroneous interpretation of the "struggle for existence" to justify social discrimination.

Galleani therefore judged Darwin's work positively and at the same time criticized the instrumental interpretation of Darwinism, which made the "struggle for existence" the sole law of life.[11] Galleani also knew that in his *Anarchist Morality*, Kropotkin clearly maintained, specifically against vulgarizations of Darwin, that solidarity is the predominant characteristic of animals that live socially. Even if there was a struggle for existence between species, within each species the dominant factor was mutual aid. First and foremost this was a moral instinct.[12] This applied equally to humans. This was what he demonstrated in *Mutual Aid*, which continued and deepened a theme that was dear to him.[13] For Kropotkin, in the struggle for existence, victory goes to the species that shows the greatest capacity for collaboration. What the theory of mutual aid disputed, as *Cronaca Sovversiva* did too, was Malthusianism. This had already been a target of criticism by William Godwin, Pierre-Joseph Proudhon, Elisée Reclus, Mechnikov, and Kropotkin himself. This theory, put forward by Thomas Malthus in his 1798 work, *An Essay on the Principle of Population*, asserted that poverty did not depend on institutional factors, but on natural causes resulting from the structural disequilibrium between limited growth in the means of subsistence and unlimited growth of the population. Galleani also addressed this several times, arguing that it was a false pretext that the ruling class used to avoid redistributing wealth.

The theory of mutual aid was not, however, the exclusive fruit of individual reflection by Kropotkin: it was a collective development by a group of anarchists and geographers that included Elisée Reclus and Mechnikov, another important theoretical reference for Galleani. Lev Mechnikov was born in St. Petersburg in 1838 to an official of the Russian army and had been a student of medicine in Kharkov. He was initially a Garibaldist and then internationalist, and he had collaborated with Elisée Reclus from the 1870s. As someone with direct knowledge of Japan, he played an important role in preparing the volume of *Nouvelle géographie universelle* on Western Asia. In 1886, about fifteen years before the theory became better known with the publication of Kropotkin's *Mutual Aid*, he published an article in which he discussed the theme of cooperation as a "main characteristic of social life" and basis of progress.[14]

During his stay in Egypt, Galleani had carefully studied both this article and Mechnikov's main work, *La Civilisation et les grandes fleuves historiques* [Civilization and Major Historic Rivers], a work of general geography published posthumously in Paris in 1889 with an introduction by Reclus. He appreciated the fact that Mechnikov directly applied scientific method to the study of society, combining biology and sociology. What had intrigued him most was how the principle of cooperation had been introduced into a theory of progress. According to Mechnikov, organisms, from the simplest to the most complex, had an increasing tendency towards cooperation. The history of humanity, he argued, had gone through successive stages: the ancient era, the middle ages, the modern period, culminating in a "universal" era, contemporary with the author. Social relations and space and time worked together in an orderly and regular way. Civilization was born around large rivers, becoming Mediterranean, then Atlantic, finally universal. The first stage was characterized by despotism, as with Imperial Rome and Eastern despotism, the second by oligarchy, typified by feudal society, the third by equality between men, which put an end to differences in social status.[15]

This approach was in line with the neo-enlightenment theories of Reclus and Kropotkin, and had its roots in the ideas of Spencer, of whom Galleani was a passionate reader.[16] Spencer had anticipated the principle of the struggle for existence as a factor of evolution subsequently developed by Darwin. He was among the first to argue that there was an analogy between biological and social development. In his *System of Synthetic Philosophy* (1862–1897) he developed a narrative according to which the evolutionary process held together an organic world, human nature, and political and social forms. The latter went through a progressive development that began with military societies based on appropriation and hierarchy and ended with industrial societies, where compulsion disappeared in favor of cooperation based on free exchange.

This theory of progress was intrinsically linked to the positivism of Auguste Comte, the philosopher of the first half of the 1800s, former collaborator of Henri de Saint-Simon and another essential theoretical source for Galleani's anarchism. Comte created a philosophy of history articulated into three eras, theological, metaphysical, and scientific, to which corresponded three stages of the sciences and three different social orders. The social reorganization that was needed had to come from an equally necessary mental renewal that was to be founded on scientific and positive thought. Therefore science was the motor of potential emancipation.

Galleani returned to these ideas countless times in his speeches and articles, although with several modifications and elaborations. He held that human history progressed through three phases—religious, political, and finally industrial—and through three stages of emancipation. Humankind was first liberated from God (hence the centrality of positive science, of Jean-Baptiste Lamarck and Darwin); then from monarchy (with the fundamental watershed of the French Revolution). Now, said Galleani, it was time to liberate ourselves from privilege, by means of social revolution. This would be "the greatest step ever recorded in the thick book of human evolution."[17] To reach this stage, the active and voluntary intervention of subversives was required. However they must not act as the avant-garde or as guides, but only as agents to kindle the independent action of the masses. "We can prepare arms and warriors for revolution," said Galleani, "but we cannot make the Social Revolution."[18]

CHAPTER XXIII

The Mexican Revolution

Cronaca Sovversiva followed social and political events abroad as well as in the United States. In addition to Italy, there were frequent reports and analyses from France, Switzerland, Germany, Spain, and Russia, as well as Argentina, Canada, Japan, China, Mexico, Brazil, Turkey, New Zealand, and Australia. Galleani strongly desired this deliberately internationalist perspective, and, in 1910, he added international news through a column called "Note sovversive dai due emisferi" [Subversive Notes from Both Hemispheres], which appeared in almost every issue of the paper, though under slightly different titles.

Starting in 1908, increasing space was given to discussions of Mexican politics. These were critical of the despotic government of Porfirio Díaz and supported Ricardo Flores Magón and his comrades, who had led a number of insurrections and tried to remove Díaz from office during the previous years. They were subsequently exiled to St. Louis, where they created the Junta organizadora del Partido liberal mexicano [Organizing Board of the PLM, Mexican Liberal Party], before moving to Los Angeles.[1] In the fall of 1910, members of the PLM crossed back over the Mexican border and took up arms to overthrow the regime at the same time as did other political groups opposing Díaz, among which Francisco Madero's Partido antirreeleccionista [Anti-Reelection Party] predominated.

In January 1911, several hundred Magonist rebels—mostly from the United States and concentrated in Baja California—liberated the villages of Mexicali, Los Algodonales (in February), Tecate (in March), and Tijuana (in May). The PLM was known as a libertarian force and its organ, *Regeneración* [Regeneration], had for some time invited anarchists and subversives to hurry up and come south, in order to provide military assistance and follow up on the widespread expropriations of the means of production. It was like a light switching on. The call was seized upon by several hundred IWW members and anarchists, including several dozen Italian activists who read *Cronaca Sovversiva* and *L'Era Nuova* [New Era]. Without hesitation, they decided to cross the border and throw themselves into the ordeal. The anarchists who went to Mexico shared the idea that they could create a local social revolution, a sort of liberated zone, from which they could trigger a more general insurrectionary process.[2] *Cronaca Sovversiva* believed that even within a strategic alliance of diverse political groups, among which the Madero faction stood out, the ideas and practices of the Magonists could prevail and succeed in expropriating the land and the means of production. They therefore called upon activists to participate in order to inject the most advanced social content into the revolution.[3]

In May 1911, Díaz abdicated, and in July, Madero triumphantly entered Mexico City. However, the PLM was not satisfied with what seemed like a mere change at the top of the government and decided to continue fighting for *tierra y libertad*. A few weeks later, *Cronaca Sovversiva*, after some vacillation, decided to publish a letter signed by eight activists who had rushed to support the Mexican rebels, a letter that reported that, in the liberated areas, such as Tijuana and its environs, the PLM was implementing a program that did not redistribute the land—not even the most arid and difficult to cultivate—nor institute social advancements. It therefore seemed to be deceiving subversives and did not deserve military, political, or financial support. Moreover, the ranks of the rebels were being corrupted by bandits and opportunists who had come to the area for adventure or to gain personal wealth, rather than to help with social emancipation.[4]

In *Cronaca Sovversiva*, there was thus a gradual change in perception and judgment, with analyses of the facts becoming increasingly critical. The newspaper reaffirmed its respect for Flores Magón and his comrades and stated that it had first supported them as refugees persecuted by the Díaz regime, and then in their political actions against him. However, it admitted the political rift and rebuked the PLM for having fallen into line with Madero's position. Gradually the paper's point of view— Galleani's primarily—was revealed. Mexico was an underdeveloped country, an overwhelming majority of its population were illiterate and sanctimonious. The conditions for a social revolution did not exist.[5] Since 1906, it was argued, the PLM had adopted a substantially bourgeois and liberal reformist program, both politically and economically. This assessment was not far from the one made by Flores Magón a few years later when he described the 1906 program as a "timid socialist program."[6] Furthermore, in calling upon revolutionaries to unite with them, the PLM imposed the condition of aligning with this program.[7] According to Galleani, anarchists could not do that without distorting their own ideals.

Others saw things in a completely different way, and believed that it was the duty of the libertarians to participate in a revolutionary process that could lead to an improvement in social conditions. Among these were Vittorio Cravello and Ludovico Caminita, organizers of the expedition of Italian anarchists to Mexico and editors of two periodicals, *L'Era Nuova* from Paterson and *Regeneración* (Italian version). They defended the gradualist strategy of the Magonists, according to which it was necessary not to appear explicitly as anarchists in the Mexican context, to avoid the risk of unpopularity among the exploited. Within the anarchist movement in Europe and in the United States, a discussion began that became very bitter and led to confrontations at two congresses.

The first was held in Brooklyn, planned by the local Club Avanti, and affirmed the value of anarchist participation in Mexican affairs. The second was organized by Gruppo autonomo of East Boston, and Galleani participated in it. It concluded by contrast that, "in Mexico, there is no social or economic movement," that it was a bourgeois, not an anarchist movement.[8] In the meanwhile, a few weeks after Díaz's removal from office, the Mexican army, under the orders of the new president, Madero, attacked and defeated two divisions of the PLM in Mexicali and

Tijuana. Thus the defeated and disappointed libertarians crossed back over the border, and some of them ended up being arrested by US authorities.

For Galleani, the Mexican revolution was a total failure from a social perspective, and this judgment did not change, either with the gradual emergence of Emiliano Zapata, who according to Galleani did not have an agrarian program significantly different from Madero's, or with the launch of a new political program by the PLM in September 1911, which called for expropriation and "solemnly declared war on capital, authority, church."[9]

CHAPTER XXIV

From Vermont to Massachusetts

During 1911, the movement connected with *Cronaca Sovversiva* debated, in the pages of the newspaper and in local meetings, the need to move its editorial headquarters. There were two main reasons for a transfer. In Barre, political friction had emerged between the periodical's historical nucleus and other Italian anarchists, who published a magazine entitled *Il Contropelo* [Against the Grain], which indulged in personal attacks on Galleani. In addition, some believed that in order to have greater influence on the lives of manual workers, it was essential to move to a more central location closer to centers of mining and industry. Groups from Pittsburgh, New York, Utica, Chicago, and Boston all offered to host the new offices, and fundraising was begun to cover transportation costs for the printing presses. In the end, the choice fell upon Lynn, Massachusetts, the most important center of the American footwear industry.

Galleani moved in August 1911 and was soon joined by Maria and the children, including the most recent addition, Mentana, born in 1909. The entire family settled in Wrentham (at 85 West Street), in the countryside between Boston and Providence, in a "cabin without doors and with broken windows and that [hosts], along with the new tenants, a cow, chickens, and many persecuted comrades." There was also an adjoining stone building that functioned as a library, built by Fernando Tarabelli, carpenter and reader of *Cronaca Sovversiva*.[1]

After several months, all of the printing equipment had been transferred to Lynn, and, from February 1910, it officially replaced Barre as the place of publication. Several groups of activists provided local support to the editorial staff, including the Lynn Circolo educativo sociale [Social Education Circle] and the Gruppo autonomo of East Boston, which were part of a numerous and active anarchist colony. As in Barre, Italian-language activists gathered together in various places within and outside of the town, including the Tony Citera Land, a tract of woodland owned by a local activist where meetings were regularly held. Here, too, there were picnics accompanied by raffles, musical entertainment, and dances with the Mentana Mandolin Orchestra and Quincy Filodrammatica, as well as target practice using images of the Czar, theatrical productions (Gori's *Primo Maggio* [May First] and *Senza Patria* [Without Homeland] were never missing), rallies with Galleani, and other meetings.

The Italian-language anarchists in Boston kept a close eye on what was happening in the United States and elsewhere, and particularly on the social struggles in Italy, using the triple perspective constantly put forth in the newspaper: approval of spontaneous actions, particularly when these transformed into open revolts; criticism of legalitarian socialists, who were regarded as the pawns of government; and denunciation of the repressive activities of the forces of order. This perspective kept the movement connected strongly to its roots. Cultural traditions were preserved through the nearly exclusive use of the Italian language. *Cronaca Sovversiva* was written in Italian, as were its books, pamphlets, manifestos; and its meetings, theatrical productions, and concerts were conducted in Italian as well.

With the headquarters transferred to Lynn, New England became the stronghold of a movement that widened its influence among Italian workers, galvanizing them with greater energy to attack state authoritarianism and systemic violence from employers. New social studies circles were formed and the number of anarchist groups that referred to the newspaper increased. Some of these had evocative names: Demolizione [Demolition], 11 novembre [November 11, the date the "martyrs of Chicago" were executed], 29 luglio [July 29, the date Umberto I was murdered], La Canaglia [The Scoundrel], Gli Insorti [The Rebels], Pietro Gori, Francisco Ferrer, Pensiero e azione [Thought and Action], Diritto all'ozio [Right to Idleness], La Rivolta [Revolt], Arte e libertà [Art and Freedom], Aurora, Carlo Marx, D'Alba, Gli Sbandati [The Degenerates], I Liberi [The Free], Volontà [Will], Gli Iconoclasti [The Iconoclasts], Bakunin, etc.

Alongside *Cronaca Sovversiva*, the continual work of oral propaganda became increasingly important. People near and

Luigi Galleani and his partner Maria Rallo in front of their house in Wrentham

far requested Galleani's presence. Every year he spent several months on tour in the United States, experiencing first-hand many of the most bitter union conflicts and leaving the editorship of the paper in the hands of Cavallazzi—who also moved to Boston—and then, after Cavallazzi's death in 1915, to other activists such as Postiglione, Costantino Zonchello, and Raffaele Schiavina.

The second decade of the 1900s was extraordinarily full of conflicts. The so-called Progressive Era, which extended from the beginning of the century until World War I, brought about legislative reforms intended to improve working conditions. Yet this did not alter the fact that still, in 1910, an estimated two million children were forced to work, and that, particularly in the railway, iron, and steel sectors, working hours were up to twelve hours a day, seven days a week, for wages of fifteen dollars a week.[2]

There were events that, due to their tragic nature, revealed the extent of exploitation. On March 25, 1911, 146 workers, mostly young women, forty-two of whom were Italian and for the most part from Sicily, died in a fire at the Triangle Shirtwaist Company, a well-known textile factory in the heart of Manhattan. To avoid being engulfed by flames, some of the victims flung themselves out of the building's windows. What remains, to this date, the most serious workplace accident ever to happen in New York revealed the contradictions of American society, and left a deep impression on the working world and public opinion. The subsequent trial absolved the owners of responsibility, despite the fact that, according to the charges, they had kept the workers locked in to prevent breaks in production.[3] The same year will also be remembered for the publication of Frederick Taylor's *The Principles of Scientific Management*, in which the entrepreneur devised a system to increase production and profits through the division of labor, mechanization, and the use of piecework, thus increasing exploitation of the labor force and eliminating any form of worker control over production.

Also of great importance were the events in Lawrence, where, between December 1911 and January 1912, twenty five thousand textile workers, mostly Italian, Polish, and Lithuanian, went on strike, protesting a wage cut. Two union organizers, Joseph Ettor and Arturo Giovannitti, came to support the strikers and were quickly arrested by the police. They were held responsible for the death of a striker, Anna Lo Pizzo, who was killed during clashes with the police. To support the rebelling workers and to demand the liberation of Ettor and Giovannitti, other well-known organizers from the IWW, such as Elizabeth Gurley Flynn, James Thompson, and "Big Bill" Haywood, came to Lawrence. In March, the workers achieved significant wage increases from the American Woolen Company, but the battle to free Ettor and Giovannitti continued.

Galleani followed the affair closely and, in meetings held in spring and summer 1912 in Lawrence, Plymouth, Philadelphia, Boston, and Lynn, he accused the police of murdering Anna Lo Pizzo and demanded the liberation of the two union leaders.[4] The columns of *Cronaca Sovversiva* carried articles to support the rebelling workers and to coordinate fundraising and protest actions. It was *Cronaca Sovversiva* that proposed and then organized hospitality for the children of strikers among groups of supporters in New York and Barre, a watershed event for the uprising, as it permitted the strike to be prolonged beyond all expectations.

As was often the case, Galleani and his comrades distinguished themselves by their attempts to radicalize the uprising. They called for a mass uprising in order to achieve the liberation of Ettor and Giovannitti. Against the judgment of the IWW and Tresca, who was very active in this dispute, Galleani, with the support of activists such as Postiglione and Calogero Speziale and the groups close to them, tried to force the matter. Using their influence over the Italian-language workers, who were the backbone of the uprising, the anarchists convinced them to go out on strike again in anticipation of the opening of the trial in Salem, and they called for street protests. These groups of anarchists waved black and red flags with "no gods no masters" inscribed on them and had a following among the most rowdy workers. They alone managed to bring several thousand workers out on strike, forcing the IWW in turn to declare a twenty-four-hour general strike on September 30, the opening day of the trial.

The Italian anarchists wanted the strike to continue indefinitely, but Tresca and the IWW insisted on limiting it to one day, and for it to be merely retaliatory and not involve street fighting. In the end Ettor and Giovannitti were cleared, which constituted an undeniable victory for the entire movement.[5]

The Lawrence strike showed the complex dialectical relationship between the anarchists and the IWW that persisted in the following years. This was a relationship of collaboration, certainly, but also of criticism from the anarchists who accused the upper echelons of the Wobblies of not wanting strikes to develop into open revolts. After the events of Lawrence, this criticism was also directed at Tresca. He faced harsh condemnation by Galleani, who believed that "Carluccio" had made a mistake by softening the IWW's positions and proclaiming a strike of just twenty-four hours when a mass of workers were ready for action.[6]

This was also what happened in Paterson in February the next year, when the IWW, again with Tresca's support, managed to organize an impressive strike of twenty-five thousand workers against the effects of mechanization in textile production. As well as giving daily help to the strikers and participating in the struggle, activists close to *Cronaca Sovversiva* supported the search for bold forms of action and did not hold back from criticizing those who judged such methods too risky and renounced them. Instead, the strike remained substantially peaceful, and ended in August with a decisive defeat, resulting in a return to work under the same conditions as before, and the rapid decline of the IWW in that area. In Galleani's eyes, it was a worse outcome than what had happened in 1902, when the movement was divided but had given proof of its own determination and desire to revolt, thus serving as an example for all rebels.

In summer 1913, miners in Colorado—mostly Greek, Italian, and Serbian—demanded reduced hours, better working conditions, and the freedom to organize themselves into a union. They went on strike, and to exert pressure, camped out with their families near the entrances to the coalmines in Ludlow, on the land of the Colorado Fuel and Iron Company owned by John Rockefeller. They were subjected to repeated searches, violence, and even gunfire from the men of a private police agency. Then, in April 1914, the National Guard set fire to their makeshift camp, killing about twenty people, including women and children. A young John Reed, who arrived at the site the next day, expressed his shock at seeing that "the tent colony, or where the tent colony had been, was a great square of ghastly ruins."[7]

Cronaca Sovversiva took part in this struggle. It had several loyal readers in the mining area. It organized initiatives to collect funds and to support the strikers. It created propaganda to extend the strike to Wyoming, and it was on the side of the United Mine Workers during the often bloody clashes with scabs. It also carried reports of acts of sabotage that damaged mining equipment. It recommended its readers arm themselves and go to Ludlow, as had happened in Denver and Colorado Springs.[8] It was an unequal struggle and at the end of the year the strikers, weakened by numerous arrests in September 1914, had to capitulate to federal troops. They paid the price with over seventy dead and loss of work for about eleven thousand (out of a workforce of thirteen thousand).

For the left, Ludlow became the ultimate symbol of capitalist brutality in a period of severe economic depression and rampant unemployment among workers. Rockefeller was seen as the leader of the reaction. In response, there were many public protests, particularly in New York, where they were led by anarchists. A number of Italian-language anarchists stood out, distinguishing themselves with their black flags, upon which "destruction" was embroidered in red letters.[9] On July 4, 1914, with the Ludlow dispute in full swing, three members of the Ferrer Center of New York blew themselves up while making a bomb to use against Rockefeller. Twenty thousand paid tribute to them in Union Square. During the following months, churches, courts, and police stations were attacked. Taking stock of the situation, Galleani described the "tasks of the moment" as follows:

> It is a well-known fact that there are daily bombings in New
> York [...]. Thus for about six months the city's chronicle of

dynamite attacks has been complicated by extraordinary threats, extraordinary attacks, attacks that in their causes, in their commitments, in their objectives, clearly and precisely outline the revolt [...]. An uninterrupted series of more or less serious, more or less successful attacks, but so characteristic that we can unquestionably celebrate them. Reasonably-minded subversives cannot classify them as ploys used by the police [...] They are so characteristic that for once the brutal yet foolish police cannot take refuge in the mysterious inscrutability of the legendary black hand and must get involved with this unexplored world of "reds" without Churches, without the Ten Commandments, without priests, rippling from the Battery to Harlem, between the two rivers, irrepressible, as inexorable as the sky or as destiny [...].

What is to be done? Continue the good war, the war to exterminate the vampires of capital, the ogres of order, in every lair, the war that knows neither fear, nor doubt, nor pity, nor truce, even if, through the daily experience of being ambushed, and in the face of the overwhelming forces of the enemy, boldness and courage must surround themselves with prudence and caution.[10]

CHAPTER XXV

Facing the World War

In the pages of *Cronaca Sovversiva*, Galleani critically analyzed the wars of the early-twentieth century, starting with the Russian-Japanese conflict of 1904 to 1905. Opposition to the war in Libya, which started in 1911 and involved the Italian army, found him incredibly busy writing a large number of articles that were often reproduced in periodicals and pamphlets printed in Italy, and giving lectures from Massachusetts to California.

He edited three issues of the periodical *Balilla* during 1912. It had a strongly anti-militaristic character and contained "biweekly libertarian propaganda for children." It was also useful for the "extremely large number of workers who remain in intellectual infancy."[1] The newspaper published "parables, sketches, brief novellas [that are] clear and meaningful, a few poems, a few suggestive illustrations, together with methods and functional exercises for reading and writing in Italian."[2] Galleani created the biweekly in its entirety, although Maria Rallo was officially its publisher. In its pages he found space to denounce the Libyan campaign and for some of his typical themes: the central importance of labor struggles, the function of acts of rebellion, and the example of figures such as Bresci.

The campaign against the Tripoli expedition went hand in hand with denunciation of those primarily responsible for it, above all the Bank of Rome, and with agitation for the liberation of Augusto Masetti, a young draftee with libertarian sympathies who had been arrested for turning his weapons against his own colonel at the Cialdini barracks in Bologna in order to avoid being sent to Africa. He had become the symbol of protests against militarism in Italy that had united the anarchists with other forces of the left and to which Galleani also contributed a large number of leaflets and pamphlets. Among these, "Alle madri d'Italia" [To the Mothers of Italy], a pamphlet issued under the name of "Mentana" was particularly successful. It explained the Masetti affair and demanded his freedom, and was widely distributed on both sides of the Atlantic.[3]

In Italy, anti-militaristic rebellion found the outlet Galleani had been hoping for during the "Settimana Rossa" [Red Week]. This was an insurrection with an epicenter of Le Marche and Romagna, though other areas of Italy were also involved.[4] The anarchist movement in Italy at this time benefited from the presence of Malatesta, who had returned from London and received encouragement and economic support from *Cronaca Sovversiva*, which considered his presence to be essential, because he was able to revive the scattered libertarian forces and do the work of "conciliation."[5]

The Settimana Rossa, as *Cronaca Sovversiva* saw it, showed that "the masses are always ready for action" and that party and union organizations remained a major problem, since once again they restrained popular energies and constrained the general strike within the limits of peaceful demands.[6]

The theme of anti-militarism had already gained importance with the war in Libya and, starting in 1914, with sharp criticism of American imperialism in the Caribbean. It became a priority for the movement a few weeks after the end of the Settimana Rossa with the outbreak of the First World War.

Galleani's opposition to the war was clear and had a certain influence on the anti-interventionist policy of the international anarchist movement. His writings on the subject were carried in several Italian-language periodicals printed in Europe, including Geneva's *Il Risveglio* and *Volontà* in Ancona. Galleani expressed no surprise at the fact that socialist parliamentary representatives in France and Germany had voted for war credits. In his eyes, this was an inevitable consequence of their strategy of conquering public power gradually, and the corruption that this strategy entailed.

However the problem was that some anarchists, including Kropotkin, who had most influenced Galleani's thought in the preceding decades, believed it was necessary to support the Allies to oppose Prussian aggression and guarantee the conditions for future social development in Europe. For the group around *Cronaca Sovversiva* this was a hard blow. In December 1912, for the Russian's seventieth birthday, a special eight-page illustrated issue was published in his honor, and a little while earlier the Italian translation of *La morale anarchiste* had been reprinted.

Moreover, Kropotkin's position was shared by other activists with whom Galleani was very close, from Cipriani to James Guillaume, Grave to Malato, Paul Reclus to Cherkezov, Herzig to

Balilla, the periodical edited by Galleani in 1912

Gross. In February 1916, some of these published the *Manifeste des Seize* [Manifesto of the Sixteen] and incited the French to fight the central powers. Malatesta answered these "Entente-supporting" or "government" anarchists emphatically, first in London's *Freedom* and then with a leaflet published clandestinely in Paris in 1916, entitled *Réponse de Malatesta au "Manifeste des Seize" Anarchistes de gouvernement* [Malatesta's Response to the "Manifesto of the Sixteen." Pro-Government Anarchists], thus making himself the spokesperson for the anti-militaristic outlook of the majority of the movement.[7]

BALILLA   5

— Guarda! quelli ch'egli affama passano al largo sbigottiti, quelli che egli ingansa si recano a gloria di levarlo, alto, sulle spalle, e cingerlo d'artai e d'armati. Chi può dirmpere di lassù sua maestà il da-naro?
— Coloro che l'hanno innalzato e possono deprimerlo, coloro che gli danno le armi e possono levar-gliele e spianarle contro di lui.
— Se comprendessero....
— Quelli che non comprenderanno andranno schiacciati quando mascheranno al sostegno i più intel-ligenti ed i più forti.

Galleani had long been clear that the concept of homeland had transformed into a lie for the proletariat. It was inconceivable for him to justify the conflict, and in a long series of articles he spelled out his reasons. Kropotkin was wrong to support war even if to oppose German militarism, as he did not distinguish between those, in every country, who benefit from war, namely, the bankers and industrialists, and those who suffer from it, whether French, German, or of any other nationality. Pitting the France of thought and culture against militaristic Germany, as Kropotkin did, was a "reckless misunderstanding." Germany too has its thinkers and its culture, its Goethe and Schiller, and if revolutionary France had always received Galleani's sympathy, this did not apply to France as such.[8] Galleani's position was also made clear in *Cronaca Sovversiva*, in whose columns over the previous weeks there had been accounts of the debate between those, like Cavallazzi, who were completely opposed to the war and others, like Postiglione, who were swayed by Kropotkin's arguments.[9]

Even though opposition to the European war was a central theme of repeated and numerous "propaganda tours" from 1914 onward, it was also a topic of conflict among Italian anarchists in the United States. Galleani was opposed to those in the movement who tried to form a temporary strategic alliance with socialists and syndicalists opposed to the war. This was proposed in *La Questione Sociale* that, after an interruption, resumed publication in October 1914 in New York, under the direction of Aldo Felicani.

Thus two opposing visions collided. On the one hand, there were those like Galleani who were opposed to an alliance with non-anarchists, and on the other hand, others like Felicani who wanted to work with other anti-militarists, just as the Italian anarchists were doing in Italy. As had happened in the past, the political argument descended into personal attacks, with Galleani being accused of making *Cronaca Sovversiva* a personal instrument and posturing as the "great pontiff" of the anarchist movement.[10]

As the conflict continued, his priority objective, apart from these disputes, was to obstruct the war machine, encourage soldiers to desert, and work so that the revolution would bring an end to the "horrendous carnage" and robbery by the possessing classes. In 1916, the battles of Verdun and the Somme alone resulted in about a million and a half dead, and left a deep and terrible scar upon the survivors. Galleani wrote, "225 billion francs have fallen into the bottomless pit of war" in only two years (August 1914–August 1916). This was the amount spent by the warring powers with the aid of bank loans that would later have to be repaid by the people, particularly the lower classes.[11]

In 1915, he began publishing letters from youth called to the front, who wrote to their parents and friends expressing their consternation, and letters from those who remained at home alone, particularly women, often condemned to poverty. The column was called "Dalle trincee e dai focolari" [From the Trenches and From the Hearths]. Here is an example:

> It is enough, my dear, to be going to die for these scoundrels and cowards! [...] The war is horrific [...]. May those who created this horrendous human slaughterhouse be cursed a thousand times [...]. If you could see the plundering, the bloody mess! The other week here in Rubino they unloaded another four hundred wounded, and if you could only see how pitiful they were: some were missing an arm, some a leg, some both, many were blind, many had two feet amputated because of the freezing cold. What horror! [...] The Italian army wants to beat the "record" in its thirst to rid the ranks of subversives. Deserters who come here tell us that no means are overlooked to harm comrades and none who, in peace time, were marked in the black book are spared now. All subversives are marked and officials have orders to assign them the most arduous tasks from which it is difficult if not impossible to come out alive.[12]

In addition to these, from summer 1915 on, letters appeared more frequently from relatives of Italian immigrants to the United States, that described the worst aspects of the war, the massacres and the poverty, and exhorted their own loved ones to "not come back." Indeed "Figli, non tornate!" [Children, Don't Come Back!] was the title of another dedicated column in the weekly. This was also the title of a leaflet signed by the "Mothers of Italy" to people who immigrated to North and South America, actually written by Galleani himself. It was branded as German propaganda by the bourgeois press, but was received enthusiastically in subversive circles, and one hundred thousand copies were printed. It aimed to make deserters out of the immigrants called back to serve in the military. It was distributed wherever there were Italian-language anarchists, It read:

> Children, don't come back!
> They will seize you like thieves, like slaves on the docks, and without allowing you to see again, to embrace, perhaps for the last time, the old folks who gave you life, sincere hearts, and fertile strength, they will sacrifice you up there in the canyons of Ampezzo or on the high plain of the Carso to bring about the triumph of a terrible and bloody deception: the homeland![13]

These were difficult years, but also years of intense activity and growth for the anarchist movement in the United States, especially from summer 1915, when Italy entered the war and the campaign in the press began to favor intervention by the United States. There were proposals, which were not taken up, to make *Cronaca Sovversiva* into a biweekly or even daily paper, and plans were made for a new monthly magazine which was to be called *Pane e Libertà* [Bread and Freedom].

"Against the war, against peace, for revolution!" was the slogan of a popular article written by Galleani, which the movement on either side of the Atlantic made its own, and which summarized anarchist thinking at this time. It read: "Insurrection will precede the truce, and will barge in to prevent peace from reestablishing the social order, which unleashed such horrors and abomination, on the ruins of war."[14] This was not just a wish, it was a clear indication of the work to be done by all activists.

CHAPTER XXVI

Nulla dies sine linea

You need to stay with the crowd.[1] There's no need to give in to reformism. Propaganda. Rebellion. Action. Our characteristic action: anti-opportunistic. Anti-religious. Anti-state. Anti-ownership. Anti-authority [...]. First destroy then educate, civilize, improve: anarchism. The others: first conquer then liberate; conquer public power. Anarchists: individuals in society. Socialism: society over the individual [...]. Bourgeoisie: the few over the many. Socialism: the many over the few. Anarchism: the autonomous individual in a free society [...]. Syndicalism is agnostic. It does not consist of the conscious class but of the composite and amorphous mass. Its reformist action. Its attitude. Inconsistency [...] Solidarity [*vs*] organization. Spontaneous cohesion [*vs*] disciplined organization.[2]

These fragmentary *Notes on Syndicalism* established the outlines of Galleani's ideas, according to which individual conscience and conscious solidarity, typical of anarchists, contrasted with the socialists' concepts of organization and discipline. A gulf between organization and solidarity that grew increasingly large, in his view, after the great strikes of Paterson and Lawrence.[3] The anarchist acted not out of discipline but from the "impulse of his own conscience."[4]

He used these notes as the outline for a series of lectures he delivered in West Virginia, Ohio, Michigan, Indiana, Illinois, and Missouri, during which he swept down like a whirlwind on the war and redefined the order of priorities for the anarchist movement. From 1915 on, the struggle against militarism and the class struggle were inextricably intertwined, and opposition to the war became a central theme in meetings, articles, and actions.

At the beginning of the conflict, the American economy, through new federal agencies such as the War Industries Board, became a planned state system that tended to restrict workers' rights. The war was financed by rampant inflation, so that the cost of living practically doubled from August 1915 through late 1919. By its end, the cost of the conflict exceeded the sum of all federal expenditures incurred by the country in its 130 year history. Social inequalities became more evident. In 1915 the Commission on Industrial Relations reported that seventy-five percent of the American population owned only five percent of the national wealth.[5]

Galleani analyzed this dynamic by studying the most emblematic dynasty of American capitalism, the Morgans. Upon the death of the patriarch J.P. Morgan, the greatest embodiment of American financial and industrial power, he wrote:

> J.P. Morgan built the privileges that allowed him to dictate his own wishes to emperors, kings, and parliaments on top of panic, poverty, adversity, ruin, frightening cracks, the chasm in which weak and rash competitors have fallen into the abyss of poverty, abandonment, anguish in which a million fall every day, slaves of his prisons, his mines, his steel mills.[6]

His son, John Pierpont Morgan Jr., in turn played an essential role in pushing President Woodrow Wilson to enter the war. Starting in September 1915, his trust provided one loan after another to the English and French and earned 270 billion dollars, a clear sign of the increased profits that the war guaranteed to large corporations.[7]

The Morgan and Rockefeller families, the subversives wrote in their newspapers, controlled state governments, bent the law to their own ends and had a monopoly over the media. Also in this field, the government created the Committee on Public Information, tasked with providing media support for enlistment and the obligation to purchase Liberty Bonds, securities issued to finance the war.[8]

Faced with such marked inequalities, the social struggle intensified. Between 1916 and 1918 the number of strikes was on average two and a half times greater than in 1915, with the proclamation of four general strikes in different areas of the country. In 1917 alone there were over four thousand strikes involving over two million workers, who often disobeyed their own federations and unions.[9]

In this situation, Italian-language anarchists played an active part and were to be found in many of the centers of worker rebellion. Galleani often and willingly gave speeches. During WWI, he crisscrossed the United States, visiting Ohio, Michigan, Wisconsin, Minnesota, Iowa, Illinois, Missouri, Arizona, Oklahoma, Kansas, Colorado, Wyoming, Montana, Idaho, Washington, Oregon, and California. He then concentrated on the Eastern states. He gave numerous lectures in small and large centers from Maine to Florida. He was repeatedly invited by groups in Boston, New York, Philadelphia, Tampa, as well as Portsmouth, Albany, Utica, Syracuse, Rochester, Buffalo, Pittsburgh, Fall River, Bridgeport, Stamford, Newark, Trenton, Norfolk, et cetera.

He often gave several lectures in the same place, as in Philadelphia, where in January 1915 local groups organized three lectures, each a week apart, on the following themes: syndicalism and anarchism, the proletariat and the war, toward the greater dawn. Wherever there was a factory or mining camp experiencing an uprising and with an active anarchist group, Galleani was asked to speak. In January and February 1916, he went several times to the Cordage Company of Plymouth, at the request of Bartolomeo Vanzetti and other comrades active in Massachusetts, to support the strike of about two thousand workers.[10]

That January, a struggle began at the steel mills of Youngstown, Ohio. The company guards opened fire on the workers, causing three deaths, and the crowd burned several plants, causing millions of dollars' worth of damage before the National Guard arrived to stop the workers.[11] In April something similar happened in Pittsburgh, where the steel mills were mobbed. Troops intervened and two workers were killed. In both cases, unskilled workers from Southern and Eastern Europe took on leading roles, rebelling against the exploitation and discipline of the factory.

Labor struggles overlapped with protests against militarism. The streets of major American cities were filled both with radicals opposing the war, who held meetings and demonstrations that were often attacked by the police, and also with patriotic advocates of intervention, against whom there was no shortage of objectors, sometimes violent. On May 1, 1916, Union Square in New York was besieged by anarchist and anti-militarist demonstrators, who gave new stimulus to that special day for all subversives.[12] But the most striking episode took place the following July 22 in San Francisco, where a procession supporting the feared US intervention in the worldwide conflict was bombed, causing ten deaths and numerous injuries. Several anarchists and socialists were arrested, including well-known union organizers Warren Billings and Tom Mooney, who, according to the workers' newspapers, were framed. To free them, the entire movement, including *Cronaca Sovversiva*, began collecting funds and mounting protest actions that lasted for months, but the two were convicted and spent over twenty years in prison.

In 1916, the mines were the theater of further agitation, especially in Ohio and Minnesota. During the summer, an iron miners' strike in the Mesabi Iron Range of Minnesota dominated the attention of revolutionaries. The strike was led by the IWW due to the work of Ettor, Elizabeth Gurley Flynn, and Tresca. Tresca was arrested during this struggle and condemned in December to a year in prison. *Cronaca Sovversiva* took part in this struggle and there were demonstrations and meetings in several cities. Galleani repeatedly gave speeches in Boston where, on December 17, a bomb caused considerable damage to a police station on Battery Street.

Then, in the autumn, coalminers in Pennsylvania by-passed

the IWW and started a wildcat strike. No fewer than three hundred Italian miners, including several active anarchists, were involved. They were supported by Galleani. Afterward he was arrested at Dupont together with four of his comrades for inciting rebellion. He was released several weeks later only after paying a $1,500 bail. The strike grew anyway until it involved about forty thousand workers. As a first objective it aimed to put an end to the practice of variable contracts, which depended on the yields of different mines, and demanded the same contract for all miners.[13]

It was a tense and exciting period. In November 1916, once free, Galleani returned to Lynn, from where he followed the events in Everett, Washington. Everett was a town known for its sawmills, where vigilantes prevented the landing of two steamboats from Seattle. Several hundred IWW activists were on board to defend a strike and freedom of speech and association. There were rifle shots from the pier. Five workers and two private guards were killed, and there were about seventy arrests.[14]

The attention of the Italian-language anarchist movement was taken up with mounting, continual solidarity campaigns for activists who were arrested after limited skirmishes with the police. In December, Galleani was suspected of having injured a police officer's hand with a knife. The event allegedly took place during an anti-military demonstration in Boston, in which the anarchists had a rough confrontation with the police and suffered several arrests.[15]

CHAPTER XXVII

The Land of the Free

In many cases, political intolerance was compounded by racial prejudice. In the major news outlets, Italians had for some time been portrayed as violent, criminal, and as biologically inferior, treated little better than African Americans at the time. As *Cronaca Sovversiva* described this treatment: "The *dago* is not just the foreigner or the barbarian, he is below both in the anthropological classification, on the lowest level: some sort of hybrid between man and gorilla, a surviving *anthropithecus*, unresponsive to all social revolutions."[1]

Due to this, they were frequently lynched. When immigrants criticized American institutions or, even worse, engaged in class struggle, the reaction of the authorities was usually much more severe.

From the beginning of his time in the United States, Galleani had done a lot to expose the hypocrisies of the so-called "Land of the Free," a country that defined itself as free but that was actually distinguished by its anti-worker and racist policies. Bosses regularly responded to the demands of workers with violence, using either the National Guard or private police. Freedom of thought and expression were restricted in practice. Legislation in 1903 required applicants for naturalization to swear an oath that they were not anarchists.

In 1908, then-President Theodore Roosevelt enacted new legislation to prevent the distribution by mail of newspapers deemed immoral. *Cronaca Sovversiva* responded to this "gag rule" by increasing its size and directly attacking the president as "violent [...], an idiot [and] an aider and abettor of the Trusts."[2]

But a quantum leap was made with the 1917 Immigration Act in February of that year. The Act's provisions allowed a foreigner to be deported within five years of their entry into the country, or without a time limit if they were accused of intending to destroy property, planning to overthrow the government by force, or having killed a public official.[3]

The hatred of immigrants, particularly if they were radicals, grew more bitter following the American government's decision to enter the war in April 1917. Subversives immediately became unpatriotic, no longer just opponents of private property, religion, and the traditional family: now they were enemies of the United States.

Before the war began, *Cronaca Sovversiva* aimed its antimilitarist criticisms at American institutions, subjecting them to stinging attacks. Since 1915, Galleani had accused American capitalism of benefiting from the global conflict, with the government's blessing.[4] Italian anarchists had also collaborated actively with Emma Goldman and Alexander Berkman, promoting their first lecture tours and the publication of their newspapers *Mother Earth* and *The Blast*, which were already targets for the government's repression.[5]

On May 18, 1917, six weeks after America entered the war, in order to organize military conscription, Congress decreed that every man between twenty-one and thirty years old was required to register with their respective draft boards within two weeks, under penalty of up to one year's imprisonment.[6] This applied to immigrants as well as to United States citizens. Under the terms of the law, registration for immigrants did not necessarily mean that they would be drafted. Nevertheless, on the first page of *Cronaca Sovversiva*, Galleani published an article entitled "Matricolati!" [Registrants!] in which he exhorted readers not to register and to avoid cooperating with those who were waging war. He wrote: "They register you so they can control your life, to take it from you on the first occasion." His advice was taken by many activists, who decided to avoid registration by going underground or crossing the border to Canada or Mexico.[7] Others, however, ended up being arrested, imprisoned, or forced to register. The article was a sign of wider activity against military service, which was also supported by New York's International Anarchist Committee of Revolutionary Rebellion and the No-Conscription League established by Goldman and Berkman, who organized street demonstrations against the war and distributed hundreds of thousands of copies of leaflets in English and Italian.

For the government, anarchism had crossed the line. Throughout the country, anarchist offices were raided, men and women beaten, premises destroyed, libraries and archives sequestered, lectures and theatrical performances suspended, newspapers and publications suppressed, and many activists arrested. This is what happened to Francesco Widmar, editor of *L'Era Nuova* in Paterson, which was silenced within a few weeks. The same happened to Hippolyte Havel and his monthly, *The Social War*, and to Goldman and Berkman and their periodicals *Mother Earth* and *The Blast*.[8]

On May 29, the offices of *Cronaca Sovversiva* were searched for the first time, with no results. Galleani was arrested and taken to Boston for interrogation, but released after a few hours. In an address to the nation on June 14, 1917, President Wilson laid down the line against radicals: "Woe to the man or group of men that seeks to stand in our way in this day of high resolution," he declared.[9] Twenty-four hours later he signed a new law, the Espionage Act, which set a penalty of up to twenty years in prison and fines of up to ten thousand dollars for those accused of helping the enemy, obstructing the draft, or encouraging disobedience within the armed forces. The next day, Galleani's home in Wrentham and the offices of *Cronaca Sovversiva* were raided by the police.

> Around 12:30 [am] an insistent thwacking upon the windows and doors suddenly wakes everyone, and before we realize what is happening around us five rogues with revolvers aimed burst into the house, forcing open the bedroom door of Luigi Galleani, to whom they shout out the arrest warrant. Our Gigi is not surprised [...] he gently

moves away the children who had clung to his neck while
Maria vents her embittered mind to the police.[10]

Galleani was arrested, as was the newspaper's typesetter,
Giovanni Eramo. They were accused of spreading propaganda
against military conscription in the article "Matricolati!" Galleani
was taken to Boston, where he was interrogated by the District
Attorney. He was held in prison until payment of a bond of ten
thousand dollars secured his release. In July he appeared before
the Federal Court in Boston, where he had to answer the charges
of insulting the president of the United States and conspiracy to
impede military conscription.

He was also brought before the Federal Immigration
Commission of Boston, which had the power to decide whether
or not he would be deported to Italy. This was a purely admin-
istrative procedure. It was used as a means to expel undesired
persons during this period, on the recommendation of the
Department of Justice, because it circumvented the safeguards of
a judicial process that was deemed to be too slow. Despite pressure from federal law enforcement agencies to deport Galleani
immediately, it was not possible because he had three children of
American nationality—and the law expressly prohibited deportation in such cases. In addition there was a lack of concrete
evidence that he was a danger to society. After the trial was postponed several times, he was finally fined three hundred dollars
and released, though subject to a six-month period of probation,
which was then extended for another six months.[11]

However, the "claws of the Holy Office," as Galleani
described the government's repressive apparatus in the columns
of *Cronaca Sovversiva*, continued to squeeze. Giobbe and Irma
Sanchini and others were arrested. Immediately after Galleani's
arrest, these two activists had begun collecting the funds needed
to get him out of prison. That July, federal agents again raided
the offices of *Cronaca Sovversiva*. In this way, the Department of
Justice tried to intimidate the editorial staff of what it described
as "the most rabid, seditious and anarchistic sheet ever published in this country" and pressured the Post Office to prohibit

its distribution.[12] They did not succeed. Although the Post Office abolished an exemption from postal charges for periodical publications, from which *Cronaca Sovversiva* had benefited, from that time on the newspaper was distributed first without exemptions as normal correspondence in sealed envelopes, and then by means of American Express private couriers. It thus kept circulating, although with some delays and rather high costs.

That summer witnessed the harshest phase of what has gone down in history as the "Red Scare." There were searches, confiscation of printed material, interceptions, surveillance, interrogations, and arrests. Eighteen leftist newspapers were banned by the Post Office Department, including *Call*, *The Masses*, and *The Appeal to Reason*, while illegal detentions, beatings, killings, and deportations affected thousands of radicals.[13]

The reverberations of the February 1917 revolution in Russia, followed by the Bolshevik revolution, also influenced events, leading to social turmoil throughout Europe and throwing the American authorities into a panic, fearful that the "insurrectionary contagion" would spread to US soil. *Cronaca Sovversiva* joyfully welcomed the February revolution and reported on the turmoil of the subsequent months. It supported the activities of the "maximalists" against and beyond the constitutional government of Alexander Kerensky. The storming of the Winter Palace in October was greeted with enthusiasm, and hopes that the uprising in Russia would spread to Germany and to other European and non-European countries. The Bolshevik revolution coincided, in the paper's view, with the activities of the soviets, a driving force that could change the course of history by promoting the guiding principle of "revolutionary defeatism," the only policy capable of ending the war through a strong international protest movement.[14] After the Bolsheviks seized power, however, Galleani did not hesitate to condemn the new party for supporting a worker's state based on a theory that had been criticized by the anarchist movement since the beginning of the century.[15]

After the events in Russia, sections of the American establishment developed a veritable obsession with insurgents trying to undermine the established order. All subversives, without distinction, were labeled Bolsheviks and targeted by the Palmer Raids, police raids ordered by the Attorney General and businessman A. Mitchell Palmer. The IWW were decimated by government repression, and Italian-language anarchist groups fared no better. Between 1917 and 1918, many study circles that counted *Cronaca Sovversiva* as an influence were raided by the police. This happened in Boston, Providence, Paterson, New York, Philadelphia, Chicago, San Francisco, Portland, Seattle, and other cities. Hundreds of arrests and deportations followed. Galleani and his comrades certainly did not intend to give up in the face of this reaction. They continued to denounce what they described as judicial tyranny with words and actions, in open defiance of the authorities. In this situation, a willingness to act and respect for the necessary confidentiality were needed.[16]

In September 1917, two members of the Milwaukee Ferrer Circle were accused of having disrupted a sermon of loyalist propaganda by Italian priest Augusto Giuliani. They were beaten to death by the police, while a third was severely injured. Two detectives were also hurt. Arrests, searches, and seizure of printed material followed.[17] In December, eleven Italian anarchists were each condemned to twenty-five years in prison. Several weeks before sentencing, a bomb was found in the basement of the Italian evangelical mission to which Giuliani belonged. When it was taken to the police station, the bomb exploded, completely devastating the building and causing the death of one civilian and ten police officers, including two who had played a role in the September conflict.[18]

This is an example of the violence that erupted in response to terror from police and bosses. As this reaction spread through the country in 1917, three episodes are worth mentioning. In July, in Bisbee, Arizona, and in Gallup, New Mexico, the authorities repressed strikes by forcing more than one thousand miners into cattle cars and then abandoning them in remote areas. In August, IWW trade unionist Frank Little was kidnapped in his hotel and hanged. This followed the murder of another well-known wobbly, Joe Hill, a poet and agitator of Swedish origin who was accused of homicide and put to death in November 1915.

Cronaca Sovversiva led an energetic campaign in his defense.[19] In November, in Tulsa, Oklahoma, seventeen oil workers (twelve of them IWW members) committed to unionizing the workers were arrested and then handed over to the Knights of Liberty, a faction of the Ku Klux Klan, which tied them to trees, whipped them, and then tarred and feathered them as a form of humiliation.

The ring around *Cronaca Sovversiva* was also growing ever tighter. In October 1917, a law was passed requiring non-English language newspapers to present translations of each article concerning the war to the Post Office Department, while agents prevented anyone from joining or leaving the editorial board. On February 22, 1918, both Galleani's house and the offices of *Cronaca Sovversiva* were again raided. A list of five thousand addresses to which the newspaper was sent was seized, in addition to correspondence and several articles including excerpts from Duval's *Memorie Autobiografiche*. In the same month, American Express yielded to pressure from the Department of Justice and refused to deliver *Cronaca Sovversiva*. Despite everything, the newspaper held out. Editorial material, names, and addresses were hidden in private homes, while distribution was undertaken by trusted activists who used their own means, even though it became less widespread and suffered major delays and expenses.

In March, Raffaele Schiavina, the director of the newspaper since April 1916 and one of Galleani's main collaborators, was put on trial and sentenced to one year of forced labor in the East Cambridge prison for not having registered for the draft. This was the first of a long series of arrests. The following May 15, during an extensive sting, over sixty activists considered to be collaborators of *Cronaca Sovversiva* were arrested. They were accused of being undesirable aliens by the immigration authorities who intended to expel them from the country on the basis of the Immigration Act. Again, however, concrete evidence was lacking and one by one they were released. This also happened to Galleani the next day. He was arrested, brought to the East Boston immigration office, interrogated, and then released.

On May 16, the room to maneuver for radicals was further reduced. The government passed the Sedition Act, by which it established a penalty of up to twenty years in prison and fines up to ten thousand dollars for those who hindered the sale of Liberty Bonds, discouraged military recruitment, or wrote things against the government or the war effort. With this Act, the authorities imposed general censorship of the press, while the combined application of the Espionage Act and the Sedition Act led to mass trials and imprisonment of roughly a thousand socialist, syndicalist, and libertarian activists.[20]

Squeezed from every side, *Cronaca Sovversiva* was no longer able to maintain regular releases from spring 1918. Eramo stepped down, as did some distributors and subscribers. Arrested or persecuted, many were no longer able to support the newspaper. After April, publication was intermittent. Two further issues, one in June and one in July, were entirely produced by Galleani. In the June issue, he wrote: "They're drowning us! They're tightening the noose around our throat with hands shaking from the double rage of fear and hypocrisy."[21] In the July issue, he published a long article on the first page. Inside there was a translation of several of the amendments most hostile to liberty approved by Congress. It concluded with the unchanged call: "Long live anarchy. Long live the social revolution!"[22] Then silence. *Cronaca Sovversiva* was declared illegal and ceased publication.

As if that was not enough, in October 1918 Congress passed another law, developed by the immigration authorities together with the Department of Justice, that expressly provided for the deportation of anyone who belonged to a libertarian organization, possessed anarchist literature for propaganda purposes, or who subscribed, collected subscriptions for, distributed *Cronaca Sovversiva*, or wrote articles for it (Article 5).[23] Everything was in place for the mass expulsion of undesirables. The list on the desk of the Department of Justice contained about seven thousand names. Close to the top of the list was the name Luigi Galleani. In January 1919, a deportation order was served against him.

End of the story? Not quite.

CHAPTER XXVIII

Adversus hostem aeterna auctoritas!

Galleani and the groups that were left did not intend to keep their heads down, all the more so because, once the global conflict was over, the intensity of worker demands increased in the United States and in many parts of Europe.[1] Between late October and early November 1918, insurrectional uprisings exploded in Hungary and Bavaria, and the armistice put an end to years of brutal war paid for with millions of lives. In the United States, about 350,000 people were classified as draft dodgers, and the entire left gained increasing support. Membership of the Socialist Party of America grew and, following repeated divisions, two new parties were founded: the Communist Party and the Communist Labor Party.

In November, in New England and in New Jersey, there were widespread demonstrations for an eight-hour workday in the textile industry. With the beginning of the new year, fueled by the unexpected rise in the cost of living, social disorder took the form of a wave of general strikes in major US cities. In Seattle, for five days in February, there was a general strike throughout the city. In the spring, railroad workers downed tools throughout the country. They were followed in the summer by 350,000 iron and steel workers and by coalminers in Illinois. In many cases, the workers bypassed their unions in favor of wildcat strikes, making 1919—*The Nation* wrote—a year of "unprecedented revolt," heavily repressed by the forces of order.[2]

The funds remaining in the coffers of *Cronaca Sovversiva* were used to finance the publication of other papers that supported workers' demands and denounced the US government, coordinated by Zonchello and Roberto Elia: *Cronache Rosse* [Red Chronicles], *L'Anarchia* [Anarchy], *Il Diritto* [Law], and *Il Refrattario* [The Refractory One].

Although a deportation order had been served to Galleani, he managed to delay its implementation through legal moves. On February 27, he gave a fiery lecture in Taunton, Massachusetts, in which he denounced and challenged the American system as a whole. That same evening, twenty-five miles away in Franklin, an explosion killed four Italian anarchists as they tried to plant a bomb in a factory of the American Woolen Company. In the meanwhile, the machines for printing *Cronaca Sovversiva* were dismantled and moved secretly from Lynn to Providence. There, thanks to the support of Alfonso Coniglio, a Sicilian living in Tampa, and other activists who were still free, two further issues were printed and released secretly in March and May 1919. The voice of the anarchists was not yet extinguished. Rather it was ready to make itself heard by any means necessary, all the more so because the death of Pietro Marucco, an anarchist living in Latrobe, Pennsylvania, had to be condemned. In March, Marucco had lost his life at sea during deportation from the United States to Italy. His comrades demanded revenge.[3]

In the days immediately before May 1, 1919, about thirty explosive packages were sent to leading figures in the government—judges, police officers, mayors—as well as industrialists and newspaper editors. Most were intercepted at various post offices and defused. There was just one injury. Starting with Palmer, the intended targets were all sworn enemies of the insurgents and particularly of the groups close to *Cronaca Sovversiva*. The persons responsible were never found. The impression left by these bomb packages on public opinion was enormous, particularly because patriotic fervor was at its peak. That same May 1, in many cities, including Boston, New York, and Cleveland, groups of nationalists and former soldiers, supported by sailors in uniform and police, attacked the left's demonstrations, and hundreds of arrests were made.[4]

In May, in this incendiary climate, Galleani continued to give lectures in New London, Pawtucket, and Providence, while

Schiavina did the same in other locations, trying to rouse the resistance, which seemed increasingly necessary to them. Less than a month later, something resounding happened: at midnight on Monday, June 2, 1919, in seven cities of the United States (Boston, New York, Paterson, Philadelphia, Pittsburgh, Cleveland, and Washington, D.C.) powerful explosions were set off less than an hour and a half apart. Kilos of dynamite blew up the residences of eminent people, all known for their anti-radical records, again including judges, inspectors, congressmen, industrialists, and mayors. The most sensational target was again Attorney General Palmer, whose home in Washington was heavily damaged. Hit by a shower of shattered glass, Palmer remained uninjured, like all the other recipients of the bombs.[5] However, one bomber was killed together with the guard of the New York home of Judge Charles Nott, Jr. The bomber was Carlo Valdinoci, a close collaborator of *Cronaca Sovversiva*, who investigators had been hunting in vain for the previous two years.

Responsibility for the bombs of both May 1 and June 2 was claimed through flyers aggrandizing revenge against the authorities and triggering a wave of anger throughout the country. Historically, this campaign was described as "the most extensive, best organized, and carefully planned operation of its type ever undertaken by Italian anarchists anywhere," and it was thought that the people responsible were about sixty Italian activists living mostly in New England and the state of New York.[6] On June 4, 1919, the *New York Tribune* wrote: "Nation-wide Search for 'Reds' Begins."[7] The mayor of Cleveland, the target of one of the June 2 attacks, expressing the general feelings of the authorities, proclaimed: "We will get them out of Cleveland, but we want to see the country rid of them. Such things as happened last night and the sending of bombs by post must waken the federal government to the necessity also for tightening up on immigration. This country cannot be made the dumping ground for the Red propagandists of Europe."[8]

After these events, the US authorities made a decisive effort to deport Galleani. In May, Galleani decided to marry Maria, probably to try to further delay deportation.

The Department of Justice was convinced that he was behind the assassination attempts, and within a few days he was arrested and brought to the East Boston immigration office.[9] He knew that deportation to Italy awaited him. The judge offered him the chance to leave for Europe by his own volition in exchange for cancellation of the deportation order. He refused, and in response

Galleani in a mugshot

asked to be sent to Egypt. He received a visit from his family. Ilia was interrogated by agents, to whom she responded scornfully. He was transferred to Ellis Island on June 24, 1919 and forced to board the *Duca degli Abruzzi* together with eight other activists, including Schiavina, Fruzzetti, and the Sanchinis with their two children. At fifty-eight years old, after eighteen years in the United States, he was returning to Italy. He left behind Maria and the six children, including three who had American citizenship. He knew that he might never see them again.[10]

EPILOGUE
Return to Italy

CHAPTER XXIX

In the Thick of the *Biennio Rosso*

On July 10, after a stop in Naples, the *Duca degli Abruzzi* docked in the port of Genoa. Upon disembarkation, Galleani was searched and locked up in the prison of the tower of Palazzo Ducale, but he was released the next day with a deportation order for Vercelli, after the Federation of Sea Workers threatened to stop work. This was a clear sign of his enduring popularity among workers, even on the other side of the ocean.[1] He felt physically weak, as he was increasingly suffering from the effects of diabetes, a disease that had affected him since his time in Pantelleria and that had grown worse in recent times.

He passed part of the summer in Camburzano, a municipality in the province of Biella at an altitude of 1,380 feet. He did so again the next summer, before returning to Vercelli, where his sister Carolina still lived. Here, he led what appeared to be a secluded life, yet he actually began to organize a local anarchist group and established increasingly close connections with activists in Turin, where Schiavina was also active, and in Liguria.

In early October, he participated in the Ligurian anarchist congress in Sampierdarena. In the middle of the month, he spoke in Sampierdarena before an audience of 1,500 people. He gave two more lectures, one in Carrara and another in Piazza Carignano in Genoa in late December, before a very large crowd that welcomed and praised Malatesta, who was finally free to return from London. Galleani was the one who warmly welcomed the old warrior on behalf of the entire Italian-language anarchist movement. He spoke again at a roundtable of activists, "with a fine and lofty eloquence, studded with luminous images" in the presence of Borghi, Pasquale Binazzi, and Giuseppe

Giulietti, secretary of the Federation of Sea Workers.[2] Three days later, Malatesta and Galleani met again privately in Vercelli to discuss the most urgent issues of the day.[3]

Many activists believed that Galleani could make a major contribution to the movement in the central phase of the *Biennio Rosso* [Two Red Years] and wanted him to resume his usual lecturing and propaganda activities. He was invited to speak in Romagna, and he thought he could complete a long tour throughout Italy. However, the precarious state of his health prevented him from doing so, and reluctantly he had to decline the invitation. He no longer had the strength necessary to command the stage.[4] He therefore concentrated his activities in Turin, where he came into conflict with the communist group L'Ordine Nuovo [New Order].

In Turin, in January 1920, a new series of *Cronaca Sovversiva* began to appear. *La Frusta* [The Whip], an anarchist bimonthly from Pesaro directed by Giobbe Sanchini, hailed the return of what they considered "the intellectual bread of the anarchist," while Pisa's *L'Avvenire Anarchico* [Anarchist Future] described its return as "a major event in the labor and anarchist world."[5] This new series lasted for nineteen issues and was edited by Galleani himself with the help of Schiavina, who was the director and *factotum*. Its release was made possible thanks to financial assistance from the United States and the effective collaboration of two other periodicals, *Il Cavatore* [The Quarryman] from Carrara and *L'Avvenire Anarchico* of Pisa, from which it received a list of addresses where the first trial issue was sent.

The periodical was also sent to the United States, with the same content but under a different title—*A Stormo* [To the Flock], with the subtitle: "Revolutionary Libertarian Weekly"—in an attempt to circumvent the prohibition on *Cronaca Sovversiva* in that country. In the paper, it was requested that all correspondence be sent to Giuditta Zanella at Via Giorgio Pallavicino 16 in Turin. Zanella was very active in local anarchist groups. Thus, in a completely unexpected manner and under a new guise, the paper that had so infuriated the US authorities, returned to circulating on US soil, just when Palmer ordered a brutal police operation that resulted in the arrest of about ten thousand trade union members. Later, almost all of them were released from prison or acquitted due to a lack of any evidence of guilt.[6] In the following months, the anti-labor offensive reached its peak together

In Lipari, almost seventy years old

with the economic crisis that caused a twenty-five to fifty percent reduction in wages and that put thirteen million out of work.[7]

A few weeks after the new series of *Cronaca Sovversiva* started, a new anarchist daily began publication. The editorship of *Umanità Nova* [New Humanity] had been offered to Galleani in vain, but he welcomed its appearance warmly. His confidence was shared by groups in America, which signed up for subscriptions in numbers sufficient to guarantee the purchase of printing machines and to cover its running costs. Galleani was confident that, under the direction of Malatesta, it would be a newspaper "of anarchists" and not "of the anarchist party."[8] This subtle distinction indicated how reassured he was by the return of Malatesta, who possessed "experience," "daring," and "an incomparably gentle spirit and lucidity of thought." But he also wanted to clarify his own position as compared to the prevalent position in the anarchist movement, of which Malatesta remained, without doubt, the recognized leader.[9]

During this period, in fact, the strategy of Malatesta and his comrades was to strengthen relations as much as possible with other sections of the labor movement, pushing it in a more revolutionary direction. This strategy, Galleani believed, involved risks. An alliance with the leaders of socialist and syndicalist organizations might not push the reformists to make revolution, but rather the revolutionaries to make reforms. To prevent this from happening, he maintained, agreements must remain exclusively practical and basic, not ideological or concerning the people at the top of the various organizations: "Malatesta is for a united front. Agreed. We too are for a united front, which, unless I am mistaken, means only: all of the proletariat in all the different sections of the avant-garde against all of the bourgeoisie."[10]

This distinction was a sign of Galleani's difficulty in adjusting to a movement that, at this time, not only advocated a united front, but was mostly involved in the construction of a national, formal, and structured organization. To him it appeared that the creation of an "anarchist party" was more a sign of "weakness" than strength, since he was convinced that the strength of anarchism was not to be found in organizing into well-defined factions that carried more weight within the alliance of the left, but rather in blending in "with the anonymous crowd [...], a decisive force that cannot be organized [and which] evades party frameworks" to push it toward the path of revolution.

He saw another bad sign in the fact that some parts of the movement sought to limit participation in the congress of the UAI [Unione anarchica italiana, Italian Anarchist Union], which was held in Bologna in July 1920, to so-called "organizer" groups that were allowed in the Union, rather than opening it to all anarchists regardless of their specific currents. Another issue that caused considerable difficulty was the excessively close relationship that had existed up to then between anarchists and unions, whether the CGL [Confederazione generale del lavoro, General Labor Confederation], or the USI [Unione sindacale italiana, Italian Syndicalist Union], which was also regarded as an essentially reformist body. He warned the libertarians about collaborating too closely with the USI, which he feared could develop into a mutual dependence, for two reasons: first because he already believed that syndicalist action and anarchist action were in principle contradictory; second because the USI, which at this point was a member of the Third International, in his eyes had fallen into line with Bolshevik policies that were far from libertarian ideals.

Although spreading anarchist propaganda among the syndicalists was justified, therefore, the opposite was unacceptable, he emphasized. A similar argument applied to the CGL and its experiments, such as factory councils. Based on his experience in the field, he absolutely rejected them as bodies that wanted to succeed the bourgeois government and postpone the "violent expropriation of the bourgeoisie."[11] The same applied also to the Socialist Party, which he regarded as an "enemy of the social revolution" and particularly the maximalist camp leading the party, represented by Serrati, with whom he had often argued in the past and who was now the most popular socialist leader.[12] Galleani denounced the party's concepts of power, the State, and the dictatorship of the proletariat, the latter accepted now by several anarchist groups, blinded by Lenin and the success of Bolshevism.

His all-round intransigence was considered by many to be excessive, but that did not inhibit him from action. Galleani's criticism was absolutely internal to the anarchist movement and influenced its behavior, accentuating its autonomy and its difference from other currents of socialism.[13] *Cronaca Sovversiva* provided detailed reports on the Bologna congress, to which Galleani added his own judgment in line with his already-established political position on congresses. On the one hand, he appreciated the opportunity for anarchists to meet nationally to exchange impressions and ideas about the social situation and to reach concrete agreements. But on the other hand, he criticized the fact that the meeting was held using delegates, creating resolutions, and a situation of majorities and minorities.

Once the conference of the UAI was over, he anxiously lived through July 21, 1920, in Turin, where the general strike was disorderly and where, on a few occasions, workers sent the police running. On this occasion, a "very dear friend" of several collaborators of *Cronaca Sovversiva*, the young Gugliemo Musso, was seriously wounded in the hand as he tried to throw a bomb at the military police. Arrested with a mutilated limb, he was condemned to eighteen years in prison and died there in 1923.[14]

The publication of the new series of *Cronaca Sovversiva* did not go unnoticed by the authorities, and the newspaper immediately found itself in their sights, so that from the first issue it was partly blanked out by the censors. But what was not censored made the meaning of the periodical clear. During a time of extreme social conflict, Galleani continually called upon the proletariat to destroy the established order, going beyond and even against their representatives, and he aimed particularly at those most directly responsible for class discrimination: "In Italy Bava Beccaris and Pelloux enjoy their retirement undisturbed, forgotten. Forgotten: this is our shame. The butchers who have so much proletarian blood on their hands, on their stomachs, should not die in their beds."[15]

Siding with "the mob," beyond and against the limits set by the socialist party and the syndicalists, he recommended individual rebellion, which he considered to be a forerunner of

collective insurrection, and warned revolutionaries against con-
demning single acts of revolt even when they seemed reckless.[16]
He again denounced the "abyss" of the world war in terms of loss
of human life and squandering of wealth, in an article entitled
"Soldato, fratello!" [Soldier, Brother!], widely distributed in the
form of a leaflet, especially in prisons. He called upon soldiers to
turn their weapons against their superiors and unite with a proletariat whose anger was boiling over:

> Soldier, brother, that fateful day dawns [...]. With a tremen-
> dous crash it will batter the walls of the barracks! To tell
> you, soldier brother, that you are no longer alone: that you
> can take back your dignity and your courage; to remind you
> that the time has finally come to bathe the tyrants in blood,
> the curse and the remorse of fratricides, of which you have
> been for so long a blind and supine instrument. To finally
> ask yourself IF YOU WILL BE FOR ONCE IMPETUOUS
> AND HEART AND ARMS WITH YOUR BROTHERS or
> with them and with your tormentors; if you will be for the
> revolution or for the villains who want to suffocate the lib-
> erating breath of life.[17]

The American authorities were again the subject of his
indignant analysis in a newspaper that, from the first page, maintained an international perspective, dedicating several articles to
the social situation in various European countries and the United
States.

In May 1920, Salsedo, who Galleani had known as a young
boy in Pantelleria and who from then on had been a close comrade and become an important figure in the anarchist movement in the United States, fell from a window of the offices of
the Bureau of Investigation on Park Row, in New York, during
an interrogation. He had been illegally detained in those offices
for eight weeks, together with Elia, former manager of *Cronaca
Sovversiva*, under orders from the Department of Justice. During
that time, Bureau officials had tried to extract confessions concerning the double wave of assassination attempts in May and

June 1919. The interrogation ended tragically, for which the responsibility fell upon the Bureau Chief, William J. Flynn. He was the one that "suicided" Salsedo, after subjecting him to countless forms of torture, wrote Galleani in an article that shed light on the spirit that *Cronaca Sovversiva* approached the clash between anarchist groups and the American authorities in 1919–1920:

> The same day William J. Flynn suicided Andrea Salsedo, last May 3, in the New York Investigation Office, anticipating a scandal, they told the press the many reasons why, *without a warrant*, they had arrested Andrea Salsedo and Roberto Elia, and the most serious reasons why, *without the judicial authorities knowing and in flagrant contempt of the law and the judiciary*, they had been secretly held in cells on Park Row for two long months.
>
> *They were not charged with any offense.*[18] There is not a single accusation against them. It is known that they were connected to the anarchist movement, to *Cronaca Sovversiva*, with the terrorist groups of Galleani in Paterson and in Lynn and they wanted them to give a deposition, whether true or false, to justify the brutal persecution they suffered, and to authorize further, more extensive, and more savage persecution.
>
> The police reports are not discussed, they are scorned; and one does not argue with Flynn, one spits at his snout; but since *Cronaca* and its editor, now and in the past, are drawn in as organizers or patrons of specific assassination attempts and groups, allow me a blunt and plain word, although it is superfluous for those who know me: I never organized groups of this type, nor have I ever affiliated with any group, still less a terrorist group that probably never existed, to which Flynn (an idiot and a flint musket who, when it comes to anarchist matters and attacks, is always throwing dice or playing lotto numbers, making similarly random picks, swearing oaths on daggers and other *eiusdem farinae* tricks) attributes the aforementioned attacks.

I have learned of the attacks from the newspapers. And I say bluntly and immediately, I don't lament them at all; I have never respected one-hundredth of the lives of the half dozen professional stooge cops taken in these targeted attacks, and I did not lament and I did not regret ... the lack of success, hoping that the imminent shot—since the gallows do not disarm nor will it disarm the rebellion—reaches the mark, all of the mark, victoriously and inexorably.

It would be odd for us to wish blessings and oblivion to the scum who only sow desolation and blood and death![19]

About three months later, the Wall Street financial district suffered an unprecedented attack. On September 16, 1920 a cart full of dynamite exploded at the corner of Wall Street and Broad Street leaving thirty-eight dead, hundreds wounded, and causing enormous material damage. The device exploded between the United States Assay Office, the Sub-Treasury Building, and the J.P. Morgan & Company building, which suffered the greatest damage. The center of American capitalism was wounded.

The authorities were convinced that it was an act of revenge in response to the repression of Italian anarchists. In particular, it could have been a reaction to the indictment of two activists linked to *Cronaca Sovversiva*, Nicola Sacco and Bartolomeo Vanzetti who, as we know, were executed in the electric chair seven years later.[20]

Flynn tried everything to connect the bomb to Galleani, but without success: the guilty party was never found.[21] In recent histories it has been conjectured that the action was the work of Italian anarchists, including Mario Buda, a signature occasionally found in the pages of *Cronaca Sovversiva*, and a close comrade of Sacco, Vanzetti, and of Galleani himself.[22]

CHAPTER XXX

The Final Struggle

In the early autumn of 1920, in poor health and relieved of many editorial tasks by Schiavina, Galleani and the legal representative of *Cronaca Sovversiva*, Pietro Raineri, were served with arrest warrants for defamation of state institutions and instigation of military rebellion and class hatred, based on the content of a series of articles that appeared in the newspaper. These included "Soldato, fratello!", a copy of which had been confiscated in the barracks of Ancona, where a mutiny of the *bersaglieri* [Italian marksmen corps] occurred in June 1920 when they refused to go on a military mission to Albania.[1]

Galleani and Schiavina were arrested—with Schiavina accused of belonging to the Turin-based Arditi del popolo [The People's Daring Ones, an anti-fascist militant group]—which brought an end to the publication of *Cronaca Sovversiva*, an event that was greatly appreciated in Washington. Tellingly, this happened about ten months after the movement to occupy factories ended. This was the most intense moment of social conflict in the *Biennio Rosso* and was followed—almost seamlessly—by government reaction. Just one week after the arrest warrant for Galleani was issued, the Milan offices of *Umanità Nova* were raided and the editors, including Malatesta, were arrested.

In the meanwhile, however, Galleani succeeded in meeting up with his brother, Camillo, in Genoa, and from there he vanished. "Large build, brown eyes, oval face, salt and pepper mustache, and grizzled beard, refined bearing, insolent, balding in front, high brow."[2] This was the description that the Ministry of the Interior circulated, together with his photo, to prefectures around the country in order to track him down. But in vain.

Galleani managed to evade the police and remained at large for about two years. Still today it is difficult to know where he hid during that period. What is certain is that, in addition to the Italian police, the American police also vainly tried to follow his tracks. The Bureau of Investigation even sent an agent to Italy: Salvatore Clemente, code name "Mull," attempted to find information on Galleani's involvement in the May and June 1919 assassination attempts. Mull was unable to find anything and was left empty-handed, aside from the "revelation" that, in due course, Galleani had received news of Valdinoci's death with tears of sorrow.[3]

On the run, Galleani witnessed the rise of fascism and had the clear feeling that the masses were voluntarily subjugating themselves to the blackshirts without sufficient resistance. Rather they were stretching out their "wrists for abdication and shoulders to be beaten." He had always placed great trust in the spontaneous mobilization of the masses, making it a point of distinction from legalitarian socialism. To see the people now incapable of reacting was a hard blow. He wrote in a letter in September 1922: "I saw the blackshirts sweep aside everything and everyone; before the frenzy, the masses implore the Italian flag [...]. The filthy crowds were supported, sustained, urged by the authorities, defended by the royal guards, by the armored cars that passed under my windows."[4]

His explanation was that the proletariat was incapable of reacting because it was disciplined by the socialist party and the unions, and thus incapable of autonomous action. The rise of fascism seemed to confirm to him the illusion that large, structured and hierarchical labor organizations could constitute a real force. In his view, the socialist party's restraining of popular demands, which began with the Genoa congress in 1892, had now reached its final consequence.

In October 1922, against the advice of his closest comrades, he turned himself in to the authorities at the prison in Turin. At his trial, which began three days later, he took responsibility for all the incriminating articles, thus clearing Raineri, who was acquitted. He explained this gesture as follows: "Under investigation I took on all responsibility for the *Cronaca* articles. I want to be neither a braggart nor a good-for-nothing. Now it's time to pay, and I pay [...]. To be at war with the rest of the world disturbs me less than not being at peace with my conscience."[5]

Galleani was defended by his old childhood friend Roggeri and by Silvio Pellegrini, son of Antonio Pellegrini, previously his lawyer in the 1894 Genoa trial. Just as twenty-five thousand black-shirts staged the March on Rome, threatening to seize power violently and demanding political control of the country, he was condemned to fourteen months in prison and a fine of 645 lira.[6] From the Turin prison, he wrote an earnest letter to Schiavina, who was about to leave for France. This was his way of passing the baton to a younger comrade. In this letter he affirmed the choices he had made during his life:

> I am the old trunk that spring will not see flower again, that will not know the glory of new foliage, the joy from new nests; but I do not complain: I have lived my days: full, turgid, intense. If now, as the sun sets, I receive greetings from afar from a battle comrade, from a brother with the same passions, even the twilight is lit up with a thrill of joy, a thrill of pride, and that is enough for me.[7]

In late 1923, exhausted by ill health, which was worsened by the prison diet that exacerbated the effects of diabetes, he was released from the Turin prison and headed to Sori Ligure.[8] Some time before that, his daughter Cossyra, who had married an Italian, had moved there and now tried to help her old father, who at first settled in her home. He spent his time between Sori Ligure and Vercelli, at the home of his sister Carolina. He tried to take care of his own health. Thanks to the support of comrades residing in America and from Recchioni, still based in London, he managed to receive regular vials of insulin—then an extremely expensive medicine that was not yet available in Italy—to mitigate his illness. Yet his body was already seriously debilitated, so that in spring 1925, he was hospitalized because of diabetes for a month in Vercelli.

On leaving the hospital, he decided to return to Sori Ligure, where he managed to rent a room of his own.[9] He lived alone, with a dog and several crates of books as his only company. Meanwhile the fascist regime, helped by information from J. Edgar Hoover, director of the Bureau of Investigation since 1924, maintained surveillance of him and confiscated most of the newspapers that were sent to him by relatives and comrades.[10] As soon as he finished reading a letter from an activist he burnt it so as to leave no traces.

He sent several writings—some of which were intercepted by the police and never reached their destination—to his American comrades. In April 1922, they had begun publishing a weekly entitled *L'Adunata dei Refrattari* [The Cry of the Refractories], which was intended as the heir of *Cronaca Sovversiva*. It was published continuously until the end of the 1970s.[11] He entertained the idea of moving to France or Switzerland, but he had no passport and his physical condition did not allow him to cross the Alps clandestinely. Diabetes had also impaired his vision, so that it was very difficult for him to read. But he was not yet broken.

He edited his work, *La fine dell'anarchismo?* [*The End of Anarchism?*] for publication as a book, and finished translating Duval's *Memoires*. Despite the suffocating surveillance, he managed to propose to his remaining comrades in the United States a reprint of *Faccia a faccia col nemico* [Face to Face with the Enemy] in pamphlet form—as a warning and an example for younger activists —and advised on how to find the most appropriate measures to obstruct the regime:

> One cannot speak, one cannot write, one cannot announce a gathering or a meeting, but one can certainly silently sharpen a knife or make something better [...]. The way that is possible [is] the way of standing one's ground, matching violence with skillful violence, changing as the needs of the moment require, and above all [being] merciless.[12]

In this last phase of his life in Italy, he often frequented places he had been to before, and relived episodes from the past. On October 31, 1926, he was returning to Sori Ligure from Vercelli, where he had gone to care for his dying father. It was the day Anteo Zamboni attempted to assassinate Mussolini in Bologna. Galleani was arrested as a precautionary measure and briefly locked up in the Alexandria prison. He was put in the same cell he had occupied in 1892.

In April of the next year, his residence in Sori Ligure was searched from top to bottom. Evidently the police were not satisfied with systematically intercepting and reading his correspondence. They knew he was in contact with groups and activists from Switzerland and the United States, from whom he received newspapers and money. The police commissioner of Genoa considered him one of the "most fanatic" anarchists, "the inspiration and the inveterate propagator" of the "sect" and, "given the danger he poses to the national order of the State," decided to issue him a warning.[13] That was only the first step. Shortly after he was caught red-handed with several issues of *L'Adunata dei Refrattari*. This was enough for him to be condemned to prison for ten days to which was added a 100 lira fine. His incarceration in the Marassi prison in Genoa lasted longer than it should have. After about a month of detention, Cossyra had to write to the Director General of Public Security, asking for "the position of her old and suffering father to be clarified as soon as possible."[14]

In response, the Prefect of Genoa—in concert with the political police—proposed that he be internally exiled to a remote area. On July 9, an ad hoc commission judged that he could be a danger to the order of the state and decided to send him to an island for three years. Because of Galleani's poor health, the prison doctor recommended that the authorities send him to a "civilized location," meaning one with a temperate climate where it was possible to acquire medicine and the food required for the diet he needed to follow.

Despite this, after two months of prison, he was taken to Lipari, the island he had seen from the window of his dormitory when he had been held in internal exile on Ustica.[15] There were a large number of activists there, including Carlo and Nello Rosselli and Emilio Lussu, in addition to several comrades with whom he had shared many struggles, such as Petraroja and Giuseppe (Joe) Russo, known as *"l'Unico"* [The Only One], who had been a very energetic supporter of *Cronaca Sovversiva* in previous years.

He had not had time to settle in when, on August 4, 1927, three days after his arrival, one of his conversations with Russo was overheard by men from the Voluntary Militia for National Security. On reading the inscription on Lipari Castle, "It is necessary to respect the Head of the government His Excellency Benito Mussolini," he was said to have added, in a jeering voice, "wooden head."[16] This was enough for him to be denounced for such an insult and condemned in October to a 550 lira fine and another six months of prison, which he served in the island's prison.[17]

Il Monito [The Warning], the newspaper that Schiavina wrote in Paris together with other anarchist activists, feared that, since he was already severely ill, his life was at risk, and it directly accused the head of the government: "Mussolini will have to pay, and answer in person before inexorable Anarchist Justice [...]. With Galleani's life, know that the Hyena also plays with his own life or, failing that, the lives of his relatives. The anarchists watch and make a solemn commitment of honor. Mussolini, return the prey: release Galleani!"[18]

Even from prison, Galleani managed to stay in contact with his most trusted comrades, so that at one point the prefect of Messina ordered that money sent to him from the United States be impounded. It was there that he received the news of the execution of Sacco and Vanzetti on August 23, 1927. It was an ending he had feared for some time and that filled him with rage. Two years earlier, on this subject, in a letter to Schiavina, he had written words revealing his close relationship with the two, and the fear that neither legal action nor united committees in their defense would be successful:

> [About] the Sacco-Vanzetti affair, it is pointless and danger-
> ous to hide one's feelings: it is a humiliating and terrible
> defeat. I am afraid that E... understands the truth: com-
> mittees become a scourge when they exist for years with
> many roles, and with the entirely Yankee characteristic

by which work performed with diligence, more than with love and faith, needs fat and constant remuneration. The other way is better: on one side trust in, rely on the masses who shudder in the face of injustice, and shudders move and provoke; on the other side... well on the other side we needed incredibly direct action, not occasionally, not just once, but systematically, like the throbs of the beating pulse, and terribly and ruthlessly, as terribly and ruthlessly as the work of the half dozen buffoons in robes who sell justice to those who pay in the trading posts of the high or low courts—in fact all are incredibly low—of the mercenary and puritan republic.

Mark this well, it is a defeat of which we need to cleanse ourselves, or the tigers, perhaps better to say the jackals, in their republican judicial lairs will not leave you even eyes to cry with. It is necessary to summarize the matter in a few lines, briefly emphasizing the evidence of the innocence of the two victims, and underneath that put, in large letters, the first and last names and home addresses of all the magistrates, of all the jurors, simply inviting the workers to go there to pay their respects and thank them... as they deserve; but without any committees. In my heart I have so much bitterness, so much desolation that I wonder if it would not have been better to intervene in the debate with my usual unflinching honesty. Instead I always abstained from uttering a single word out of fear that appearing to be their friend would aggravate the legal situation for them both. However, if they had judged them to be Galleanisti they would not have treated them any worse. But then one hoped: there was so much money, and so many lawyers!

Kiss them, if you manage to see them, kiss them so much for me...

Yours always
Gigi[19]

Galleani remained in prison until February 10, 1928. Several months before his sentence was due to end, Mussolini ordered an amnesty intended partially to free up the prisons, in order to create space for new detainees. To be released, prisoners had to sign a preprinted form in which they thanked *Il Duce* for his act of clemency. Galleani had no intention of doing so and decided to serve out the remaining months of his sentence instead.

Once released, he was met by Buda, who had also been sentenced to prison and reached Lipari in November 1927. They were together on the island until summer 1929, when Buda was transferred to Ponza.[20] In the period, the two spend together on Lipari, Buda received a visit from the American journalist Edward Holton James. James had the suspicion, which many others shared, that Buda was one of those behind the kidnapping and murder for which Sacco and Vanzetti were executed, and he wanted to get information from him that would clear their names posthumously. He interviewed Buda for three hours, getting nothing except for claims of his own innocence and that of Sacco and Vanzetti. Galleani welcomed James coldly, and Buda explained this behavior in a letter to James: "Galleani often tells me about you. But he believes little in justice by those in high positions or those who use politics to serve—and be served by—those with the largest coffers."[21]

While exiled, Galleani demonstrated his solidarity with the other inmates, without regard for political differences. Thus he testified in the Messina courtroom in favor of the communist Nello Bolognini who was accused, together with Buda, of having sung subversive songs.

In February 1930, he was released four months before the end of his sentence, following another amnesty for hundreds of anti-fascists who had served two-thirds of their sentences (this time without requiring a thank you note).[22] Between exile and prison, he spent over two and a half years in Lipari, without ever asking to be transferred, or for any form of clemency. He was accompanied to Genoa under close supervision and released.

The lack of any treatment during exile had further weakened his body. He went first to Sori Ligure. There, he found Cossyra and, with her, affectionate letters from Maria and the children who had remained in the United States. Olimpio sent him dozens of vials of insulin, glasses, new clothes, and books by Henry David Thoreau and Ralph Waldo Emerson. After several weeks, the authorities gave him his identity card, which he needed to travel. He then left Sori Ligure, storing his furniture and books in a rented garage, and moved to his sister Carolina's house in Vercelli. But he did not want to be a burden on her, all the more so because police surveillance had become obsessive and he was continuously shadowed. He was exhausted and his health went from bad to worse. He thought about finding shelter in Fornovo, at the Ramiola clinic, which specialized in treating diabetes. In the end, however, he abandoned the idea and, in April 1930, took refuge in Val di Magra, accepting an offer from Binazzi and Zelmira Peroni, former editors of *Il Libertario* from La Spezia, with whom he had been friendly for a decade. They found him a rented room in the Tardiani villa, on Strada Statale 62 bordering the Magra river, a few hundred yards from Bettola di Caprigliola, where Zelmira had been born.[23]

He mostly stayed there alone, but was cheered by Binazzi's company during the summer months, when the Peronis were in the habit of leaving La Spezia to live in a house a few hundred yards from Galleani's. He spent his days reading and writing and going for walks in the surrounding area. In this period he also worked on Nietzsche's philosophy "to show how absurd it is to deduce even the most hybrid and distant affinity with anarchism."[24]

He was monitored closely by the authorities. Police and military police alternated to ensure that he was guarded continuously, around the clock. Two policemen were always present in the house during the day and two military policemen were stationed outside through the night. The forces of order followed his every move, whether to Caprigliola, where he regularly went to the pharmacy or post office, or to Albiano, where—who knows how—he secretly managed to pass a letter or a note to some local associates who then sent it where it needed to go. Old conspiratorial habits became useful under a regime more hostile to freedom than any before.

The police also had orders to be present when he met other people. Conversations had to take place in Italian and the compulsory orders from the Massa police headquarters were to stop all those who engaged in conversation with him. This police headquarters also urged officers to collect evidence that might lead to another prison sentence, so that his home was repeatedly searched. The prefecture of Massa Carrara was no less diligent. In November 1930, it suggested that the Ministry of the Interior should arrest him because Zelmira and Binazzi had received a copy of Duval's *Memoires*, which—the official noted—contained a preface by Galleani, in which he wrote that the bourgeoisie lives by robbery and that it was therefore necessary to assert the right of expropriation.[25]

His mail was read meticulously and was transcribed. This is why we now have copies of several letters received from other activists, from his sister Carolina, and from his wife and children in the United States.[26] In letters written between June and October 1930, Olimpio told his "beloved father" that he had recently moved to Needham, in Massachusetts, where he was reunited with Maria, Ilia, and Mentana. The economic crisis that hit the United States after the 1929 Wall Street crash had affected them and they all lived in a cabin in the country. Olimpio was a farmer, Ilia had started a practice as a doctor and treated some of her father's old comrades, among others. Balilla, the youngest child, was traveling in California. Olimpio's deep affection shines through, his "devotion" toward his old father to whom "unforgettable loving memories" are connected. Olimpio shared his father's ideological leanings emotionally and wrote of having been moved over the release of the translation of Duval's *Memoires*, a fact that was enough for the Italian police to put him down as an anarchist. Along with affectionate greetings from Maria and other family members, as well as from Osvaldo Maraviglia and the comrades of *L'Adunata dei Refrattari*, Olimpio sent clothes and shoes "high enough for the winter with a pair of felt shoe covers that will keep your feet warm," and packages of insulin, books, and magazines such as *Current History* and *Reader's Digest*, which the Italian police inspected and not infrequently confiscated. He also regularly sent money, which often remained in the hands of the Italian authorities.[27] The same happened to the money American activists continued to send him by means of Luigi De Cecco and Nick Di Domenico. Galleani responded warmly to Olimpio and ends one of his letters with these words: "I remember all with affection as unchanged as faith, I embrace and kiss you. Remember me to everyone at home, without reproach for anyone. Always devoted to you. Papà."[28]

In these months he also received a letter from Malatesta in Rome, where he had been forced into a sort of house arrest and constant surveillance, not unlike what Galleani was subjected to. It was a letter between two old men approaching the end of their lives, which revealed a long and deep friendship, an enduring link, and a long correspondence: "How are you? Did you find a place to live near Fornovo, as you had been looking for? I'm fairly well, although starting to feel the weight of the years. I realize this when I need to climb the stairs (I'm on the fourth floor) which I must do slowly so as not to become breathless, whereas two or three years ago I ran up them. I embrace you with much affection. Yours, Errico."[29]

The last winter of Galleani's life was marked by increasingly urgent health problems, aggravated by the cold, against which the oil stove he managed to install in the house could do little. On February 18, 1931, he was subjected to another search. The authorities were looking for evidence to connect him to Michele Schirru, a man from Sassari active in the US, arrested a few days earlier in Rome and accused of intending to kill Mussolini. He would be put to death the next May. Again they found no concrete evidence.

In spring, after an unexpected worsening in his physical condition, he moved to the home of the Binazzis, where their large family lived and where he had his own room with a kitchen. The Italian police were worried because they feared he might secretly correspond with other activists through the Binazzi relatives. In this period, he tried to resume his routine: reading for eight to ten hours a day, alternating with half-hour walks. When it rained he performed a little vendetta against the guards: he left with the intention of going to the tobacco shop at Albiano, with an umbrella and well covered, forcing the soldiers who shadowed him in shifts to follow him and get wet.

In August 1931, on the occasion of his seventieth birthday, *L'Adunata dei Refrattari* published a letter by Malatesta, who wrote:

> Great are the services that Luigi Galleani, with his vigorous pen, fascinating eloquence, and constant example of courage and abnegation, has given to the cause of anarchy. Everywhere he carried out his activities, in Europe and in America, he has aroused a wealth of energy and taught ranks of the youth, who look to him as their master and inspiration and are among the best of our hopes.[30]

He received many greetings from all the members of his family and several activists. To some of them he responded with the following: "The faith and the banner of the first day are still those of the last [...]. I am happy with myself, even if along the way they have devastated everything, my home, my family, my health, and at seventy years I feel in exile here in this wild valley, without even a dog for company."[31]

At five in the afternoon on November 4, 1931, he left for his usual walk and, at the crossroads of Caprigliola, not far from his home, he suffered a heart attack. He was saved by a doctor who lived nearby and was taken to the Binazzi's home, where he died two hours later. The police, in the meanwhile, had confiscated the letters that he had in his pocket and his wallet.

His funeral was held two days later. It was organized by the Binazzis, and attended by Carolina and Cossyra. The forces of order scrupulously monitored the funeral so that no anarchist symbols or flags were displayed. The funeral procession ended at the Albiano cemetery, where he was buried.

New York's *Il Martello*, edited by Tresca, in remembering his "compelling and powerful oratory," described him as "an anarchist in the most noble sense of the word—an educator and a warrior [who] never condemned those who rose up against the established order, however they rose up."[32]

From Montevideo, Luigi Fabbri's *Studi Sociali* wrote:

The Italian anarchist family, the global anarchist movement, have lost one of their purest spiritual representatives,
one of the most courageous standard-bearers of their propaganda, one of the most gifted apostles of their thought.[33]

After the war, the anarchists of the surrounding area erected
a marble funeral monument in the Albiano cemetery to commemorate Luigi Galleani. The monument still stands there today.

Abbreviations

a. anno [year]

AFL American Federation of Labor

ACS Archivio centrale dello Stato [Central Archive of the State]

art. article

ASM Archivio di Stato di Massa [Massa State Archives]

ASMAE Archivio storico Ministero affari esteri [Historical Archive of the Ministry of Foreign Affairs]

AST Archivio di Stato di Torino [Turin State Archives]

BI Bureau of Information

CGL Confederazione generale del lavoro [General Labor Confederation]

Cp Crescita politica [political growth]

CPC Casellario politico centrale [Central Police Registry]

Dbai (Dizionario biografico degli anarchici italiani) [Biographical Dictionary of Italian Anarchists]

fasc. Fascicolo [file]

FBI Federal Bureau of Investigation

IWW Industrial Workers of the World

no. number

vol. volume

POI Partito operaio italiano [Italian Workers' Party]

Plm Partido liberal mexicano [Mexican Liberal Party]

Ps Pubblica sicurezza [public security]

Rl Rivoluzione libertaria [libertarian revolution]

UAI Unione anarchica italiana [Italian Anarchist Union]

USI Unione sindacale italiana [Italian Syndicalist Union]

Notes

Foreword

1.   Bruce Watson, *Sacco and Vanzetti: The Men, the Murders, and the Judgment of Mankind* (New York: Viking Books, 2007), 16.

2.   Forerunner of the Federal Bureau of Investigation (FBI).

3.   F. Weiss, "In re: Bomb outrages in Washington, DC, Cleveland, Boston, Etc. (Anarchist Matter)," B.I. report June 19, 1919, 4.

4.   E.J. Hobsbawm, *Age of Extremes: The Short Twentieth Century, 1914–1991* (London: Michael Joseph, 1994), 74.

5.   Luigi Galleani, *The End of Anarchism?*, translated by Max Sartin and Robert D'Atillio (Orkney: Cienfuegos Press, 1982), 48.

6.   Usually known by its literal translation as "The health is in you!" but meaning something more like "The power is in your hands."

7.   William J. Flynn, "On the Trail of the Anarchist Bandits," *New York Herald*, March 5, 1922, section VII.

8.   Beverly Gage, *The Day Wall Street Exploded: A Story of America in Its First Age of Terror* (Oxford: Oxford University Press, 2010), Part IV.

9.   Wikipedia, Luigi Galleani: https://en.wikipedia.org/wiki/Luigi_Galleani.

10.   Dennis Lehane interviewed about his best-selling novel, *The Given Day* (New York: William Morrow, 2008), in which Galleani figures prominently as the "main orchestrator" of "urban terrorism." Chris Vognar, "Chris Vognar Column: Dennis Lehane Expands His Literary Horizon," *The Dallas Morning News*, July 14, 2008.

Chapter I: From Law Student to Labor Organizer

1.   See "A proposito di L. Galleani," *La Lotta Umana*, Paris, year II, no. 10 (April 18, 1929); Luigi Fabbri, "Luigi Galleani. 12 agosto 1861–

4 novembre 1931," *Studi Sociali,* January 10, 1932. For biographical and bibliographic information by and about Luigi Galleani, see Ugo Fedeli, *Luigi Galleani. Quarant'anni di lotte rivoluzionarie 1891–1931* (Cesena: Edizioni L'Antistato, 1956); Augusta Molinari, "Luigi Galleani: un anarchico italiano negli Stati Uniti," in Raimondo Luraghi et al., *Le lotte sociali negli Stati Uniti alla fine del diciannovesimo secolo. Saggi storici nella ricorrenza bicentenaria della rivoluzione americana* (Florence: La Nuova Italia, 1974), 261–86; Franco Andreucci and Tomoasso Detti (eds.), *Il movimento operaio italiano. Dizionario biografico 1843–1953, vol. II* (Rome: Editori Riuniti, 1976); Nunzio Dell'Erba, "Luigi Galleani," in *Dizionario biografico degli italiani,* Treccani, vol. 51, 1998; Rudolph J. Vecoli, "Galleani Luigi," *American National Biography Online,* http://www.anb.org/view/10.1093/anb/9780198606697.001.0001/anb-9780198606697-e-1501196; M. Antonioli, G. Berti, S. Fedele, and P. Iuso (eds.), *Dizionario biografico degli anarchici* italiani, 2 volumes (vol. I), (Pisa: Biblioteca Franco Serantini, 2003), 654–57; E. Gianni, *L'Internazionale in Italia tra libertari ed evoluzionisti. I Congressi della Federazione Italiana e della Federazione Alta Italia dell'Associazione Internazionale dei Lavoratori (1872–1880)* (Milan: Pantarei, 2008), 488–90; Michael Schmidt and Lucien Van der Walt, *Black Flame: The Revolutionary Class Politics of Anarchism and Syndicalism* (Oakland: AK Press, 2009), 138–41; Fabrizio Giulietti, *Dizionario biografico degli anarchici piemontesi* (Casalvelino Scalo: Galzerano, 2013), 90–94; Luigi Botta, *Figli, non tornate (1915–1918)* (Turin: Aragno, 2016), 4–6; Sean Sayers, "Luigi Galleani. 'L'Anarchico più pericoloso d'America,'" *Umanità Nova,* year 96, no. 19 (June 5, 2016). Also see C. Levi [Paolo Finzi], "L'anarchico dei due mondi," *A Rivista Anarchica,* vol. IV, no. 4 (May 1974): 22–24; Nunzio Pernicone, "Luigi Galleani and Italian Anarchist Terrorism in the United States," *Studi Emigrazione,* vol. 30, no. 111 (September 1993): 469–88; A. Senta, *Luigi Galleani e l'anarchismo antiorganizzatore – Luigi Galleani and Antiorganizationist Anarchism* (Imola: Bruno Alpini, 2012); Antonio Senta, "Sugli anarchici antiorganizzatori," *A Rivista Anarchica,* no. 373 (Summer 2012): 144–50; Paul Avrich, ed. by Antonio Senta, *Ribelli in paradiso. Sacco, Vanzetti e il movimento anarchico negli Stati Uniti* (Rome: Nova Delphi Libri, 2015).

2.   See R. Galleani D'Agliano di Caravonica Comm. di Giustizia del S.M.O. di Malta, *Origini e ramificazioni dei Galleani* (Rome: A.R.T.E., 1956).

3.   He was also fined 51 lira in the sentence of July 23, 1883, of

the Vercelli Court, see ASMAE (Archivio storico del Ministero affari esteri [Historical Archive of the Ministry of Foreign Affairs]), polizia internazionale [international police] 1880–1906, fasc. [file] Galleani, Luigi; ASM (Archivio di Stato di Massa [Massa State Archives]), Questura, g. 53, sovversivi deceduti [deceased subversives], no. 12, Galleani, Luigi.

4.   See Amaryllis [Nella Giacomelli], "Luigi Galleani alle Assisi di Torino," *Umanità Nova,* year III, no. 195 (November 25, 1922); R. Gremmo, "Il giovane Galleani a Vercelli fra duelli e lotte operaie," *Storia Ribelle,* no. 16 (Autumn 2004): 1479–91.

5.   ACS (Archivio centrale dello Stato [Central Archive of the State]), CPC (Casellario politico centrale [Central Police Registry]), envelope no. 106, dossier for Galleani, Luigi.

6.   Newesk [Luigi Galleani], "Guglielmo Castellano (un morto di fame)," *Cronaca Sovversiva,* October 31, 1908, reprinted in Luigi Galleani, *Figure e figuri* (Ragusa: La Fiaccola, 1992), 63–65.

7.   See Mariella Nejrotti, "Le prime esperienze politiche di Luigi Galleani (1881–1891)," in Fondazione Luigi Einaudi (ed.), *Anarchici e anarchia nel mondo contemporaneo* (Turin: Fondazione Luigi Einaudi, 1971), 205; P. C. Masini, "La giovinezza di Luigi Galleani," *Movimento Operaio,* year VI, no. 3 (May/June 1954): 445–508. Also see Marco Scavino, "'Alla scuola della rude esperienza.' Il Partito operaio a Torino," *Studi Storici,* year 39, no. 1 (January–March 1998): 245–76; L. Briguglio, *Il Partito operaio italiano e gli anarchici* (Rome: Edizioni di storia e letteratura, 1969); M. G. Meriggi, *Il Partito operaio italiano* (Milan: Franco Angeli, 1985); Gastone Manacorda, *Il movimento operaio italiano. Dalle origini alla formazione del Partito socialista (1853–1892)* (Rome: Editori Riuniti, 1973). Also see Aldo Agosti and Gian Mario Bravo (eds.), *Storia del movimento operaio del socialismo e delle lotte sociali in Piemonte, vol. I, Dall'età preindustriale alla fine dell'Ottocento* (Bari: De Donato, 1979).

8.   Luigi Galleani, "Frammenti," *L'Adunata dei Refrattari,* December 23, 1950.

Chapter II: *La Boje!*

1.   Luigi Galleani, "Chi siamo?," *La Boje!,* May 25, 1885.

2.   Ibid., "Tra capitale e lavoro."

3.   G.L. [Luigi Galleani], "La malattia dei miserabili," *La Questione Sociale,* May 17, 1885.

4.   G.g. [Luigi Galleani], "Correspondence," *La Questione*

Sociale, December 13, 1885; "Correspondence of G. G. from Vercelli," *La Questione Sociale*, January 10, 1886.

5.   G.L. [Luigi Galleani], "Correspondence," *La Questione Sociale*, May 10, 1885 and May 24, 1885.

6.   ACS, CPC, envelope no. 106.

Chapter III: The Redemption of Labor

1.   Il riscatto del lavoro
     de' suoi figli opra sarà;
     o vivremo del lavoro
     o pugnando si morrà!

2.   Emilio Franzina, "Canzoniere anarchico e socialista," in Mario Isenghi (ed.), *Gli italiani in guerra. Conflitti, identità, memorie dal Risorgimento ai nostri giorni, vol. II, Le tre Italie. Dalla presa di Roma alla "vittoria mutilata" (1870–1914)* (Turin: Utet, 2008), 187–99.

3.   Renato Zangheri, *Storia del socialismo italiano, vol. II, Dalle prime lotte nella Valle Padana ai fasci siciliani* (Turin: Einaudi, 1997), 263.

4.   "Relazione del nostro rappresentante Luigi Galleani al Congresso del Partito Operaio tenuto a Bologna nei giorni 8, 9 e 10 settembre 1888," *La Nuova Gazzetta Operaia*, September 30 and November 7, 1888.

5.   "Il Partito Operaio," *La Questione Sociale*, June 17, 1888; "Il Partito Operaio e gli anarchici," *La Questione Sociale*, August 5, 1888. Also see Felice Anzi, *Il Partito Operaio Italiano 1882–1891. Episodi e appunti. Cronistoria autobiografica di un giornalaio giornalista* (Milan: Edizioni dell'ANS, 1933), 66n, 74.

6.   Paolo Spriano, *Storia di Torino operaia e socialista. Da De Amicis a Gramsci* (Turin: Einaudi, 1972), 10–13.

7.   Nejrotti, *Le prime esperienze politiche di Luigi Galleani (1881–1891)*, 212–14. Also see M. Scavino, *Con la penna e con la lima. Operai e intellettuali nella nascita del socialismo torinese (1889–1893)* (Turin: Paravia, 1999).

Chapter IV: From *Il Nuovo Combattiamo!* to *L'Attaque*

1.   For further information, see P. Galleani [Gaetano Perillo], "Il settimanale degli anarchici genovesi negli anni 1889–90," *Movimento Operaio e Contadino in Liguria*, year IV, no. 1–2 (January–April 1958): 51–59.

2.   Fedeli, *Luigi Galleani. Quarant'anni di lotte rivoluzionarie 1891–1931*, 26.

3.   Giampietro Berti, *Errico Malatesta e il movimento anarchico italiano e internazionale 1872–1932* (Milan: Franco Angeli, 2003), 149.

4.   The editors, preface to L. *Galleani, Una battaglia* (Rome: Biblioteca de L'Adunata dei Refrattari, 1947), VII.

5.   ASMAE, polizia internazionale, 1880–1906.

6.   Ettore Croce, *Domicilio coatto* (Casalvelino Scalo: Galzerano, 2000), 235; Giorgio Mangini, "La scienza per l'anarchia (Ettore Molinari)," *A Rivista Anarchica*, March 2016.

7.   L. Galleani, *Figure e figuri*, 179–88; Guglielmo Natalini, *Amilcare Cipriani la vita come rivoluzione* (Florence: Firenze Libri, 1987); L. Campolonghi, *Amilcare Cipriani. Memorie* (Pescara: Samizdat, 1996).

8.   Antonio Senta, *L'altra rivoluzione. Tre percorsi di storia dell'anarchismo*, (Bologna: Bradypus, 2016), 109–12.

9.   Charles Malato, *Philosophie de l'anarchie (1888–1897)* (Paris: Stock, 1897).

10.   Circolo internazionale degli studenti anarchici, *Agli studenti; Ai soldati* (Paris: Imp. Grave, 1890).

11.   The anarchists to the people on May 1, Paris, 1890, Service Historique de la Défense, Paris, Archive N (IIIeme République 1872–1940), 7/1363.

Chapter V: With Reclus on Lake Geneva

1.   Fedeli, *Luigi Galleani. Quarant'anni di lotte rivoluzionarie 1891–1931*, 29. On Jacques Gross, see M. Enckell, G. Davranche, R. Dupuy, H. Lenoir, A. Lorry, C. Pennetier, and A. Steiner (eds.), *Les anarchistes. Dictionnaire biographique du mouvement libertaire francophone* (Ivry-sur-Seine: Les Editions de l'Atelier/Les Editions Ouvrières, 2014), 228–29; *Cantiere biografico degli anarchici in Svizzera*, www.anarca-bolo.ch/cbach/biografie.php?id=407. For more information on the basis of the relationship between Galleani and Gross, see the Jacques Gross Papers, International Institute of Social History, Amsterdam.

2.   Luigi Galleani to Jacques Gross, Clarens, August 17, 1890, Jacques Gross Papers.

3.   El vecc [Luigi Galeani], "Eliseo Reclus. Impressioni e ricordi," *Cronaca Sovversiva*, Barre, July 29, 1905, also in Galleani, *Figure e figure*, 38–45 and in Elisée Reclus, *Scritti sociali I* (Naples: Immanenza: 2014), 9–14.

4.   Elisée Reclus, "Pourquoi somme-nous anarchistes?," *La Societé Nouvelle*, year V, no. 66 (August 31, 1889): 153–54.

5. Elisée Reclus, *Natura e società. Scritti di geografia sovversiva* (Milan: Elèuthera, 1999), 161.

6. Elisée Reclus, preface to Peter Kropotkin, *La conquête du pain* (Paris: Tresse & Stock, 1892), XI.

7. On anarchist geographers, and particularly Elisée Reclus see Federico Ferretti, *Il mondo senza la mappa. Elisée Reclus e i geografi anarchici* (Milan: Zero in Condotta, 2007); Ferretti, *Anarchici ed editori. Reti scientifiche, editoria e lotte culturali attorno alla Nuova Geografia Universale di Elisée Reclus (1876–1894)* (Milan: Zero in Condotta, 2011); Ferretti, "The Correspondence between Elisée Reclus and Pëtr Kropotkin as a Source for the History of Geography," *Journal of Historical Geography* no. 37 (2012): 216–222; Philippe Pelletier, *Geographie & anarchie. Elisée Reclus, Pëtr Kropotkin, Léon Metchnikoff et d'autres* (Paris: Editions du Monde libertaire & Editions libertaires, 2013); Philippe Pelletier and Federico Ferretti, "Spatialités et rapports de domination dans l'œuvre des géographes anarchistes Reclus, Kropotkine et Metchnikoff," in A. Fleury, J. Rebotier, and S. Weber (eds.), *Espace et rapports de domination* (Rennes: Presses Universitaires de Rennes, 2015), 23–34.

Chapter VI: Come, oh May

1. Ugo Fedeli, *Errico Malatesta. Bibliografia* (Naples: RL, 1951), 10.

2. "Peraskiev Stojanoff," in *Cantiere biografico degli anarchici in Svizzera*, http://www.anarca-bolo.ch/cbach/biografie.php?id=772; Cemal Selbuz, *Un anarchico sulle strade della libertà. Biografia dell'anarchico armeno Alexander Atabekian*, https://www.anarkismo.net/article/5214.

3. Ricardo Mella, *Primo maggio. I martiri di Chicago (La tragedia di Chicago)* (Milan: Zero in Condotta, 2009); Martin Duberman, *Haymarket, Chicago* (Santa Maria Capua Vetere: Spartaco, 2005); Claudia Baldoli, *Il nostro maggio. All'origine della festa dei lavoratori: autobiografie e testimonianze da Chicago* (Santa Maria Capua Vetere: Spartaco, 2005).

4. ASMAE, polizia internazionale 1880–1906; "Service télégraphique. Bern, December 16," *Journal de Genève*, December 17, 1890.

5. Conféderation Suisse. "Anarchistes," *Gazette de Lausanne*, December 22, 1890, 2.

6. Errico Malatesta, *La politica parlamentare nel movimento*

socialista (London: Tipografia dell'Associazione, 1890), 28.

7.   Ibid., 16, 21.

8.   Partito socialista rivoluzionario anarchico italiano, *Manifesto ai socialisti ed al popolo d'Italia e Programma. Risoluzioni del Congresso socialista italiano di Capolago 5 gennaio 1891* (Castrocaro: Barboni e Paganelli, 1891), 2.

9.   Malatesta, *La politica parlamentare nel movimento socialista*, 27.

10.   Errico Malatesta, *L'anarchia* (Florence: Clichy, 2016).

11.   ACS, CPC, envelope no. 106.

12.   "Whomsoever publicly justifies an act that the law establishes as a crime, or encourages disobedience of the law, or encourages hatred among the various social classes in a way dangerous to public tranquility, shall be punished with detention from three months to one year and with a fine from fifty to one thousand lira," Penal Code of the Kingdom of Italy (Zanardelli Code), Regional Decree June 30, 1889, no. 6133, Title V: Crimes against the public order, Paragraph I: Instigation to commit crimes, art. 247.

13.   See Luigi Galleani to Jacques Gross, Vercelli, July 4, 1891. On the events of May 1, 1891 in Rome and, more generally, on the rationale and coherence of insurrectionary activity by the Italian-language anarchist movement during the last decade of the century, see Davide Turcato, *Making Sense of Anarchism: Errico Malatesta's Experiments with Revolution, 1889–1900* (Oakland: AK Press, 2015).

Chapter VII: "The Helm Remains to be Built"

1.   Luigi Galleani to Jacques Gross, Vercelli, July 21, 1891, Jacques Gross Papers; also see Berti, *Errico Malatesta e il movimento anarchico italiano e internazionale 1872–1932*, 176.

2.   ASMAE, polizia internazionale 1880–1906, biographic account of March 1892.

3.   ASMAE, Questura, sovversivi deceduti, biographic account of June 1894.

4.   Luigi Fabbri, "Luigi Galleani," *Studi Sociali*, year III, no. 1 (January 10, 1932).

5.   Luigi Galleani to Jacques Gross, Sampierdarena, October 23, 1893, Jacques Gross Papers.

6.   Croce, *Domicilio coatto*, 237. Amleto Fabbri, an Italian activist residing in the United States and secretary of the Committee for the Defense of Sacco and Vanzetti, used similar terms: "He was austere and

generous at the same time, implacable with enemies and adversaries in bad faith, excessively scrupulous in the dignity of his mission of sacrifice and adamantine integrity, admirer of men of character even if they were adversaries or enemies," Amleto Fabbri, "Luigi Galleani. Impressioni e ricordi," *L'Adunata dei Refrattari*, November 7, 1942. On Amleto Fabbri see Senta, *L'altra rivoluzione. Tre percorsi di storia dell'anarchismo*, 127–30.

7.   Luigi Galleani to Jacques Gross, Clarens, August 17, 1890, Jacques Gross Papers.

8.   Peter Kropotkin, *La morale anarchica* (Ragusa: La Fiaccola, 1994). Also see Peter Kropotkin, *L'etica* (Ragusa: La Fiaccola, 1980), 296; and Giacomo Cortesi, "L'Etica di Pëtr Kropotkin tra scienza, natura e politica," *Bollettino Filosofico* no. 26 (2010): 110–25.

9.   Jean-Marie Guyau, *Abbozzo d'una morale senza obbligo né sanzione* (Turin: Paravia, 1999), 216.

10.   Ibid., 141, italics in the original.

11.   Ibid., 220.

12.   Jean Maitron, *Ravachol et les anarchistes* (Paris: Gallimard, 1992), 39–76; G. Guilleminault and A. Mahé, *Storia dell'anarchia* (Florence: Vallecchi, 1974), 47–80.

13.   Galleani, *Figure e figure*, 19–23; Alexander Berkman, *Prison Memoirs of an Anarchist* (New York: Mother Earth Publishing Association, 1912).

Chapter VIII: Against Legalitarian Socialism

1.   E. De Amicis, *Pagine allegre* (Milan: F.lli Treves, 1912), 16–17.

2.   Gaetano Perillo, "Socialismo e classe operaia nel Genovesato dallo sciopero del 1900 alla scissione sindacalista," *Il Movimento Operaio e Socialista in Liguria*, year VI, no. 4 (July–August 1960): 103. By Perillo see also "Il Primo Maggio del 1890 e del 1891 in Liguria," *Movimento Operaio e Contadino in Liguria*, year II, nos. 3–4 (May–August 1956): 76–89; and "Il settimanale degli anarchici genovesi negli anni 1888–1890," *Movimento operaio e contadino in Liguria*, year IV, no. 1–2 (January–April 1958): 51–59.

3.   G. Pimpino [Luigi Galleani], "Pietro Gori," *Cronaca Sovversiva*, January 21, 1911.

4.   On the need for this change in direction, openly discussed before the assembly, see "La Critica Sociale, Congresso Operaio," *Critica Sociale*, August 10, 1892.

5.   Il Congresso nazionale del Partito dei lavoratori in Genova, *Lotta di Classe*, Milan, August 20–21, 1892, cited in Luigi Cortesi, *Il socialismo italiano tra riforme e rivoluzione. Dibattiti congressuali del Psi 1892–1921* (Bari: Laterza, 1969), 18. For further reports and interpretations of the congress from both the socialist and anarchist side, see Ugo Fedeli Papers, International Institute of Social History, Amsterdam, folders nos. 379, 830–835. Also see M. Scavino, "Tanti rancori, tante calunnie, tante piccinerie da una parte e dall'altra! Considerazioni sulla rottura tra anarchici e socialisti alla fine dell'Ottocento," in M. Antonioli, F. Bertolucci, and R. Giulianelli (eds.), *Nostra patria è il mondo intero. Pietro Gori nel movimento operaio e libertario italiano e internazionale* (Pisa: Biblioteca Franco Serantini, 2012), 89–101; Zangheri, *Storia del socialismo italiano*, 459–89.

6.   ACS, CPC, folder no. 106.

7.   "Luigi Galleani nei ricordi di Max Nettlau," *L'Adunata dei Refrattari*, January 17, 1932.

8.   On the insurgency for the release of the two and their expulsion, see Luigi Galleani to Max Nettlau, Sampierdarena, September 5, 10, and 14, 1893, in Max Nettlau Papers, International Institute of Social History, Amsterdam, folder no. 457.

9.   ACS, CPC, folder no. 106.

10.   Luigi Galleani to Jacques Gross, Sampierdarena, October 11, 1892, Jacques Gross Papers.

11.   ASM, Commissariato di PS di Carrara [Carrara Committee of the Socialist Party], 1900, folder 21, fascicolo Riunioni pubbliche [public meetings sheet], telegram from the PS Inspector of Carrara Defecondo to the Prefect of Massa of October 2, 1892.

12.   Luigi Galleani to Jacques Gross, Sampierdarena, November 9, 1892, Jacques Gross Papers.

13.   Ibid. Also see Dora Marucco, "Processi anarchici a Torino tra il 1892 ed il 1894," in Fondazione Luigi Einaudi (promoted by), *Anarchici e anarchia nel mondo contemporaneo. Atti del Convegno (Turin, December 5, 6, and 7, 1969)* (Turin: Fondazione Luigi Einaudi, 1971), 217–41.

14.   Luigi Galleani to Jacques Gross, Sampierdarena, October 11, 1892, Jacques Gross Papers. See Peter Kropotkin, *Paroles d'un révolté* (Paris: Marpon et Flammarion, 1885); *La conquête du pain*. Also see the articles that appeared during the same period in *Freedom*, now in *Act for Yourselves, Articles from Freedom 1886–1907*, ed. by Nicolas Walter (London: Freedom Press, 1998).

15.   Luigi Galleani to Jacques Gross, Sampierdarena, October 11, 1892.

16.   Fabbri, "Luigi Galleani." Also see Niall Whelehan, "Political Violence and Morality in Anarchist Theory and Practice. Luigi Galleani and Peter Kropotkin in Comparative Perspective," *Anarchist Studies* vol. 13, no. 2 (2005): 147–68.

17.   *Fasces* or peasant cooperatives and industrial unions.

18.   Ugo Fedeli, *Anarchismo a Carrara e nei paesi del marmo. Dall'Internazionale ai moti del 1894* (Carrara: Tipolitografica, 2004); Gino Vatteroni, *"Abbasso i dazi, Viva la Sicilia". Storia dell'insurrezione carrarese del 1894* (Sarzana: Zappa 1993); L. Gestri, "Incombenze e tribolazioni incorse a un propagandista libertario in un anno di grazia di fine '800," *Rivista Storica dell'Anarchismo*, year I, no. 2 (July/December 1994): 7–44; Learco Zanardi, *Luigi Molinari. La parola, l'azione, il pensiero* (Mantova: Sometti, 2003). Note also that, in early January 1894, Charles Malato, alias Charles Keller, a companion of Galleani's in Paris, crossed the border with the objective of attempting insurrection in the countryside of Biella, but his plan failed.

19.   ACS, CPC, folder no. 106.

20.   *Il Caffaro*, year XX, no. 142, May 22, 1984, supplement, Ugo Fedeli Papers, folder no. 830.

21.   ACS, CPC, envelope no. 106, cit., biographical account to 1895.

22.   Pietro Gori, *Gli anarchici e l'art. 248. Difesa innanzi al Tribunale di Genova* (Rimini: L'Iniziativa, 1907), 14, now in Gori, *Opere*, vol. V, *Le difese. Pronunciate innanzi ai Tribunali e alle Corti di Assise* (Milan: Editrice Moderna, 1947).

23.   Ibid., 19.

24.   Ibid., 26–27.

25.   Ibid., 35.

26.   Ibid., 38.

Chapter IX: In Prison

1.   Emile Henry, *Colpo su colpo* (Treviolo: Vulcano, 1978).

2.   *L'Indipendente*, January 13, 1894; *Les Temps*, July 22, 1894; *Le Radical*, July 23, 1894.

3.   ACS, CPC, biographic account to 1895.

4.   Galleani, *La fine dell'anarchismo?*, 72.

5.   Elisée Reclus to Jacques Gross, October 7, 1894, in E. Reclus, *Correspondance. Tome III et dernier. September 1889–July 1905* (Paris:

Alfred Costes, 1925), 126.

6.   Giuseppe Galzerano, *Paolo Lega. Vita, viaggio, processo, "complotto" dell'anarchico romagnolo che attentò alla vita del primo ministro Francesco Crispi* (Casalvelino Scalo: Galzerano Editore, 2014); Gianluca Vagnarelli, *Fu il mio cuore a prendere il pugnale. Medicina e antropologia criminale nell'affaire Caserio* (Milan: Zero in Condotta, 2013); Roberto Gremmo, *Sante Caserio. Vita, tragedia e mito di un anarchico lombardo* (Biella: ELF, 1994).

7.   Daniela Fozzi, *Tra prevenzione e repressione. Il domicilio coatto nell'Italia liberale* (Rome: Carocci, 2010); Antonio Senta, "'Siamo coatti e baldi'. Le leggi antianarchiche del 1894," in Giorgio Sacchetti (ed.), *'Nel fosco fin del secolo morente'. L'anarchismo italiano nella crisi di fine secolo. Atti del convegno di studi storici (Carrara, 29 ottobre 2011)* (Milan-Venice: Biblion, 2013), 35–52. Also see R. Canosa and A. Santosuosso, *Magistrati, anarchici e socialisti alla fine dell'Ottocento in Italia* (Milan: Feltrinelli, 1981); S. Di Corato Tarchetti, *Anarchici, governo, magistrati in Italia 1876–1892* (Rome: Carocci, 2009).

8.   Errico Malatesta, "Le candidature proteste. Lettera aperta ad Adamo Mancini," *L'Associazione*, January 23, 1890.

9.   "Lotta elettorale," *Avanti!*, March 19, 1897; "Echi della lotta elettorale. A Vercelli," *Avanti!*, March 24, 1897.

10.   Luigi Galleani to Jacques Gross, Parma, August 30, 1896, Jacques Gross Papers.

11.   Galleani, *La fine dell'anarchismo?*, 72.

12.   Fabbri, "Luigi Galleani. August 12, 1861–November 4, 1931."

Chapter X: Internal Exile and the Question of Protest Candidates

1.   Luigi Galleani to Jacques Gross, Pantelleria, December 5, 1896, Jacques Gross Papers.

2.   For a description of this prison location, see Amedeo Boschi, *Ricordi del domicilio coatto* (Turin: Seme Anarchico, 1954), 35–37; T. Corniglia [Tito Lubrano], *Brani di vita: ricordi e novelle* (Rome: Industria e Lavoro, 1907).

3.   "Il domicilio coatto (Impressioni di Jessie White Mario)," *Il Domicilio Coatto. Pubblicazione unica dei socialisti, socialisti-anarchici e società operaie*, Forlì, November 14, 1897.

4.   Luigi Galleani to Jacques Gross, Ustica, March 28, 1897, Jacques Gross Papers. Favignana too had previously been a site of collective protests. In February 1896, following one of these uprisings,

the authorities had made seventeen arrests, while in May some of the prisoners, including Francesco Pezzi and Palla, had managed to escape by sea.

5.   "Running Luigi Galleani against Guido Baccelli, we have not fostered the illusion that his name can triumph at the ballot box. We intend only that today socialists, anarchists, republicans, and all goodhearted men of the third voting constituency, make a solemn affirmation of freedom and justice in the name of Luigi Galleani, so that he and all other victims of political reaction have their rights as citizens reinstated and can again circulate freely under this beautiful Italian sun, which warms and nourishes so many official wrongdoers. Vote for Luigi Galleani." "I nostri candidati. III Collegio. Luigi Galleani," *Avanti!*, March 21, 1897. Also see "Dépêche télégraphique des correspondants particuliers du Temps," *Les Temps*, March 8, 1897, 1; "I candidati nei 5 Collegi di Roma," *Avanti!*, March 12, 1897; "Lotta elettorale. Piemonte," *Avanti!*, March 15, 1897.

6.   "Roma. La riunione dei socialisti," *Avanti!*, March 16, 1897; "Roma. Il comizio a favore della candidatura Galleani. Chiare provocazioni della polizia e arresti," *Avanti!*, March 20, 1897.

7.   F.S. Merlino, "Contro l'astensione," *Avanti!*, March 9, 1897. Note that even Andrea Costa sought to make a case for Galleani and other prisoners before the Chamber, see Chamber of Deputies, *Parliamentary Acts*, Legislature XX-1 sessions-discussions-votes of April 13, 1897 and of May 17, 1897 and 2 sessions-discussions-votes of February 20, 1899, 205, 742, and 2166.

8.   Errico Malatesta and F.S. Merlino, *Anarchismo e democrazia* (Ragusa: La Fiaccola-Candilita, 2015).

9.   Errico Malatesta, "Le candidature di protesta," *L'Agitazione*, March 14, 1897, now in E. Malatesta, *Opere Complete*, "'Un lavoro lungo e paziente...'. Il socialismo anarchico dell'Agitazione 1897–1898," edited by Davide Turcato (Milan-Ragusa: Zero in Condotta-La Fiaccola, 2011), 18–19.

10.   "Candidature di protesta," *L'Agitazione*, March 21, 1897; L. Damiani and G. Molinelli, "Rome. March 16. 'Una lettera di Luigi Galleani,'" *Avanti!*, March 17, 1897.

11.   In Turin I, where Benedetto Brin was elected with 1,181 votes, he was first among the non-elected, as well as in Rome III, where Guido Baccelli was elected with 1,237 votes. See *Statistica delle elezioni generali politiche, 21 e 28 marzo 1897*, Tipografia nazionale Bertero, Rome 1887, 71, 80, and 97.

12.   Elisée Reclus to Jacques Gross, January 6, 1897, Jacques Gross Papers, Centre international de recherches sur l'anarchisme, Lausanne, cited in Ferretti, *Anarchici ed editori*, 177.

13.   Natale Musarra, "Andrea Salsedo da Pantelleria," *Sicilia Libertaria*, October 2016.

14.   Nemo [Emidio Recchioni], "'Gigi' Galleani," *L'Adunata dei Refrattari*, March 12, 1932.

15.   Gianni Oliva, "Illusioni e disinganni del volontariato socialista: la Legione Cipriani nella guerra greco-turca del 1897," *Movimento Operaio e Socialista*, year V, new series, no. 3 (September/December 1982): 331–487.

16.   "Infamie spagnuole. Anarchici torturati. Barcellona," *Avanti!*, January 5, 1897. Also see Federazione anarchica italiana, *Michele Angiolillo. Il suo eroico atto e ciò che di lui si scrisse* (Foggia: Gruppo Anarchico Michele Angiolillo, n.d.).

Chapter XI: From Island to Island

1.   Luigi Galleani to Jacques Gross, Ustica, July 3, 1898, Jacques Gross Papers.

2.   The prisoners succeeded in denouncing the inhumane conditions of this prison site, which led to the death of about fifteen of them. These facilities were closed by the Pelloux government during 1899, see "Altro che la Cajenna!," *Avanti!*, January 17, 1899, 2; "Tortura e morte a domicilio coatto," *Avanti!*, January 24, 1899, 2. Also see Marco Lenci, *All'inferno e ritorno. Storie di deportati tra Italia ed Eritrea in epoca coloniale* (Pisa: Biblioteca Franco Serantini, 2004).

3.   Boschi, *Ricordi del domicilio coatto*, 35.

4.   Luigi Galleani to Jacques Gross, Alexandria, Egypt, March 1900, Jacques Gross Papers.

5.   Leonardo Bettini, *Bibliografia dell'anarchismo. Periodici e numeri unici anarchici in lingua italiana pubblicati in Italia (1872–1971)* (Florence: CP, 1972), 127, 139–42, 144, 149, 158; other single issues and periodicals on internal exile are recorded in Leonardo Bettini, *Appendice ai primi due volumi*, http://blab.racine.ra.it/index.php/cataloghi.

6.   Armando Borghi, "Fermezza anarchica," *Umanità Nova*, April 3, 1960.

7.   Luigi Galleani, "Manet immota fides!," *I Morti*, November 2, 1899, now in *Gli anarchici del 1899* (Pistoia: RL, 1974). Other signatories in the newspaper are Giovanni Gavilli, Luigi Fabbri, and Rodolfo Felicioli.

8.   See Natale Musarra, "Una storia d'amore e di anarchia," *Sicilia Libertaria*, April 2007.

Chapter XII: In Egypt

1.   Fedeli, *Luigi Galleani*. *Quarant'anni di lotte rivoluzionarie 1891–1931*, 70. On the intrinsically transnational nature of the Italian-language anarchist movement, see Davide Turcato, "Italian Anarchism as Transnational Movement, 1885–1915," *International Review of Social History* 52, no. 3 (December 2007): 407–44; G. Berti and C. De Maria (eds.), *L'anarchismo italiano. Storia e storiografia* (Milan: Biblion, 2016), 291–367. See two examples of the transnational historiographic approach: Benedict Anderson, *Sotto tre bandiere. Anarchia e immaginario anticoloniale* (Rome: Manifestolibri, 2008); Constance Bantman, *The French Anarchists in London, 1880–1914: Exile and Transnationalism in the First Globalisation* (Liverpool: Liverpool University Press, 2013). On the subject of anarchism as a network, also see Bert Altena, "Anarchism as a Social Movement 1870–1940," *Social.Geschichteonline* no. 18 (2016): 15–62. Also see Maurizio Degl'Innocenti (ed.), *L'esilio nella storia del movimento operaio e l'emigrazione economica* (Manduria: Lacaita, 1992).

2.   Luigi Galleani to Jacques Gross, Alexandria, Egypt, May 9, 1900, Jacques Gross Papers.

3.   Elisée Reclus to Luigi Galleani, Brussels, April 6, 1900, in E. Reclus, *Correspondance, tome III et dernier*, 220.

4.   Furio Biagini, *"Il Risveglio" (1900–1922) Storia di un giornale anarchico dall'attentato di Bresci all'avvento del fascismo* (Manduria-Bari-Rome: Lacaita, 1991).

5.   Luigi Galleani to Jacques Gross, Alexandria, Egypt, October 6, 1900 and November 11, 1900, Jacques Gross Papers.

6.   Gigi [Luigi Galleani], "Fu ben altro!," *La Questione Sociale*, June 6, 1902; L'Eretico [Luigi Galleani], "Gaetano Bresci." *Cronaca Sovversiva*, July 26, 1913. Also see Giuseppe Galzerano, *Gaetano Bresci. Vita, attentato, processo, carcere e morte dell'anarchico che "giustiziò" Umberto I* (Casalvelino Scalo: Galzerano, 2001); Massimo Ortalli, *Gaetano Bresci, tessitore, anarchico e uccisore di re* (Rome: Nova Delphi Libri, 2011).

7.   Léo Campion, *Le drapeau noir, l'équerre et le compas. Les maillons libertaires de la chaîne d'union* (Paris: Alternative Libertaire, 2004).

8.   Anthony Gorman, "Anarchists in Education: The Free Popular University in Egypt (1901)," *Middle Eastern Studies* 41, no. 3 (May 2005): 303–20; Bettini, *Bibliografia dell'anarchismo. Periodici*

e numeri unici anarchici in lingua italiana pubblicati all'estero (1872–1971), 281–88.

9.   Gorman, *Anarchists in Education*; Elisée Reclus to Luigi Galleani, Brussels, April 6, 1900, 221.

Chapter XIII: On the Move Again

1.   Elisée Reclus to Luigi Galleani, Brussels, April 6, 1900, 221.

2.   Luigi Galleani to Jacques Gross, Alexandria, Egypt, May 9, 1900.

3.   Luigi Galleani to Jacques Gross, Alexandria, Egypt, May 9, 1900. On the whole question and the different interpretations, see in particular M. Antonioli, G. Berti, S. Fedele, and P. Iuso (eds.), *DBAI*, vol. I, 393–96; Berti, *Errico Malatesta e il movimento anarchico italiano e internazionale 1872–1932*, 286–88; Nunzio Pernicone, "Malatesta e La Questione Sociale," in E. Malatesta, *"Verso l'anarchia." Malatesta in America 1899–1900*, edited by Davide Turcato (Milan-Ragusa: Zero in Condotta-La Fiaccola, 2012), XV–XXXI; Giuseppe Ciancabilla, *Un colpo di lima* (Barcelona: Gratis, 2011), 5–26; Ugo Fedeli, *Biografie di anarchici* (Pescara: Samizdat, 2002), 9–60; Mario Mapelli, "Giuseppe Ciancabilla: uno sguardo sull'anarchismo italoamericano. I gruppi anarchici italiani attivi in USA tra il 1899 e il 1904," *Bollettino dell'Archivio Giuseppe Pinelli* no. 14 (December 1999): 9–14.

4.   Il Circolo di Studi Sociali di Barre, "Programma?," *Cronaca Sovversiva*, June 6, 1903; Luigi Galleani, *L'Adunata dei Refrattari*, November 5, 1931.

5.   Pietro Di Paola, *The Knights Errant of Anarchy: London and the Italian Anarchist Diaspora (1880–1917)* (Chico, CA: AK Press, 2017); Errico Malatesta, *"Lo sciopero armato." Il lungo esilio londinese 1900–1913*, edited by Davide Turcato (Milan-Ragusa: Zero in Condotta-La Fiaccola, 2015).

6.   Report by Virgilio [Ennio Belelli], London, November 4, 1901, in ACS, CPC. Note that Galleani later publicly restated his deep respect for Malatesta several times and defended him whenever necessary, coming to regard him as an activist "gifted with superior abilities"; see G. Pimpino [Luigi Galleani], "Purulenze," *Cronaca Sovversiva*, Barre, June 3, 1905.

7.   [Luigi Fabbri], "L'attentato di Buffalo," *L'Agitazione*, September 13, 1901; E. Malatesta, "Arrestiamoci sulla china: a proposito dell'attentato di Buffalo," *Il Risveglio Socialista-Anarchico*, September 28, 1901, now in E. Malatesta, *Lo sciopero armato*, 56–58.

Chapter XIV: The Revolt of the Dyers

1.   Luigi Galleani to Jacques Gross, Montreal, July 1902, Jacques Gross Papers.

2.   Francesco Rigazio, "Alberto Guabello, Firmino Gallo e altri anarchici di Mongrando nella catena migratoria dal biellese a Paterson N.J.," *Archivi e Storia* no. 23/24 (January–December 2004): 143–252.

3.   "Dagli Stati Uniti. New York," *La Questione Sociale*, October 26, 1901.

4.   Ggi [Luigi Galleani], "I gruppi femminili di propaganda," *La Questione Sociale*, November 23, 1901.

5.   Galleani and Gross, no date [1910], Jacques Gross Papers.

6.   Constantino Zonchello, "Il propagandista e l'uomo," *L'Adunata dei Refrattari*, December 19, 1931. For further considerations on his speaking talent, see Senta, "Luigi Galleani e l'anarchismo antiorganizzatore." Report presented at the European Social Science History Conference (Glasgow, April 11–14, 2012), B. Alpini, Imola 2012, now in Senta, *L'altra rivoluzione*, 95–108. To this end also see the significant testimonies collected in Paul Avrich, *Anarchist Voices, An Oral History of Anarchism in America* (Oakland: AK Press, 2005), 107, 111, 113, 117, 129, 130, 132, 138, 142; and finally B. Biaschi, "Gori, Malatesta e Galleani," *La Frusta*, June 15, 1922, in which the author, after comparing the eloquence of the three leading representatives of the Italian libertarian movement, writes: "Listening to their speeches, with Gori one exclaims: it's beautiful; with Malatesta one says: it's true; with Galleani one yells: now's the time."

7.   Giobbe Sanchini, "Galleani oratore," *Umanità Nova*, May 1, 1946.

8.   "The propaganda of Comrade G. Pimpino. Milford, Worcester," *Cronaca Sovversiva*, September 8, 1906.

Chapter XV: La Questione Sociale

1.   Élie Reclus, *Les primitifs. Études d'ethnologie comparée. Hyperboréens orientaux et occidentaux, Apaches, monticoles des Nilgherris, Naïrs, Khonds, Chamelot* (Paris, 1885). The study of anthropology, a discipline to which Elie Reclus dedicated himself, and which also comes into play in the work of his brother Elisée and of Kropotkin, was also of interest to Galleani, as he considered it capable of demonstrating the concrete possibility of non-state societies.

2.   Ggi [Luigi Galleani], "Fu ben altro!"; Gigi [Luigi Galleani], "Compari! Da Berra a Giarratana," *La Questione Sociale*, November 8,

1902. On June 27, 1901, in Berra, the forces of order and the military opened fire on field hands, causing two deaths. On September 8, 1902, in Candela, the military police shot at striking farmers, killing eight. On October 13, 1902, in Giarratana, there were clashes between field hands and the military police: one worker, an agent, and a child died. For a specific judgment on Enrico Ferri, see G. Pimpino [Luigi Galleani], "Al pettine," *Cronaca Sovversiva*, January 1, 1910.

3. El vecc [Luigi Galleani], "Gli ultimi avvenimenti d'Italia. Modeste considerazioni," *Cronaca Sovversiva*, November 5, 1904.

4. Ggi [Luigi Galleani], "L'episodio di Tampa," *La Questione Sociale*, October 26, 1901.

5. Luigi Galleani in the memoirs of Max Nettlau.

Chapter XVI: Strike!

1. Vittorio Cravello, "Le tintorie di seta," *Cronaca Sovversiva*, May 19, 1907.

2. C. Pimpino [Luigi Galleani], "Lo sciopero generale," *Cronaca Sovversiva*, November 9, 1907. It is curious to note that Galleani traced the birth of the general strike back to the times of the Roman Republic, when around 500 BC the plebeians withdrew to Mons Sacer, refusing to take up arms against the Aequi and Volsci, to achieve the abolition of debt. The uprising was successful, marking the abolition of private debt and the institution of the plebeian court, organs of inviolable and sacred rights; see Luigi Galleani, "Uno sciopero generale. Duemilaquattrocentododici anni fa," *Il Risveglio*, May 1, 1908; Balilla [Luigi Galleani], "Uno sciopero d'altri tempi," *Il Diritto*, February 15, 1919.

3. Ggi [Luigi Galleani], "Minatori della Pennsilvania e tintori di Paterson," *La Questione Sociale*, May 31, 1902.

4. Ggi [Luigi Galleani], "Scioperi e unioni di mestiere," *La Questione Sociale*, August 23, 1902.

5. Ggi [Luigi Galleani], "Unioni di mestiere e propaganda anarchica," *La Questione Sociale*, September 13, 1902.

6. Errico Malatesta, "Gli anarchici e le società operaje," *La Questione Sociale*, October 14, 1899, now in *Verso l'anarchia*, 77.

7. Errico Malatesta, "Dopo la sconfitta," *Lo Sciopero Generale*, March 18, 1902, now in *Lo sciopero armato*, 65.

8. "Lo sciopero armato," *Lo Sciopero Generale*, June 2, 1902, now in "Lo sciopero armato," 71–72.

9. Luigi Galleani, "Lo sciopero generale," *Il Risveglio*, May 1, 1910.

10. On William MacQueen, see a brief biographical account at   https://libcom.org/history/articles/1875-1908-william-macqueen. On Rudolf Grosmann and German anarchism in New York, see Tom Goyens, *Beer and Revolution: The German Anarchist Movement in New York City, 1880–1914* (Chicago: University of Illinois Press, 2007), 190–93; Hans Müller-Sewing, "Rudolf Grosmann alias Pierre Ramus," *Bollettino dell'Archivio Giuseppe Pinelli* no. 24 (December 2004): 21–22.

11. P. Ghio, *L'anarchisme aux Etats-Unis* (Paris: Librairie Armand Colin, 1903), 138.

12. Ibid., 141–42.

13. La moglie di Cesare, "I fatti di giugno alla corte," *La Questione Sociale*, November 1, 1902.

14. See Report of the Italian Consul in the United States to the Department of Foreign Affairs of June 20 and 24, 1902 in ASMAE, polizia internazionale 1880–1906; "Militia Called out to Suppress Rioting of Paterson Strikers. Anarchists Blamed. Chief of Police Deposed. Firemen Rout Big Mob with Streams of Water," *The Boston Herald*, June 20, 1902; "State Troops are now in Paterson to Keep Peace," *Trenton Times*, June 20, 1902. See also *Cronaca Sovversiva*, May 18, 1907.

Chapter XVII: A Spaniard in Montreal

1. Luigi Galleani to Jacques Gross, Montreal, July 1902.

2. ASMAE, polizia internazionale 1880–1906; Luigi Galleani to Jacques Gross, Montreal, Jacques Gross Papers, September 2, 1902.

3. Luigi Galleani to Jacques Gross, November 2, 1902, Montreal.

4. Ibid.

5. Luigi Galleani to Jacques Gross, 1902, Montreal, Jacques Gross Papers.

6. "Welcome!," *La Questione Sociale*, September 27, 1902; see the complete text in Malatesta, *Lo sciopero armato*, 75–77.

7. Errico Malatesta, "Gli Anarchici nelle Società Operaje," *La Rivoluzione Sociale*, London, November 1, 1902, also in *Lo sciopero armato*, 105.

8. He continued: "Chemistry and mechanics must not only be developed for the oppressors [...]. Strikes, resistance to the government's orders, protests against an injustice that has upset the public can be, or can be made, occasions to provoke conflict with authority and push the people to revolution. But the reason this succeeds is that there are groups that possess arms or know where to go and get them; groups that already have a battle plan ready and are prepared to implement

it; groups that know how to appropriately use iron, fire, explosives," Errico Malatesta, "L'insurrezione armata," *La Rivoluzione Sociale*, London, April 5, 1903, also in, *Lo sciopero armato*, 151.

9.   United States Police Service, January 7, 1903, in ASMAE, polizia internazionale 1880–1906.

10.   "Ai compagni," *La Questione Sociale*, February 28, 1903.

Chapter XVIII: Among the Quarry Workers of Vermont

1.   G. Vatteroni, *Anarchici da Carrara a Barre*, unpublished, a work from which I gathered much of the information provided in this section.

2.   Nevesk [Luigi Galleani], "Ieri ed oggi. Saggi di...patologia Coloniale," *Cronaca Sovversiva*, March 20, 1909.

3.   Roberto Cappelli, *Cronaca Sovversiva. Ebdomadario anarchico di propaganda rivoluzionaria (Barre Vermont-Lynn Mass.)*, graduate thesis in literature, Faculty of Education, Università degli studi di Firenze, 1969–1970; Augusta Molinari, "I giornali delle comunità anarchiche italo-americane," *Movimento Operaio e Socialista* (January–June 1981): 127–30; Antonio Senta, "Ut redeat miseris, abeat fortuna suberbis. I primi anni del settimanale 'Cronaca Sovversiva,'" *Il Presente e la Storia*, no. 91 (June 2017): 19–37; Luigi Galleani, *Alcuni articoli da Cronaca Sovversiva (Barre Vermont, Stati Uniti d'America 1904–1906)* (Pistoia: Edizioni Archivio Famiglia Berneri, 1984). Ettore Zoccoli, in his work *L'anarchia. Gli agitatori le idee i fatti* (Turin: F.lli Bocca, 1907), 357–58, defines the periodical as "individualistic" and "doctrinaire" and praises its technical composition "envied by every legalitarian party." *Cronaca Sovversiva* can be accessed here: http://chroniclingamerica. loc.gov/lccn/2012271201/issues.

4.   Andrew Hoyt, "Methods for Tracing Radical Networks: Mapping the Print Culture and Propagandists of the Sovversivi," in J. Meléndez Badillo and N. Jun (eds.), *Without Border or Limits: An Interdisciplinary Approach to Anarchist Studies* (Cambridge: Cambridge Scholars Press, 2013), 75–106. By Hoyt also see: "The Whole World Is Our Homeland: Italian Anarchist Networks in Global Context, 1870–1939," *Zapruder World* no. 1 (2014) and *The Black Ink of the Subversive Press: Italian Propaganda Networks and Radical Print Culture in the Atlantic World (1903–1920)*, PhD dissertation, University of Minnesota, 2017.

5.   Berti, *Errico Malatesta e il movimento anarchico italiano e internazionale 1872–1932*, 102–103.

6.   Errico Malatesta, "La fine dell'anarchismo? di Luigi Galleani," *Pensiero e Volontà*, June 1, 1926. Also see G. Rose, *Presentazione a L. Galleani, La fine dell'anarchismo?* (Cesena: L'Antistato, 1966), 10.

7.   "Anniversario," *Cronaca Sovversiva*, June 2, 1906.

8.   "Post fata resurgo," *Cronaca Sovversiva*, January 21, 1905.

9.   "I manifesti, I pirati dell'anarchismo," *Cronaca Sovversiva*, September 29, 1909; "Ai compagni non alle oche," *Cronaca Sovversiva*, December 13, 1909.

10.   Marcella Bencivenni, *Italian Immigrant Radical Culture: The Idealism of the Sovversivi in the United States 1890–1940* (New York: New York University Press, 2011); Philip Cannistraro and Gerald Meyer (eds.), *The Lost World of Italian-American Radicalism: Politics, Labor, and Culture* (Westport-London: Praeger, 2003); Donna Gabaccia, *Militants and Migrants: Rural Sicilians Become American Workers* (New Brunswick-London: Rutgers University Press, 1988); Rudolph Vecoli, "The Italian Immigrants in the United States Labor Movement from 1880 to 1929," in Bruno Bezza (ed.), *Gli Italiani fuori d'Italia. Gli emigrati italiani nei movimenti operai dei paesi di adozione (1880–1940)* (Milan: Franco Angeli, 1983), 257–306.

11.   "Il nostro avvenire," *Cronaca Sovversiva*, October 24, 1903.

12.   *Cronaca Sovversiva*, July 29, 1905. Excessive consumption of alcohol among the anarchists and socialists of Barre was not a recent problem. Activists, Galleani confided, "drink a lot of wine, beer and whiskey, making every house a tavern," Luigi Galleani to Jacques Gross, no date [1910], Jacques Gross Papers.

13.   "La donna schiava," *Cronaca Sovversiva*, September 12, 1903. On women's participation in the Italian anarchist movement in the United States, with particular attention to the environment of Paterson's *La Questione Sociale*, see Jennifer Guglielmo, "Donne Ribelli: Recovering the History of Italian Women's Radicalism in the United States," in Cannistraro Meyer, (ed.), *The Lost World of Italian-American Radicalism*, 113–41.

14.   "La donna e la famiglia," *Cronaca Sovversiva*, October 17, 1903; R.C., "La schiava," *Cronaca Sovversiva*, March 26, 1910.

15.   G. M., "La Rivoluzione in sé stesso," *Cronaca Sovversiva*, September 17, 1904.

16.   For a complete list of texts available during 1905, see *Cronaca Sovversiva*, March 11, 1905.

17.   Carlo Abate was the creator of several drawings and portraits in the newspaper's pages, and from issue no. 17 became its publisher.

See Andrew Hoyt, "Santi e martiri anarchici. La ritrattistica in 'Cronaca Sovversiva,'" *Bollettino Archivio G. Pinelli* no. 44 (2014): 34–39.

18. Sébastien Faure, "Per l'insegnamento. Monopolio o libertà?," *Cronaca Sovversiva*, August 1, 1903.

19. "La patria," *Cronaca Sovversiva*, February 20, 1904.

20. Alcuni anarchici, "Una diga contro l'oscurantismo," *Cronaca Sovversiva*, November 10, 1906. On the important theme of education in the United States with regards to anarchism and the modern school movement, see Paul Avrich, *The Modern School Movement: Anarchism and Education in the United States* (Oakland: AK Press, 2006); Giuliana Iurlano, *Da Barcellona a Stelton. Ferrer e il movimento delle Scuole Moderne in Spagna e negli Stati Uniti* (Milan: M&B Publishing, 2000); G. Fornaciti, "Mezzo secolo di contro educazione: la Ferrer Association da St. Mark's Place a Stelton," *Bollettino Archivio G. Pinelli* no. 47 (2016): 26–31.

21. See the special issues dedicated to him on October 23, 1909, October 15, 1910, and October 14, 1911; several articles by Galleani on Ferrer are now reprinted in Luigi Galleani, *"Scuola Moderna" di Francisco Ferrer (1902–1909)* (Turin: Luigi Assandri, 1978).

Chapter XIX: *Cronaca Sovversiva*

1. Pimpino [Luigi Galleani], "Un uomo," *Cronaca Sovversiva*, June 3, 1905.

2. Il Circolo di Studi Sociali di Barre, "Ai compagni," *Cronaca Sovversiva*, Barre, year I, no. 1, June 6, 1903.

3. Ibid., "Programma?," *Cronaca Sovversiva*, June 6, 1903.

4. Tropie, "Sintesi anarchica," *Cronaca Sovversiva*, May 6, 1905; "Il governo," *Cronaca Sovversiva*, October 3, 1903.

5. Red [Luigi Galleani], "L'anarchia sarà!," *Cronaca Sovversiva*, June 27, 1903. Over the years Galleani made positive evaluations of several aspects of Stirner's thought, while he remained fundamentally opposed to Nietzsche's philosophy. In 1910–11 *Cronaca Sovversiva* published a long piece in installments by Massimo Rocca entitled "La crisi dell'anarchismo," and several groups close to the newspaper arranged lectures by him. Rocca was an individualist, a former editor of a periodical entitled *Il Novatore* [The Innovator], and strongly influenced by Nietzsche. This collaboration ended in summer 1911 because of irreconcilable political differences. See Maurizio Antonioli and Pier Carlo Masini, *Il sol dell'avvenire. L'anarchismo in Italia dalle origini alla Prima Guerra mondiale* (Pisa: Biblioteca Franco Serantini, 1999), 76–79.

Also see L. Tancredi [Massimo Rocca], *L'anarchismo contro l'anarchia (Studio critico documentario)* (Pistoia: Rinascimento, 1914); C. Berneri, "Uomini e idee. Libero Tancredi," *Rivoluzione Liberale*, March 18, 1924.

6.   D. M., "L'idea del progresso e l'anarchismo," *Cronaca Sovversiva*, March 25, 1905.

7.   Armando Borghi, *Del nostro e dell'altrui individualismo. Riflessioni storicocritiche su l'anarchia* (Brisighella: Servadei, 1907), VIII, 58.

8.   La Cronaca Sovversiva, "No!," *Cronaca Sovversiva*, January 18, 1908; Stenko Razine [Luigi Galleani], "Lo scisma liberatore," *Cronaca Sovversiva*, April 9, 1910.

9.   "L'onorevole anarchico," *Cronaca Sovversiva*, September 10, 1904.

10.   El vecc [Luigi Galleani], "Una Conferenza Anarchica," *Cronaca Sovversiva*, August 8, 1903; G. Pimpino [Luigi Galleani], "Convegno di St. Louis," *Cronaca Sovversiva*, March 19, 1904; A. Cavallazzi, "Per un congresso internazionale," *Cronaca Sovversiva*, September 30, 1905; Id., "Congressomania," *Cronaca Sovversiva*, October 20, 1906; Santuzza [Luigi Galleani], "Congressi, congress," *Cronaca Sovversiva*, July 6, 1907; L'Eretico [Luigi Galleani], "S'incomincia male," *Cronaca Sovversiva*, 1913; n.d.r., "Pro e contro un convegno," *Cronaca Sovversiva*, October 6, 1917.

11.   "All'anarchia si arriverà passando per lo Stato socialista?," *Biblioteca di Studi Sociali* (Barre 1905).

12.   "Dal nostro corrispondente speciale in Svizzera, Legalitari ed anarchici nelle agitazioni operaie," *Cronaca Sovversiva*, June 6, 1903. The "special correspondent in Switzerland" was Jacques Gross.

13.   Diogene [Luigi Galleani], "Sulla via di Damasco. Dall'anarchia al socialism," *Cronaca Sovversiva*, July 25, 1903. The articles in the *Mandateli lassù!* column are now collected in Luigi Galleani, *Mandateli lassù!* (Cesena: L'Antistato, 1954).

14.   *Cronaca Sovversiva*, November 7, 1911; *Il Proletario*, August 23, 1903.

15.   *Cronaca Sovversiva*, October 10, 1903 and following issues; P. Valera, "Giacinto Menotti Serrati direttore dell'Avanti!," *La Folla* (Milan, 1920). Galleani's writings on the issue are collected in Luigi Galleani, *Metodi della lotta socialista* (Sora: Biblioteca de l'Adunata dei Refrattari, 1972).

16.   "Alcuni anarchici di Losanna, Ancora per un Rettile," *Giacinto Menotti Serrati*, October 1904, Max Nettlau Papers. For the

genesis of this manifesto, see Luigi Galleani to Jacques Gross, Barre, May and June 1903, Jacques Gross Papers. Also see Valera, "Giacinto Menotti Serrati direttore dell'Avanti!," 46–47.

17. See "Barre Italians Protest. Hold Indignation Meeting Over Arrest of Luigi Galleani," *St. Albans Daily Messenger*, January 3 and 10, 1907.

18. See "Paterson Anarchist Free. Galleani Friends Raise $6,000 Cash Bail for Him," *New York Times*, January 18, 1907; "Anarchist Meeting in Barre. Emma Goldman and Luigi Galleani Speak in Opera House," *St. Albans Daily Messenger*, February 27, 1907.

19. See "Fund of $37,000 Raised there and in Boston to Defend Galleani," *The Boston Herald*, January 5, 1907. To read part of the trial see *Cronaca Sovversiva*, May 18, 1907 (special issue).

Chapter XX: The End of Anarchism?

1. "L'anarchismo muore," *Cronaca Sovversiva*, July 20, 1907; G. Pimpino [Luigi Galleani], "La fine dell'anarchismo?," *Cronaca Sovversiva*, August 17, 1907 and following issues.

2. Galleani, "La fine dell'anarchismo?" English translation: *The End of Anarchism?*, translated by Max Sartin and Robert D'Atillio (Cienfuegos Press, Orkney, 1982), 5 (emphasis original).

3. Ibid., 12.

4. "Dall'estero. Russia," *Cronaca Sovversiva*, June 6, 1903.

5. Maurizio Antonioli, *Figli dell'officina. Anarchismo, sindacalismo e movimento operaio tra Ottocento e Novecento* (Pisa: Biblioteca Franco Serantini, 2012), 51. For France see Jean Maitron, *Le mouvement anarchiste en France I. Des origines à 1914* (Paris: Gallimard, 1992), 265–330.

6. Malatesta, *Lo sciopero armato*, 181. On the convention see Maurizio Antonioli, *Dibattito sul sindacalismo. Atti del Congresso internazionale anarchico di Amsterdam (1907)* (Florence: CP, 1978).

7. Galleani returned to this theme several times, restating that syndicalism could not "suffice in itself," see Corrado [Luigi Galleani], "Del sindacalismo," *Cronaca Sovversiva*, June 18, 1910.

8. Malatesta, *Lo sciopero armato*, 182. In one of his articles entitled "Anarchism and Syndicalism" which ran in *Freedom* of London in November 1907 and was republished in Italian by *Il Risveglio Socialista-Anarchico*, Malatesta observed the trend toward degeneration inherent in unions and institutions in general with these words: "every institution has a tendency to extend its functions, to perpetuate itself,

and to become an end in itself," reprinted in Malatesta, *Lo sciopero armato*, 201–205.

9.   "I fachiri dell'Unione," *Cronaca Sovversiva*, December 12, 1903.

10.   Balilla [Luigi Galleani], "Neanche una," *Cronaca Sovversiva*, June 22, 1907.

11.   Richard Boyer and Herbert Morais, *Storia del movimento operaio negli Stati Uniti* (Bologna: Odoya, 2012); Elisabetta Vezzosi, "Sciopero e rivolta. Le organizzazioni operaie italiane negli Stati Uniti," in P. Bevilacqua, A. De Clementi, and E. Franzina (eds.), *Storia dell'emigrazione italiana* (Rome: Arrivi, Donzelli, 2009), 271–82; Gino Cerrito, "Sull'emigrazione anarchica italiana negli Stati Uniti d'America," *Volontà*, year XXII, no. 4, July–August (1969): 269–76; Daniel Guérin, *Il movimento operaio negli Stati Uniti 1867–1970* (Rome: Editori Riuniti, 1975); Ferdinando Fasce, "Gli Industrial Workers of the World e il movimento socialista americano 1905–1913," *Movimento Operaio e Socialista*, year XII, no. 1–2 (January–June 1976): 23–50; Ferdinando Fasce, "Alle origini del sindacalismo d'industria negli Stati Uniti," in M. Antonioli and L. Ganapini (eds.), *I sindacati occidentali dall'800 ad oggi in una prospettiva storica comparata* (Pisa: Biblioteca Franco Serantini, 1995), 93–115; Patrick Renshaw, *Il sindacalismo rivoluzionario negli Stati Uniti* (Bari: Laterza, 1970); Renato Musto (ed.), *Gli IWW e il movimento operaio americano. Storia e documenti* (Naples: Thélème, 1975); Louis Adamic, *Dynamite. La storia della violenza di classe in America* (Milan: Collettivo Editoriale Libri Rossi, 1977); Filippo Manganaro, *Senza patto né legge. Antagonismo operaio negli Stati Uniti* (Rome: Odradek, 2004); Bruno Cartosio (ed.), *Wobbly! L'Industrial Workers of the World e il suo tempo* (Milan: ShaKe, 2007); also see the historical novel of Valerio Evangelisti, *One Big Union* (Milan: Mondadori, 2011). For the influence of anarchist immigration on the origins of the IWW and its cultural character, see Sal Salerno, *Red November Black November: Culture and Community in the Industrial Workers of the World* (Albany: State University of New York Press, 1989); Salvatore Salerno, "No God, No Master: Italian Anarchists and the Industrial Workers of the World," in Cannistraro and Meyer, (eds.), *The Lost World of Italian American Radicalism*, 171–87.

12.   In this connection, see the statistics collected by Galleani on the number of miners killed at work in the United States: 3,881 from 1883 to 1907, *Cronaca Sovversiva*, December 28, 1907; 7,919 in the three-year period of 1910–1912, *Cronaca Sovversiva*, January 3, 1914.

There are other lists in *Cronaca Sovversiva*, March 12, 1910. This issue also reported five hundred thousand disabling accidents per annum in the workplace. According to the Commission on Industrial Relations, in 1914 there were thirty five thousand fatal accidents at work and seven hundred thousand injuries. See Howard Zinn, *Storia del popolo americano. Dal 1942 a oggi* (Milan: il Saggiatore, 2010), 227.

13. Richard Boyer and Howard Morais, *Storia del movimento operaio negli Stati Uniti 1861–1955*; William Haywood, *La storia di Big Bill (autobiografia del principale rappresentante degli Industrial Workers of the World)* (Milan: Iskra, 1977).

14. On the relations between *Cronaca Sovversiva* and Tresca's camp see Nunzio Pernicone, "War among the Italian Anarchists: The Galleanisti's Campaign against Carlo Tresca," in Cannistraro and Meyer (eds.), *The Lost World of Italian American Radicalism*, 77–97; Travis Tomchuk, *Transnational Radicals: Italian Anarchists in Canada and the U.S. 1915–1940* (Winnipeg: University of Manitoba Press, 2015); Oreste Veronesi, "Un movimento delle differenze: Galleani e Tresca nella storia degli anarchici," *Bollettino Archivio G. Pinelli*, no. 48 (2016): 22–26. On Carlo Tresca, see Nunzio Pernicone, *Portrait of a Rebel* (Oakland: AK Press, 2010); Dorothy Gallagher, *All the Right Enemies: The Life and Murder of Carlo Tresca* (New Brunswick: Rutgers University Press, 1988); Antonioli, Berti, S. Fedele, and P. Iuso (eds.), *DBAI*, Vol. 2, 623–26; Carlo Tresca, *Autobiografia* (Palombara Sabina: Anicia, 2006); Stefano Di Berardo, *La poesia dell'azione. Vita e morte di Carlo Tresca* (Milan: Franco Angeli, 2013). On *Il Martello*, see Adriana Dadà, "Il Martello," in Bettini, *Bibliografia dell'anarchismo. Periodici e numeri unici anarchici in lingua italiana pubblicati all'estero*, 201–205.

Chapter XXI: *La salute è in voi*

1. "Tattica d'azione," *Cronaca Sovversiva*, June 27, 1903.

2. Balilla [Luigi Galleani], "La forca alla riscossa," *Cronaca Sovversiva*, January 7, 1905.

3. Conselice and Santa Susanna are sites of peasant massacres.

4. *La salute è in voi!* (Bari: Biblioteca di Studi Sociali, 1906), now an appendix to Anarchici cuneesi (ed.), *La salute è in voi. Sacco, Vanzetti e la dimensione anarchica* (Villafalletto: Il Picconiere-El Rùsac-Cassa Antirep delle Alpi Occidentali-El Paso Occupato, 2017). A transcription is contained in ACS, Ministry of the Interior, Pubblica Sicurezza [Public Security], H2, B1, file 1911.

5. "Tra libri e giornali," *Cronaca Sovversiva*, February 10, 1906.

6.   G. Pimpino [Luigi Galleani], "Dinamitiamoli!," *Cronaca Sovversiva*, January 16, 1904.

7.   Red [Luigi Galleani], "L'anarchia sarà!," *Cronaca Sovversiva*, June 27, 1903; "Demoliamo," *Cronaca Sovversiva*, July 23, 1904. "Sgherri" is an archaic term: it refers to something along the lines of "thugs with a mandate," or private armed guards with less-than-honorable assignments.

8.   Malatesta, *Lo sciopero armato*, 183, also see 193–200.

9.   Ibid., 187.

Chapter XXII: A Little Bit of Theory

1.   *Cronaca Sovversiva*, May 20, 1905, in which the preface to Elisée Reclus's work, *L'homme et la terre* was published; J.G. [Jacques Gross], "Rivoluzione catastrofica," *Cronaca Sovversiva*, July 4, 1903. As regards the writings of Elisée Reclus, I am referring here to the anthologies *Natura e società. Scritti di geografia sovversiva* and *Scritti sociali I, II*.

2.   "Le conferenze del compagno L. Galleani a Philadelphia, Pa.," *Cronaca Sovversiva*, November 4, 1905.

3.   "Il contraddittorio Caroti-Pimpino a New London," *Cronaca Sovversiva*, August 5, 1905; Il Circolo di Studi Sociali di Barre, "Ai compagni," *Cronaca Sovversiva*, June 6, 1903.

4.   "Il terrorismo," *Cronaca Sovversiva*, December 14, 1907.

5.   L. Pimpino [Luigi Galleani], "Clemente Duval," *Cronaca Sovversiva*, June 15, 1907; on Vittorio Pini, see Gigione [Luigi Galleani], "Vittorio Pini è morto," *Cronaca Sovversiva*, January 16, 1904.

6.   L. Galleani, *Faccia a faccia col nemico. Cronache giudiziarie dell'anarchismo militante* (Casalvelino Scalo: Galzerano, 2001).

7.   L'Eretico [Luigi Galleani], "Contro la violenza, la violenza!," *Cronaca Sovversiva*, June 1, 1912. Also see Corrado [Luigi Galleani], "L'utilità della violenza," *Cronaca Sovversiva*, August 2, 1913.

8.   Mentana [Luigi Galleani], "Può venire, l'attendiamo di piè fermo!," *Cronaca Sovversiva*, April 16, 1916.

9.   "Il mutuo appoggio nell'evoluzione," *Cronaca Sovversiva*, November 28, 1903; Peter Kropotkin, "Verso la felicità," *Cronaca Sovversiva*, November 26, 1904.

10.   Peter Kropotkin, *Il mutuo appoggio. Un fattore dell'evoluzione* (Rome: Salerno, 1982).

11.   "La lotta per l'esistenza e l'anarchismo," *Cronaca Sovversiva*, May 23, 1908.

12. Kropotkin, *La morale anarchica*.

13. Kropotkin, *Il mutuo appoggio. Un fattore dell'evoluzione*.

14. L. Mechnikov, "Revolution and Evolution," *The Contemporary Review* no. 50 (1886): 412–37. Also see Federico Ferretti, "The Correspondance between Elisée Reclus and Pëtr Kropotkin as a Source for the History of Geography," *Journal of Historical Geography* no. 37 (2011): 216–22.

15. L. Mechnikov, *Les grands fleuves historiques*, Imprimérie de la société typographique (Neuchâtel 1888); Mechnikov, *La civilisation et les grands fleuves historiques* (Paris: Hachette, 1889); Also see Ferretti, *Il mondo senza la mappa*, 117–47.

16. "In morte di H. Spencer," *Cronaca Sovversiva*, December 19, 1903.

17. "Per la vita e per l'Idea. Stati Uniti. Stafford Spring, Conn.," *Cronaca Sovversiva*, October 14, 1905.

18. "Le conferenze del compagno L. Galleani a Philadelphia, Pa.," *Cronaca Sovversiva*, November 4, 1905.

Chapter XXIII: The Mexican Revolution

1. *Cronaca Sovversiva*, February 22, 1908. On anarchism in the Mexican Revolution, see Pietro Ferrua, *Ricardo Flores Magón e la rivoluzione messicana* (Ragusa: La Fiaccola, 1975); Pietro Ferrua, *Gli anarchici nella rivoluzione messicana: Praxedis G. Guerrero* (Ragusa: La Fiaccola, 1976); Claudio Albertani, "Ricardo Flores Magón," *Bollettino dell'Archivio Giuseppe Pinelli* no. 14 (December 1999): 45–47; Pier Francesco Zarcone, *La libertà e la terra. Gli anarchici nella rivoluzione messicana* (Bolsena: Massari, 2006); Michele Presutto, *La rivoluzione dietro l'angolo. Gli anarchici italiani e la Rivoluzione messicana 1910–1914* (Foligno: Editoriale Umbra, 2017).

2. Liane [Luigi Galleani], "Messico rosso," *Cronaca Sovversiva*, April 1, 1911.

3. Ricardo Flores Magón et al., "Ai lavoratori di tutto il mondo," *Cronaca Sovversiva*, May 20, 1911; Liane [Luigi Galleani], "Per i rivoluzionari del Messico," *Cronaca Sovversiva*, June 3, 1911.

4. E. Teodori et al., "Gli anarchici e la rivoluzione messicana da quelli che ci sono stati," *Cronaca Sovversiva*, June 18, 1911.

5. Luigi Galleani, "La tormenta messicana," *Cronaca Sovversiva*, August 18, 1911.

6. Ricardo Flores Magón, *La revolución mexicana* (Mexico City: Editorial Grijalbo, 1970), 145. Also see Luigi Galleani, "Lo vogliono

proprio?," *Cronaca Sovversiva*, September 2, 1911.

7.   Luigi Galleani, "Poiché lo vogliono proprio...," *Cronaca Sovversiva*, September 23, 1911.

8.   "La questione messicana al Convegno di East Boston," *Cronaca Sovversiva*, January 6, 1912.

9.   Flores Magón, *La revolución mexicana*, 138–48, 150. Also see Margarita De Orellana, *Villa e Zapata. La rivoluzione messicana* (Milan: Fenice 2000, 1993); Edgcumb Pinchon, *Zapata l'invincibile* (Milan: Feltrinelli, 1956); John Womack Jr., *Morire per gli indios. Storia di Emiliano Zapata* (Milan: Mondadori, 1973); Frank McLynn, *Villa e Zapata. Una biografia della rivoluzione messicana* (Milan: Il Saggiatore, 2003); "Il 'compagno' Emiliano Zapata," *Cronaca Sovversiva*, January 13, 1912. For a summary of the anarchist debate and intervention in the Mexican Revolution, see Kenyon Zimmer, *Immigrants Against the State: Yiddish and Italian Anarchism* (Chicago: University of Illinois Press, 2015), 124–30; Presutto, *La rivoluzione dietro l'angolo*.

Chapter XXIV: From Vermont to Massachusetts

1.   Sanchini, *Galleani oratore*; also see Avrich, *Anarchist Voices*, 130.

2.   Boyer and Morais, Storia del movimento operaio negli Stati Uniti, 246.

3.   L'Eretico [Luigi Galleani], "Italian Black Hand," *Cronaca Sovversiva*, April 6, 1912; Zinn, *Storia del popolo americano*, 226–27; Marcella Bencivenni in Michele Presutto (ed.), "Noi e loro: Sacco e Vanzetti novant'anni dopo. Tavola rotonda con Marcella Bencivenni, Luigi Botta, Salvatore Salerno," *Frontiere*, year XVIII, no. 34 (2017): 17; Filippo Manganaro, *Un sogno chiamato rivoluzione* (Rome: Nova Delphi Libri, 2012).

4.   G. Pimpino [Luigi Galleani], "L'orgia cosacca," *Cronaca Sovversiva*, March 2, 1912; L'eretico [Luigi Galleani], "Ai tessitori di Lawrence," *Cronaca Sovversiva*, May 18, 1912; G.S., "Pro Ettor e Giovannitti. La grande manifestazione di Boston," *Cronaca Sovversiva*, July 13, 1912.

5.   G. Pimpino [Luigi Galleani], "Una grande battaglia proletaria a Lawrence, Mass.," *Cronaca Sovversiva*, January 20, 1912; Cronaca Sovversiva, "Lo sciopero di Lawrence, Mass.," *Cronaca Sovversiva*, January 27, 1912; L'Eretico [Luigi Galleani], "Né un giorno, né un'ora, più!," *Cronaca Sovversiva*, August 10, 1912; Antica Cossira [Luigi Galleani], "Faccia a faccia col nemico. Vigilia d'armi," *Cronaca Sovversiva*,

September 28, 1912. Also see Renshaw, *Il sindacalismo rivoluzionario negli Stati Uniti*, 99–123; Pernicone, *Carlo Tresca*, 54. On this event, and generally on the role of the Italian-language anarchist movement in the United States from 1912–1916, starting with the life of one of its major representatives, Umberto Postiglione, see E. Puglielli, *"L'Autoeducazione del maestro." Vita di Umberto Postiglione*, forthcoming from the Istituto storico abruzzese per la storia della Resistenza e dell'Italia contemporanea.

6. Ggi [Luigi Galleani], "Questa no, Carluccio!," *Cronaca Sovversiva*, March 20, 1915; Mentana [Luigi Galleani], "L'equivoco è durato assai!," *Cronaca Sovversiva*, September 18, 1915; L'altissimo. Dagli empirei de la Cronaca Sovversiva [Luigi Galleani], "Le bizze di Carluccio," *Cronaca Sovversiva*, October 2, 1915; l'Altissimo [Luigi Galleani], "Le bizze di Carluccio," *Cronaca Sovversiva*, December 4, 1915.

7. John Reed, "The Colorado War," *Metropolitan Magazine*, July 3, 1914. Also see Spartaco, "La guerra sociale nel Colorado," *Cronaca Sovversiva*, May 9, 1914.

8. See L'Eretico [Luigi Galleani], "Non disarmate!," *Cronaca Sovversiva*, May 16, 1914; F. B., "Indarno! Guerra sociale nel Colorado," *Cronaca Sovversiva*, May 23, 1914; [Ugo Fedeli, Raffaele Schiavina], *Un trentennio di attività anarchica, 1914–1945* (Cesena: L'Antistato, 1953), 121–22; Zinn, *Storia del popolo americano*, 244–47.

9. See Paul Avrich and Karen Avrich, *Sasha and Emma: The Anarchist Odyssey of Alexander Berkman and Emma Goldman* (Cambridge: The Belknap Press of Harvard University Press, 2012), 217; Pernicone, *Carlo Tresca*, 80–82.

10. Mentana [Luigi Galleani], "Il trionfo di Mardocheo," *Cronaca Sovversiva*, March 13, 1915, now partially in [Ugo Fedeli, Raffaele Schiavina], *Un trentennio*, 125–26. Also see Beverly Gage, *The Day Wall Street Exploded: A Story of America in Its First Stage of Terror* (New York: Oxford University Press, 2010); Ronald Creagh, *Sacco & Vanzetti, un delitto di Stato* (Milan: Zero in Condotta, 2017), 79–81; Avrich, *The Modern School Movement*, 203–39. Following these attempts, police agent Amedeo Polignani infiltrated the Circolo Bresci of New York. Polignani arrested two young activists, Frank Abarno and Carmine Carbone, while they were placing a bomb near the St. Patrick Cathedral on the anniversary of Francisco Ferrer's execution. A united protest campaign was organized for their liberation.

Chapter XXV: Facing the World War

1.   *Balilla*, July 15, 1912.

2.   La redazione, "Venia cortese," *Balilla*, June 5, 1912.

3.   Mentana [Luigi Galleani], "Madri d'Italia!," *Cronaca Sovversiva*, October 4, 1913 and subsequent issues.

4.   Luigi Lotti, *La Settimana Rossa* (Florence: Le Monnier, 1965); Antonio Senta (ed.), *La rivoluzione scende in strada. La Settimana Rossa nella storia d'Italia 1914–2014* (Milan: Zero in Condotta, 2016). Papers from the conference organized by the Archivio storico della Federazione anarchica italiana, Imola, Saturday September 27, 2014.

5.   L.C.S. [Luigi Galleani], "Malatesta in Italia," *Cronaca Sovversiva*, November 25, 1911, now in Galleani, *Figure e figuri*, 207–12. Also see Errico Malatesta, "La guerra e gli anarchici," *Cronaca Sovversiva*, May 11, 1912, reproduced in the single issue *La Guerra Tripolina*. *Cronaca Sovversiva* also organized the collection of funds to finance both Malatesta's lecture tour in Italy, as well as his new publication, *Volontà*.

6.   Yosto, "Ha divampato," *Cronaca Sovversiva*, June 20, 1914; Corrado [Luigi Galleani], "Romagna docet," *Cronaca Sovversiva*, July 19, 1914 and subsequent issues.

7.   Luigi Fabbri, *Malatesta l'uomo e il pensiero* (Naples: RL, 1951), 169–70. *Cronaca Sovversiva* definitively severed relations with several activists who, in previous years, had occasionally worked with the newspaper and who now lined up with interventionist positions, including revolutionary syndicalists Pulvio Zocchi and Edmondo Rossoni, with whom the first major disagreements dated back to 1910 and 1913, respectively.

8.   Mentana [Luigi Galleani], "Per la guerra, per la neutralità o per la pace?," *Cronaca Sovversiva*, November 7, 1914 to January 2, 1915, now reprinted in L. Galleani, *Una battaglia*, 1–43.

9.   Saraceno [Umberto Postiglione], "La guerra europea," *Cronaca Sovversiva*, August 15, 1914; Corrado, "I due imperatori," *Cronaca Sovversiva*, August 29, 1914.

10.   La redazione, "Vigliaccheria," *La Questione Sociale*, October 16, 1915; La redazione, "I nostri calunniatori alla sbarra," *La Questione Sociale*, February 12, 1916; La Questione Sociale, "La 'débacle' morale di Luigi Galleani," *La Questione Sociale*, April 1, 1916.

11.   Mariuzza [Luigi Galleani], *La voragine. La grande guerra – Quello che costa–Chi paga*, Tipografia della Cronaca Sovversiva (Lynn 1916), 4, 21. Also see Mariuzza, "La voragine," *Cronaca Sovversiva*, May

6, 1916 to May 20, 1916, now in L. Galleani, *Una battaglia*, 118–31.

12.   Botta, *Figli, non tornate (1915–1918)*, 292, 293, 297, 391, 482.

13.   Le madri d'Italia ai figli emigrati nelle due Americhe, "Figli non tornate!," *Cronaca Sovversiva*, July 24, 1915; Madri d'Italia [Luigi Galleani], *Pei nuovi richiamati. Figli non tornate!* [pamphlet, no location, no date], now in Galleani, *Una battaglia*, 69–72.

14.   Mentana [Luigi Galleani], "Contro la guerra, contro la pace, per la rivoluzione," *Cronaca Sovversiva*, March 18, 1916, now in Galleani, *Una battaglia*, 97–109 and in Luigi Galleani, *Contro la guerra, contro la pace per la rivoluzione sociale* (Catania: Centrolibri, 1983). Also see Mentana [Luigi Galleani], "Contro la guerra, per la rivoluzione sociale!," *Cronaca Sovversiva*, April 3, 1915, now in Galleani, *Una battaglia*, 55–65.

Chapter XXVI: *Nulla dies sine linea*

1.   *Nulla dies sine linea* is a Latin saying that can literally be translated as "never a day without a line," and that Galleani also translated as "a word every day." Used by Pliny the Elder to characterize Apelle's habit of painting every day, it indicates the necessity of working, day after day, to reach a specific goal.

2.   L. Galleani, "Appunti sul sindacalismo," *L'Adunata dei Refrattari*, October 28, 1950.

3.   L'eretico [Luigi Galleani], "Un problema," *Cronaca Sovversiva*, March 22, 1912.

4.   Galleani, "Appunti sul sindacalismo."

5.   Boyer and Morais, *Storia del movimento operaio negli Stati Uniti*, 247–49.

6.   L'Eretico [Luigi Galleani], "Intorno alla carogna di Creso," *Cronaca Sovversiva*, April 12, 1913, also reproduced in *Il Risveglio*, May 1, 1913, now in Galleani, *Figure e figuri*, 133.

7.   Boyer and Morais, *Storia del movimento operaio negli Stati Uniti*, 260.

8.   Ferdinando Fasce, *La democrazia degli affari. Comunicazione aziendale e discorso pubblico negli Stati Uniti, 1900–1940* (Rome: Carocci, 2000), 85–92.

9.   Boyer and Morais, *Storia del movimento operaio negli Stati Uniti*, 265; Jeremy Brecher, *Sciopero! Storia delle rivolte di massa nell'America dell'ultimo secolo* (Rome: Derive Approdi, 1999), 115.

10.   Mariuzza [Luigi Galleani], "Un uovo fuor dal cesto," *Cronaca Sovversiva*, January 29, 1916; Mariuzza, "Smontando le insidie del nemico.

Le vicende dello sciopero di Plymouth," *Cronaca Sovversiva*, February 5, 1916.

    11.   Mariuzza, "Una meteora. Aspetti ed ammaestramenti d'un'agitazione," *Cronaca Sovversiva*, January 22, 1916.

    12.   Rudolph Vecoli, "Primo Maggio: teoria e pratica fra gli immigrati italiani negli Stati Uniti," in Giani Donno (ed.), *Storie e immagini del 1° Maggio. Problemi della storiografia italiana ed internazionale* (Manduria: Lacaita, 1990), 449–61; Elisabetta Vezzosi, "Le stanze della memoria: il Primo Maggio dei radicali italiani negli Stati Uniti del primo Novecento," in Donno (ed.), *Storie e immagini del 1° Maggio. Problemi della storiografia italiana ed internazionale*, 481–95.

    13.   "Un minatore, Nei feudi cosacchi della Grande Repubblica," *Cronaca Sovversiva*, September 23, 1916; Mentana [Luigi Galleani], "La guerra sociale nei bacini dell'antracite," *Cronaca Sovversiva*, September 30, 1916.

    14.   Corfinio [Umberto Postiglione], "Sotto il giogo della realtà," *Cronaca Sovversiva*, November 25, 1916. For a summary of the trial see Va-nu-pieds [Luigi Galleani], "Il caso di Everett," *Cronaca Sovversiva*, March 10, 1917, now in Galleani, *Aneliti e singulti*, 312–17; Va-nu-pieds, "Il processo di Everett," *Cronaca Sovversiva*, March 24, 1917 to April 21, 1917.

    15.   Gallagher, *All the Right Enemies*, 89.

Chapter XXVII: The Land of the Free

    1.   Marcolfa [Luigi Galleani] "Dagoes!," *Cronaca Sovversiva*, August 28, 1915. Also see Gavino, "Negri, bianchi e noi," *Cronaca Sovversiva*, April 8, 1916. "Dago" is a derogatory epithet used in the United States and Canada to indicate immigrants of Latin origin, mostly Italian, but also Spanish or Portuguese.

    2.   G. Pimpino [Luigi Galleani], "Viva l'anarchia!," *Cronaca Sovversiva*, April 18, 1908. Also see Nevesk [Luigi Galleani], "Verre," *Cronaca Sovversiva*, April 14, 1907.

    3.   Roy Garis, *Immigration Restriction: A Study of the Opposition to and Regulation of Immigration into the United States* (New York: MacMillan, 1927), 126; E. P. Hutchinson, *Legislative History of American Immigration Policy, 1798–1965* (Philadelphia: University of Pennsylvania Press, 1981), 444–45.

    4.   Mentana [Luigi Galleani], "La Repubblica di Sant'Ignazio," *Cronaca Sovversiva*, January 9, 1915, now in Galleani, *Una battaglia*, 48–52.

5. Avrich and Avrich, *Sasha and Emma*, 269–72.

6. For this phase in the life of the Italian-language anarchist movement in the United States (1917–1920) see Avrich, *Ribelli in paradiso*.

7. Mentana [Luigi Galleani], "Matricolati!... Nulla dies sine linea," *Cronaca Sovversiva*, May 26, 1917, now in L. Galleani, *Una battaglia*, 197–203.

8. Avrich and Avrich, *Sasha and Emma*, 272–78.

9. Harriet Peterson and Gilbert Fite, *Opponents of War, 1917–1918* (Madison: University of Wisconsin Press, 1957), 14.

10. E. Coda, "L'arresto di L. Galleani," *Cronaca Sovversiva*, June 23, 1917.

11. La Cronaca Sovversiva, "Ci siamo?," *Cronaca Sovversiva*, June 16, 1917; Department of Justice, National Archives, Washington, D.C., 186233-444; R. Finch, April 6, 1918, Bureau of Investigation, National Archives, Washington, D.C., Bi Og 20713; ASM, Questura, sovversivi deceduti.

12. William Young and David E. Kaiser, *Postmortem: New Evidence in the Case of Sacco and Vanzetti* (Amherst: University of Massachusetts Press, 1985), 15; F. F. Weiss, Boston, September 3, 1918, Department of Justice, 9-12-276.

13. William Preston, Jr., *Aliens and Dissenters: Federal Suppression of Radicals, 1903–1933* (New York: Harper & Row, 1963); Robert Murray, *Red Scare. A Study in National Hysteria, 1919–1920* (New York: McGraw-Hill, 1955); Robert Justin Goldstein, *Political Repression in Modern America: From 1870 to the Present* (Cambridge: Schenkman Publishing Co., 1978). For a reconstruction of the "infamous hypocrisy" of the US government, following twenty years of class struggle, see Sigfried, "Nelle fauci della 'giustizia americana'. Storia di sangue e di terrore antiproletario," *Umanità Nova*, February 11, 1922 to April 13, 1922.

14. Mariuzza [Luigi Galleani], "Baleni precursori," *Cronaca Sovversiva*, March 24, 1917, now in Galleani, *Aneliti e singulti*, 318–22. "Revolutionary defeatism" refers to the idea that workers could gain by exploiting their countries' defeat in a capitalist war, moving from civil war at home to international revolution.

15. A. Arnauld, "Lo Stato operaio," *Cronaca Sovversiva*, August 8, 1903.

16. See Nonna Luisa [Luigi Galleani], "Tenetevi abbottonati. Consigli pratici d'igiene elementare," *Cronaca Sovversiva*, December 1, 1917 to December 15, 1917, now in L. Galleani, *Una battaglia*, 276–82.

17. *Milwaukee Journal*, September 10, 1917; *Chicago Tribune*, September 10, 1917.

18. *Milwaukee Journal*, November 25, 1917; *Chicago Tribune*, November 25, 1917; *Cronaca Sovversiva*, November 24, 1917; *Cronaca Sovversiva*, December 27, 1917; *Mother Earth Bulletin*, January 1918. H. Hibbard, May 20, 1918, Federal Bureau of Investigation, National Archives, Washington, D.C., 61-481-2; [U. Fedeli, R. Schiavina], *Un trentennio di attività anarchica*, 138; Robert Tanzilo, *Milwaukee 1917. Uno scontro tra italoamericani* (Foligno: Editoriale Umbra, 2006).

19. See Mentana [Luigi Galleani], "La legge del taglione," *Cronaca Sovversiva*, September 25, 1915; Mariuzza [Luigi Galleani], "L'ostaggio," *Cronaca Sovversiva*, October 23, 1915; Mariuzza, "Fucilato!," *Cronaca Sovversiva*, November 27, 1915. Also see Gibbs M. Smith, *Joe Hill. La vita (leggendaria) e le canzoni (rivoluzionarie) del "primo eroe popolare del ventesimo secolo"* (Milan: La Salamandra, 1978); Rino De Michele et al., *Never Forget Joe Hill* (Mestre: Fuoriposto-Aparte, 2015).

20. Reed, *Red America*, 225; Howard Zinn, *Vi racconto l'America. Alla scoperta del Nuovo Mondo* (Milan: Tropea, 2008), 115.

21. Noi [Luigi Galleani], "In articulo mortis," *Cronaca Sovversiva*, June 6,1918, now in L. Galleani, *Una battaglia*, 338–45.

22. La Cronaca Sovversiva [Luigi Galleani], "Viva l'anarchia!," *Cronaca Sovversiva*, July 18, 1918, now reprinted in Galleani, *Una battaglia*, 345–57.

23. Garis, *Immigration Restriction*, 138–40; Constantine Panunzio, *The Deportation Cases of 1919–1920* (New York: Federal Council of Churches of Christ, 1921), 99–100.

Chapter XXVIII: *Adversus hostem aeterna auctoritas!*

1. This chapter title refers to a law of the Twelve Tables taken from Roman law, which specifies that legal action is inapplicable against foreigners. In the final decades of the nineteenth century it was used in parliament to express the idea that it is unnecessary to compromise with enemies of the homeland. Galleani used it several times, translating it "into good vernacular" as: "all means are allowed against the enemy," see Mentana [Luigi Galleani], "Può venire, l'attendiamo di piè fermo!"

2. Brecher, *Sciopero!*, 113–50.

3. Il Diritto, "Pietro Marucco," *Il Diritto*, April 1919.

4. *Boston Herald*, May 2, 1919; *Cleveland Plain Dealer*, May 2, 1919.

5. *Boston Globe*, June 3–4, 1919; *Boston Herald*, June 3–4, 1919;

Pittsburgh Press, June 3, 1919; *Philadelphia Inquirer,* June 4–5, 1919; *New York Times,* June 3, 1919; *New York World,* June 3–4, 1919; *New York Call,* June 4, 1919; *Washington Post,* June 5, 1919.

6.   Pernicone, *Luigi Galleani and Italian Anarchist Terrorism in the United States,* 472, 484–485.

7.   Boyer and Morais, *Storia del movimento operaio negli Stati Uniti,* 282.

8.   *Cleveland Plain Dealer,* June 4, 1919; *Pittsburgh Press,* June 3, 1919.

9.   M. Valkenburgh, June 23, 1919, Boston, Bureau of Investigation, National Archives, Washington, D.C., I211793; *New York Times,* September 19, 1920.

10.   Domani, "I nostri deportati," *Domani,* June 30, 1919.

Chapter XXIX: In the Thick of the *Biennio Rosso*

1.   Fedeli, *Luigi Galleani. Quarant'anni di lotte rivoluzionarie 1891–1931,* 104.

2.   Armando Borghi, *Errico Malatesta* (Milan: Istituto Editoriale Italiano, 1947), 178.

3.   Paolo Finzi, *La nota persona. Errico Malatesta in Italia. Dicembre 1919–luglio 1920* (Ragusa: La Fiaccola, 2008), 69–74.

4.   See ACS, CPC, file no. 106.

5.   "La Cronaca Sovversiva," *La Frusta,* January 1, 1920, now in Luigi Balsamini and Federico Sora (eds.), *Periodici e numeri unici del movimento anarchico in provincia di Pesaro e Urbino. Dall'Internazionale al fascismo (1873–1922). Bibliografia e collezione completa* (Fano: Archivio-Biblioteca Enrico Travaglini, 2013), 583; L'Avvenire Anarchico, "Un grande avvenimento. L'uscita a Torino di 'Cronaca Sovversiva,'" *L'Avvenire Anarchico,* December 26, 1919.

6.   Boyer and Morais, *Storia del movimento operaio negli Stati Uniti.*

7.   Ibid.

8.   The Old Man [Luigi Galleani], "Errico Malatesta," *Cronaca Sovversiva,* January 17, 1920.

9.   Ibid.

10.   Ibid.

11.   Minin [Luigi Galleani], "Attenti ai mali passi!," *Cronaca Sovversiva,* July 10, 1920.

12.   Gaetano Arfè, *Storia del socialismo italiano (1892–1926)* (Turin: Einaudi, 1965), 284–86.

13.   Borghi, *Errico Malatesta,* 189–97; Finzi, *La nota persona. Errico Malatesta in Italia. Dicembre 1919–luglio 1920,* 158–59.

14.   R. Gremmo, "La 'Cronaca Sovversiva' di Galleani, la 'banda armata' di Raffaele Schiavina e la bomba del giovane anarchico Musso," *Storia Ribelle* no. 18 (Autumn 2005): 1657–67.

15.   "Note sovversive," *Cronaca Sovversiva,* January 31, 1920.

16.   L.C.S. [Luigi Galleani], "Colla teppa!," *Cronaca Sovversiva,* February 28, 1920.

17.   Tramp [Luigi Galleani], "Soldato, fratello!," *Cronaca Sovversiva,* May 15, 1920 [original print]; *Soldato, fratello!,* Tipografia Alleanza, Turin 1920, AST (Archivio di Stato di Torino [Turin State Archive]), Fondi processuali [Trials Collection], Corte d'Assise [Court of Assizes], file 13, sentenza [sentence] 73, January 30, 1922.

18.   In English and emphasized in the original.

19.   Luigi Galleani, "Nota bene," *Cronaca Sovversiva,* Turin, year I, no. 9, new series, June 12, 1920, now in Galleani, *Aneliti e singulti,* 358–59. See *New York Times,* May 4, 1920; Carlos Salsedo, *Andrea and Me: A Digital Autoethnographic Journey into the Past,* Dissertation Submitted to the Graduate School of the University of Massachusetts Amherst in Partial Fulfillment of the Requirements for the Degree of Doctor of Philosophy, February 2010.

20.   For a report of the extensive literature related to Nicola Sacco and Bartolomeo Vanzetti, see Luigi Botta, *Sacco & Vanzetti. Cronologia e strumenti di ricerca* (Savigliano: Associazione Cristoforo Beggiami, 2017); Creagh, *Sacco & Vanzetti, un delitto di Stato.*

21.   Gage, *The Day Wall Street Exploded;* W. Flynn, "On the Trail of the Anarchist Band-Chief Flynn," *Albuquerque Morning Journal,* March 15, 1922.

22.   Gage, *The Day Wall Street Exploded;* Michele Presutto, "'L'uomo che fece esplodere Wall Street'. La storia di Mario Buda," *AltreItalie* no. 40 (January–June 2010), 83–107.

Chapter XXX: The Final Struggle

1.   See ACS, CPC, file no. 106; AST, Fondi processuali, op. cit.; Amaryllis [Nella Giacomelli], "L'accanimento della magistratura torinese contro 'Cronaca Sovversiva,'" *Umanità Nova,* October 19, 1921.

2.   *Bollettino delle Ricerche,* year IX, no. 280 (December 1, 1921).

3.   Gage, *The Day Wall Street Exploded;* D. DiLillo, February 27, 1922, Federal Bureau of Investigation, BI 61-381.

4.   Luigi Galleani to *L'Adunata dei Refrattari,* September 22,

1922, Letters of Luigi Galleani, *L'Adunata dei Refrattari*, December 19, 1931.

5.   Luigi Galleani to *L'Adunata dei Refrattari*, October 22, 1922, *L'Adunata dei Refrattari*, New York, April 2, 1932.

6.   ACS, CPC, file no. 106; AST, Fondi processuali; r.s. [Renato Siglich], "Luigi Galleani condannato a 13 mesi," *L'Avvenire Anarchico*, November 10, 1922; Raffale Schiavina, "Il caso Galleani, 'Solidarietà pro Vittime Politiche,'" supplement to no. 67 of *Libero Accordo*, February 1923.

7.   Luigi Galleani to Raffaele Schiavina, Carceri giudiziarie, Turin, January 2, 1923, *L'Adunata dei Refrattari*, December 19, 1931.

8.   ACS, CPC, file no. 106; ASM, Questura, sovversivi deceduti; Olga Galleani [zia di Luigi e sorella di Alfonso] to Max Nettlau, Sori Ligure, May 7, 1923, Max Nettlau Papers, folder no. 458.

9.   ACS, CPC, file no. 106; ASM, Questura, sovversivi deceduti.

10.   ACS, CPC, file no. 106.

11.   G. Licheri, *L'Adunata dei Refrattari nel ventennio fra le due guerre (1922–1939)*, thesis, Faculty of Magistero, University of Florence, 1967–1968.

12.   M.S. [Raffaele Schiavina], "Galleani oratore," *L'Adunata dei Refrattari*, November 30, 1963.

13.   ACS, CPC, file no. 106; ACS, Confinati politici [political detainees], file no. 447, dossier for Luigi Galleani.

14.   ACS, Confinati politici, file no. 447.

15.   Ibid.; Luigi Galleani to Jacques Gross, Ustica, March 28, 1897, Jacques Gross Papers.

16.   ACS, Confinati politici, file no. 447; P. La Torre, "Un episodio giudiziario," *L'Adunata dei Refrattari*, April 7, 1956; Fedeli, *Luigi Galleani. Quarant'anni di lotte rivoluzionarie 1891–1931*, 120.

17.   ASM, Questura, sovversivi deceduti; "Alcuni ostaggi di casa nostra. Luigi Galleani," *Almanacco Libertario pro Vittime Politiche*, Geneva, 1929, 27–28.

18.   Newspaper clipping in ACS, Confinati politici, file no. 447.

19.   Luigi Galleani [to Raffaele Schiavina], February 6, 1925, Sori Ligure, in *L'Adunata dei Refrattari*, December 19, 1931, now in U. Fedeli, *Luigi Galleani. Quarant'anni di lotte rivoluzionarie 1891–1931*, 118–19; Anarchici cuneesi (ed.), *La salute è in voi. Sacco, Vanzetti e la dimensione anarchica*, 54–55. Raffaele Schiavina, just before execution of the two, effectively managed to give the press the important pamphlet *Sacco e Vanzetti. Cause e fini di un delitto di Stato* [Sacco and Vanzetti. Causes

and Objectives of a State Crime] (Paris: Jean Bucco, 1927), in which he outlined clearly the events and the key players in the affair.

20.   ACS, Confinati politici, file no. 162, dossier for Mario Buda.

21.   Mario Buda to Edward Holton, Lipari, November 28, 1928, ACS, Confinati politici, file no. 162. Also see M. Presutto, *L'uomo che fece esplodere Wall Street*, 91–94.

22.   ACS, Confinati politici, file no. 447.

23.   ASM, Questura, sovversivi deceduti.

24.   Luigi Galleani to O. [Olimpio Galleani], Caprigliola, May 29, 1930, *L'Adunata dei Refrattari*, November 30, 1963.

25.   ASM, Questura, sovversivi deceduti.

26.   Ibid.

27.   Olimpio Galleani to Luigi Galleani, [Needham,] June 9, 1930; July 1, 1930; October 15, 1930, in ASM, Questura, sovversivi deceduti; also see ACS, CPC, file no. 106 dossier for Olimpio Galleani.

28.   Luigi Galleani to Olimpio Galleani [Bettola di Caprigliola], March 8, 1931, in ASM, Questura, sovversivi deceduti.

29.   Errico Malatesta to Luigi Galleani, Rome, May 30, 1930, in ASM, Questura, sovversivi deceduti.

30.   Errico Malatesta, "Per Luigi Galleani," *L'Adunata dei Refrattari*, November 21, 1931. In a previous article with the same title, written on Galleani's sixty-fifth birthday, Malatesta had written: "We, his old and young brothers in arms, even during inadvertent strategic mishaps, have always felt warm friendship and sincere admiration for him," Errico Malatesta, "Per Luigi Galleani," *Pensiero e Volontà*, October 1, 1926.

31.   Luigi Galleani to *L'Adunata dei Refrattari*, August 1931, *L'Adunata dei Refrattari*, July 1, 1933.

32.   F.G., "Un cavaliere della libertà: Luigi Galleani," *Il Martello*, November 1931, clipping, Ugo Fedeli Papers, folder no. 834.

33.   La Redazione, "È morto Luigi Galleani," *Studi Sociali*, November 21, 1931.

Index

AK Press is small, in terms of staff and resources, but we also manage to be one of the world's most productive anarchist publishing houses. We publish close to twenty books every year, and distribute thousands of other titles published by like-minded independent presses and projects from around the globe. We're entirely worker-run and democratically managed. We operate without a corporate structure—no boss, no managers, no bullshit.

The FRIENDS OF AK program is a way you can directly contribute to the continued existence of AK PRESS, and ensure that we're able to keep publishing books like this one! FRIENDS pay $25 a month directly into our publishing account ($30 for Canada, $35 for international), and receive a copy of every book AK PRESS publishes for the duration of their membership! Friends also receive a discount on anything they order from our website or buy at a table: 50% on AK titles, and 20% on everything else. We have a FRIENDS OF AK ebook program as well: $15 a month gets you an electronic copy of every book we publish for the duration of your membership. You can even sponsor a very discounted membership for someone in prison.

Email friendsofak@akpress.org for more info, or visit the FRIENDS OF AK PRESS website: https://www.akpress.org/friends.html.

There are always great book projects in the works—so sign up now to become a FRIEND OF AK PRESS, and let the presses roll!